Keep The Peace At All Cost

First World War Memoirs of Private William Lees,

abridged and edited by Annette (Lees) Gray

Keep The Peace At All Cost

First World War Memoirs of Private William Lees

ISBN: 978-0-9735467-3-6

Printed and bound in Canada

Books Available from

Annette (Lees) Gray (janegray@telus.net)

4320--54 Avenue

Innisfail, Alberta T4G 1K5

FOREWORD

Across the twisted and torn countryside of war plagued France and Belgium came 93,936 Canadians to fight on foreign soil. And fight they did, from 1914-1918, for the idea that "life without liberty was nothing." Almost 60,000 of these men never returned, but with those who did, came stories of the battles across Vimy Ridge, Passchendaele, Ypres, Amiens, Arras, and Cambrai—stories that stagger the imagination.

Where once beautiful villages nestled in lush green hills and valleys, millions of bombs fell, destroying whole communities and turning the peaceful European countryside into massive shell holes so deep with water men drowned in them. Splintered wood, glass, and brick blended with the twisted remains of men, horses and mules. Soldiers lived like wild animals, crawling through muddy trenches and sleeping in rat and lice-infested holes in the ground. Often, they were wet, cold, hungry, and nauseated from the smell of raw wastes and rotting flesh. It was hell on earth!

Here is one factual account as recorded by William Lees in the summer of 1919, with help from his sister, maps and personal notes. More importantly, his first draft was written while William's memories were still fresh and painful. It is my hope that readers of this new book (especially Private William Lees's descendants), will find strength in this day-by-day account of twenty-seven months in the life of a Canadian soldier.

ACKNOWLEDGEMENTS

A huge thank you to my late father for keeping a detailed account of his life as a soldier in the First World War. I would also like to thank each of my family for their assistance in keeping our ancestors' memories alive. Special thanks to my sisters, Evelyne and Doreen for their encouragement; to William's granddaughter, Deb (Gray) Wynn for her reading and approval, and to William's grandson, Kerry Olauson (our family historian), for his contribution to *Keep The Peace At All Cost.* Kerry devoted countless hours to the project with patience, expertise and guidance. I'm much obliged, Kerry! Also, kudos to my friends at Blitz Print, Calgary for their many years of service.

Annette Gray

INTRODUCTION

William Lees, my father, was born August 31st, 1893, in Southport, Lancashire, England. Extremely quiet and shy as a boy, he received his education in All Souls Anglican and Holy Trinity Schools. His happiest hours were spent rambling in the woods near Blowick and St. Luke's Train Stations, where his fascination with trains was second only to his love of the birds and flowers he found there.

At seventeen-years-old, he was serving an apprenticeship as a typesetter to the local newspaper, the *Southport Visitor,* when his mother died. Her death, in 1910, triggered the decision to leave England. Not having enough money to join their father, who owned a haberdashery in New Zealand, the three siblings: William (18), his elder sister, Evelyne (24), and younger brother, John (16), decided to come to Canada. The three young people knew no one in Canada but were fortunate to find immediate employment: Evelyne as a teacher, and William and John as farm labourers. As money became available, John attended Stettler High School and later completed his teacher's training at Camrose Normal School. Evelyne never married but devoted her working life to teaching in Alberta's rural schools for almost fifty years.

On March 30th, 1915, Father filed on a homestead quarter, twelve and a half miles north of Leslieville, Alberta, in the Aurora-Carlos area. He lived on this land for over sixty years. In 1930, while visiting relatives in Southport, Father met and married a widow, Gertrude (Gertie Mister) Morris. Returning to Canada, they first resided in Calgary. Then, at the height of the depression, they left the city and took up residence on William's homestead. Here (from 1939 to 1963), they operated the Carlos Post Office, farmed, and logged for a living. My sisters and I grew up on the homestead: my eldest sister, Evelyne (Mrs. Elmer Heringer); myself, Annette (Mrs. Dennis Gray), and my younger sister, Doreen (Mrs. William Thomsen).

My parents retired to Red Deer in 1968, where they lived out their lives. Father passed away on June 27th, 1984, and Mother on May 16th, 1993.

Before he died, Father published *My Adventures During World War 1,* an unpretentious collection of journal entries written in the third person. His memories of the war were aided by notes jotted down in his own brand of shorthand, discernable only to himself. (According to my aunt, Father took shorthand in school when he was fourteen years old.) He wrote these dots and dashes on the backs of postcards as he marched through France, Belgium, and Germany.

For my part as a daughter, writer, and publisher of this edition of my father's memoirs, I have chosen to call this new book, *"Keep The Peace At All Cost."* This was an expression so often used by Father in the years following what he termed, "an inhumane war."

I have also differed from his approach by presenting the dialog in the first person, just as my father would speak to you, if you were visiting at our kitchen table. I am extremely proud of my dad, my Canada and our Canadian soldiers. I hope you share my pride.

Keep the Peace © Annette Gray

He was a kind and tolerant man,

my father, machine-gunner in the First World War.

Yet, when we siblings fought, as children do,

he would scold us in his gruffest voice, saying,

"Keep the peace at all cost."

He never spoke of those terrifying days in the trenches,

nor his only brother, killed near Vimy Ridge,

but when he came in from the fields,

tired from a hard day's work,

he would sit, dozing by the fire,

then suddenly spring up and yell,

"Get down, the Jerries are coming."

As a child, I laughed,

not realizing what his nightmares were about,

that he was reliving the sight of dying men,

bathed in blood and screaming,

some drowning in water-filled graters hewn out by bombs.

I had no way of knowing, so I scoffed.

When I was older, he told me he had seen a cavalry charge,

in 1918, perhaps the last:

horses on a hillside, sleek and shining in the sun.

The command given, they raced forward,

then German guns barked, and horses fell.

Not one proud cavalry man or mount survived.

Yet, flailing hooves and mangled men lived on

as horrors in his mind. They never left.

In his last years, my father wrote a book,

My Adventures During World War I,

crossing out much of what he'd written.

"Too gory," he would say.

Yet in his eyes I read the whole,

and never scoffed again,

when he woke from a dream and yelled, "Get down!"

Finally, I understood those crucial words,

"Keep the peace at all cost."

War is too evil for the human soul to bear.

CHAPTER ONE

As a child growing up in the Victorian era, I (William Lees), knew nothing of world conflicts. My life revolved around our family's elegant three-story brick home in an upper-middle class neighbourhood. So, it never entered my head that I would grow up to be a machine-gunner in World War One—the goriest of all battles—the war to end all wars, so we were told.

My parents, Thomas William (May 3, 1856–Nov. 26, 1917) and Sarah Hanna (Hopwood) Lees (Feb. 3,1857–Dec.17, 1910), were born in England and married Aug. 9,1886 in *Blackley, Lancashire*. After their wedding, the young couple sailed "down under" to *New Zealand* where they owned and operated a general store in *Auckland*. However, my mother was extremely homesick. She was one of ten children and hated being torn away from her parents and siblings. Finally, after the birth of the first of their four children, Evelyne, born on October 31,1887, Mother returned to England. Before she left *New Zealand,* Father bought her a gold ring, telling her this was to be sold should she run out of money. After my father disposed of his store and other holdings in *Auckland*, he too returned to England. Now reunited, my parents had three more children: myself born on August 31st, 1893, John Edward, born November 5th, 1895 and Roselyne born in June of 1897. Here we lived on the corner of Oak and 80 Hart Street, *Southport, Lancashire*, in a large brick house that was built in 1892, a year prior to my birth. For the next eighteen years this was to be my home.

By the standards of that day and age, it was considered a posh residence. My earliest memories were of playing hide-and-seek with my brown-eyed little brother in the many nooks and crannies of the big house. Like other young lads, it was rough and tumble as well as boyish shenanigans that sometimes got us into trouble.

One day, John and I decided to crawl through an upstairs window. Once outside, we balanced precariously on the narrow window ledge twenty-five feet above the cobbled street. I'm sure we must have given our mother the shock of her life. Had we fallen, we could very well have been crippled for life—or worse.

My parents were strict Church of England (Anglicans), and did their best to keep up appearances on the Sabbath. Each Sunday sister Evelyne was dressed in a lace-trimmed frock; Mother wore high necked, tightly corseted gowns and stylish hats, while Father, John, and I were crammed into starched white collars and tailored suits. Then, with shoes spit and polished, we'd make a dignified procession to Christ Church, a few blocks away. Here we children were ceremoniously escorted to Sunday School, while Mother and Father knelt for Morning Service with other devotees.

After church, we returned home for tea, and then, if the weather was mild, we'd go for an evening stroll to *Blowick Station* where Mother and Evelyne admired beds of multicoloured flowers and where Father, John and I turned our attention to the huge black steam locomotives, puffing their way to various towns. Looking back, those were the best of times.

Mother was exceptionally talented. She used to knit long woollen stockings for us children. For John and me, she made flannel shirts and underwear, and for Evelyne lace-trimmed dresses and nightgowns. She also crocheted bed valences, wall hangings, pillowcases, doilies and antimacassars for chairs. I remember the delicious bread, buns, pies, and puddings she made, and how she planted a white rose bush under the window in the corner of the yard, and the pretty potted plants she cosseted, both inside and out.

Mother, Father and sister Evelyne

Photo credit Kerry Olauson

William's first home, 80 Hart Street, Southport

The Lees Family, August 21ˢᵗ, 1897 (l to r): Baby Roselyne, Eve-lyne (10), William (4) in front of Mother Sarah Hanna, Father Thomas (2-year-old John missing)

I don't remember my parents quarrelling. If they did, their disputes were well hidden, but the family fortune must have taken a plunge, because our lovely front parlour was converted into a haberdashery shop. After this transition, my parents were extremely busy, selling such things as cooking pots, wash tubs, clothes props, umbrellas, and smaller items such as thimbles and thread.

Having customers wandering through our living space changed our lives from domestic bliss to hustle and bustle. Rules were stricter and we children had to tow the line. Yet the worst was yet to come when our one-year-old sister, Roselyne, died in August 1898. A day before my 5ᵗʰ birthday, Roselyne was buried in South-port Cemetery, plot #411, Sec 5, in a child's oak coffin that was lined with white and gold furnishings. A one-horse Brougham Hearse was rented for the occasion. I remember bouncing on the seat of the carriage and wondering why everyone was crying when heaven was supposed to be such a happy place.

Home life changed even more dramatically after that. I believe losing a child eroded my parents' relationship. In the Victorian era, emotions were never displayed openly; traditionally it was "keep a stiff upper lip." Yet grief filled every corner of our once happy home.

No doubt these restrained emotions were part of the reason my father left England in 1906 and went back to *New Zealand*— alone. As a youngster, he'd contracted rheumatic fever. He'd lived in *New Zealand* before his marriage, and often said the warmer climate in the Auckland area agreed with his constitution much better than the cold English dampness which tended to stir up old aches and pains.

Perhaps when Father left England, he intended to make his fortune and return to us. Who knows? Whatever his plans were, the end result was I never saw my father again.

Did he send money to Mother for our upkeep? I have no way of knowing. No one explained to us children the "whys" and "wherefores" of my father's departure. I was keenly aware that my role model was gone. As a young lad of thirteen, I missed him terribly and had a hard job forgiving him for leaving me when I needed him the most. To his credit, every so often we'd receive a postcard from him, and we could feel the love and caring in the tone of those short messages.

My father sent me this postcard on December 13th, 1908. It read:

"Dear Willie.

'Received letter from Mother three days ago, the first news from Southport for over three months. Welcome news and glad to hear of your success. The view I send (by postcard) is of the fancy end of our street. My shop is a little higher up (the street), farther than the trees on the right, the next one past where you see the man standing. My shop looks very like the one marked Shaving Saloon. 'Glad to hear shop news and the news that you are all in good health, the same blessings I enjoy.

Yours, Dad."

W. Beattie & Co., Publishers.   Queen Street, Onehunga, looking towards One Tree Hill.—547   Auckland. N.Z.

Postcard from Thomas William Lees, Queen's Street,

Onehunga, New Zealand.

Much of his correspondence to Mother seemed very formal. Letters and postcards were sometimes addressed to Mrs. Lees. On other occasions, it was S.H. Lees.

Instead of living in the city of *Auckland* as he had done before, my father took up residence in the small town of *Onehunga* in 1906. *Onehunga* was a sea-side village eight kilometres south of Auckland city centre (a few kilometres north of where *Auckland's* airport is today). Here he operated another haberdashery with merchandise similar to what Mother was selling in the front room of our house on 80 Hart Street. He also worked part-time as a dock hand. Did he regret his decision to leave England for good? I have no way of knowing.

To John from Father Thomas William—April 19th, 1910,

(via Rarotonga, and Penryn, and Iceland per the SS Ionic)

Dear John: *How are you getting on? I have not heard from you since you left school, excepting Willie's account of you rambling over the verdant fields (which made me smile). I thought you might be able to make a sketch of the Bridge on which I am crossing today (DV) having resumed my cough five weeks ago with colder weather. I am in moderate health but getting older and now have got white whiskers. Yours, Dad*

To son, William—June 21st, 1910 (via Ceylon):

Received your ST... (perhaps Southport Times) this morning. News all well. Same as self. Love to all. Just had a letter from Mr. W Covell who is at Napier. All well.

To wife, Sarah Hannah: *Dear S H ------ Received yours and Willies of the 23rd of May. Glad to hear you are all well. Self Bz (busy) today. Had headache. Will Covell arrived here on Saturday, looking for a job, but has not yet succeeded. He is lodging in Queen Street for a week. Hope he may succeed eventually. Out here, a good many are looking for jobs. At present things are not booming. Has Evelyne had her exams yet? When does Willie get an advance? and John owes me a letter.*

P.S. I sleep well and don't take my worries to bed; don't fight my pillow but lay down and kick all troubles out of the bed. I like the news and cuttings from the S Gdn (Southport Guardian) which you have sent from time to time. I always cut off the bottom and do the test.

Yours TWL

To Evelyne Lees from her father—April 7th, 1910, via Suez:

Dear Evelyne: I received Mother's letter yesterday and was very glad that your efforts and study have been rewarded by the gratifying addition of two distinctions to your certificate—the ease to your mind must also be beneficial. I put an extra-long day in today in sympathy with your amazing labour. When shall our labours have an end? "In joy and peace" as the hymn says. Your, "Dad."

One postcard to mother contained a nostalgic piece of prose about a man excitedly climbing a hill, only to gaze sadly at the country on the other side. This following message written sometime between November and December of 1910, was the last Dad wrote to our mother.

"Dear Sarah Hannah.

I received your letter of October 20th. Very sorry to hear of Mr. Diggles sudden death, quite a shock to the district. Glad to hear you are all in good health as I am at present. I conclude Birkdale has now found Southport—making a big town of nearly 70,000 while our town is now near 5,000, and Auckland is 100,000. One-hunga Theater is now built, quite an imposing structure costing 1,200 pounds. This card will show you where my shop is, next to the church on the left, the spire amongst the trees is the Roman Catholic Church.

In the above dispatch, my father mentioned the shock of losing a neighbour. Little did he know there was a greater shock in store—our mother's sudden death on December 17th, 1910. Mother had continued to run the store on the home front and was a competent businesswoman and homemaker right up to time she took to bed, three days before her passing. She was laid to rest on December 21st and shares the grave with our baby sister in Southport Cemetery. It was a devastating loss. At the time of her death, my brother, John, was fifteen; I was seventeen and my twenty-two-year-old sister, Evelyne, had just completed her teacher's training.

CHAPTER TWO

Technically, since our father, Thomas Lees, lived on the other side of the globe, my siblings and I were orphans. Now all life's decisions were ours to make, so we took what little money Mother left us and bought one-way tickets to Canada on an ocean-going liner, the Concordia.

We arrived in Canada on March 12th, 1912 and kept traveling west until we ran out of money, which happened to be in *Calgary, Alberta*.

That summer found John and I working for Mr. Hunt on a farm near *Turner Valley*. We boys kept a diary, recording our first activities in our newly adopted country. One day I would make the diary entries; the next Brother John would. Our first record began, "Monday, August 12th, 1912: John and I are thinning turnips."

This farm job was quite a change for two city-bred lads, but it afforded some on-the-job work experience. We also met many interesting characters who were employed by Mr. Hunt. Among those I remember were Harry Weidner, David Irvin (a Scotchman), John Walter (a native), Tom Claxton, Frank Paton, and men we knew as Webster, Jack, Jim, Swede, and Irish.

If we weren't too busy on Sundays, John and I would hike to Pine Creek Church or we'd wander aimlessly about, climbing hills to see the distant mountains. How we enjoyed that first spring in Canada with its unfamiliar wild birds and flowers. Later, that summer we got our first scent of newly mowed hay, and later still watched autumn's red and gold leaves float lazily to the ground.

Sunday, October 27th, I went with a co-worker, John Walter, to his house on the *Morley Reserve*. I had never been on a native reserve before, never experienced the musky scent of canvas tents and buffalo-hide tepees; never seen dark-eyed women in long cotton skirts and beaded moccasins. Nor had I heard the plaintive whine of reserve dogs or the jangling chains on hobbled horses. It was quite an experience!

While working for employer, Hunt, I had a variety of jobs, each one depending on the season. All work was done by sheer brawn and horse-drawn implements: ploughing, disking, harrowing, cutting and threshing grain, milking cows, poisoning gophers and hauling feed and lumber. Sometimes, by way of a change, we worked for Mr. Hunt on land he owned close to *Midnapore*, and on Feb. 4th, 1913, a fellow nicknamed "Irish" and I hauled green feed to *Calgary* for Pat Burns.

There was always something to keep us busy. As I recall, I didn't take a full day off work until January 6th, 1913, when I met owner Hunt in *Calgary* and was paid a $100 of the $260 dollars I had coming. A day later, my brother and I hopped the 21-3 train in *Calgary*. It was cold and windy when we changed trains in *Lacombe* on route to Botha where Evelyne was teaching in a one-room school. It was not a very long break. On Saturday, January 11th, I was back working for my boss, Mr. Hunt, hauling manure in blowing snow and a temperature of minus 38 degrees.

Finally, Monday, April 21st, 1913, I told my employer I was moving on. That evening, I caught the train in *Calgary*; got to *Olds* at 1:30 am; *Innsifail* at 10:30 am; *Red Deer* at 4 pm and with a layover, I arrived much later in *Ponoka*—almost a full day's travel.

On April 24th, 1913, I began working for Walter L. Gee, directly west of *Ponoka*. This was farm work, much as I had done for Mr. Hunt, except I was handling large Clydesdale horses, ploughing, harrowing, hauling manure, planting potatoes, painting Gee's house, building a granary and cutting logs to build a hog barn. However, the most important job I was asked to do, was help construct a huge hip-roofed barn, which has been a landmark ever since for travelers on the *Edmonton-Calgary Highway* (the *QE2*)

William pictured on top rafters of Walter Gee's large barn.

Walter and Mrs. Gee were very good to me, but their small son, Merle, was worrisome. I recall one day finding young Merle seated on a milk stool, directly behind one of the big Clydesdales. With currycomb in hand, he was combing the horse's long white fetlock. It was nothing short of a miracle that the little tyke didn't get kicked to kingdom come.

When the first World War broke out in August of 1914, I was still working on Walter Gee's farm, *Ponoka*. Evelyne was teaching school in *Stettler*, and John, was boarding with her and attending *Stettler High School*. We three young Englishmen were happy in our adopted land. Evelyne had the good teaching position she wanted. John was doing well at school.

Then, on the thirtieth of March 1915, I filed on my homestead, SE 27-41-5 W5th, in the *Carlos* district, north of *Leslieville, Alberta*. This was also the year John attended *Camrose Normal*, received his teacher's certificate and applied to teach at *Washington Heights*, a public school located a few miles south of my homestead.

William Lees on his homestead

Dad would be proud to see what his children were accomplishing. Evelyne and John were doing well academically, and I had my own home. What's more we three were going to spend Christmas together in the small house a previous resident built on my homestead.

14

John and I enjoyed our time together, but on occasions he didn't think my rough and ready ways were up to his standards and he let his pet peeves be known when he wrote to Evelyne to make arrangements for Christmas.

"Dear Evelyne," he wrote. *"I had not intended to write till next Sunday but perhaps you might not get the letter if I left it till then. It would be something like Willie's way—posting a letter to us on the way to the station.*

"Since last writing, I have found how the trains run. I will leave here (from Camrose), on the 8-11 train on Thursday (CPR) and meet you at Burbank (a CNR railway station between Lacombe and Red Deer.) *at 1-45. So, I will be able to attend the social evening on Wednesday night (if they have one). You won't have any difficulty recognizing me at Burbank. I'll be wearing the old grey coat and blue cap as you have seen me hundreds of times before.*

Don't forget to reserve a seat for me! It will be about 5 o'clock when we get to Leslieville, so we'll have four hours drive in the dark.

"However, it will be full moon on the 21st, so that if the night is clear and William has sleighs (which I doubt), it will not be too bad. I hope you will take my advice and send a plentiful supply of necessities out to Willie for I don't suppose he has anything out there, but a few rolled oats and some delicacies of his own concoction.

"The exams begin next Thursday and I'm not too optimistic in regard to them. I haven't read any of the texts thoroughly and so will be lucky if I manage to scrape through. I won't worry anyway as I don't expect to teach. One of the boys joined the 5th University Corps which left for Montreal about a week ago. He was the most popular fellow in the school and got quite a send off. There will be another University Corps formed early in the spring which I should like to join.

"..... Be sure not to miss the train and make them wait for me at Burbank if I'm not there. Yours, John Edward Lees."

On December 30th, 1915, my brother decided to apply for a teaching position at a small one-room school a few miles south of my homestead. By this time John had passed his exams with flying colors and was ready to become a teacher-farmer. He addressed the following letter to Mr. Austin, the secretary-treasurer of Washington Heights School.

"Dear Sir," he wrote. *"While at Camrose Normal, I was informed that the Washington Heights School requires a teacher and I wish to apply for that position. I have successfully completed the course at Camrose Normal and now hold a teacher's certificate. I also have the certificate of the Strathcona Trust for Physical Culture and am qualified to teach penmanship, art, and manual training to all grades by the most up-to-date methods. Having attended one of the best rural schools in this province, I have had special opportunities for observing how rural schools with all grades are conducted. Should you require any character or ability references, Mr. McNally, the principal of Camrose Normal will furnish them. As salary, I would require $720.00 per annum. I will call around to see you next Saturday afternoon regarding this matter."*

"Yours truly, John Edward Lees."

Nevertheless, John had another change of heart, and on April 7, 1916, he gave in to peer pressure and enlisted in the 196th Battalion of the Canadian Overseas Expeditionary Force (C.E.F.). Expecting the war to be over soon (before he left Canada), he filed on the NW-4-42-5 W5th on June 10, 1916. His land was about four miles northwest of mine. However, early in December 1916, the quarter section (bordering mine to the north), became vacant.

Compared to the quarter John had filed on earlier, this newly abandoned quarter had better soil and was in a more desirable location. So, I sent word to John who was now stationed in *Seaford, Sussex,* telling him he could trade the quarter section he'd filed on, for the one next to mine. As I expected, he was excited to get the news.

"By all means, the quarter next to yours is definitely more to my liking. Please send me the land transfer forms."

For my part, the thought of having my brother living so close to me was almost too good to be true. I anticipated a lifetime of John and I working together on farms of our very own. It was going to be so much better than working for strangers. With this thought in mind, on December 19th, 1916, I set off for the Land Office in *Red Deer* to get the necessary papers to send my younger brother. Little did we know the conflict in Europe would dash all such hopes and dreams.

On getting to *Red Deer*, I was surprised to see a large number of soldiers around town. They seemed to be everywhere. That evening, I stayed at the Windsor Hotel and met a returned soldier who had been wounded in *France*. In the course of conversation, he told me about his non-too pleasant experiences. This set me to worrying about John. What if anything happened to my kid brother while I was enjoying life on my farm in Alberta? Normally, I'm not a worrier. Nevertheless, sleep evaded me and sometime during the night I made up my mind. The homestead business could wait until the war was over. I would enlist.

I discovered the 191st Battalion were making their headquarters at the Red Deer Armouries. So, the next day, December 20th, I went to the armouries, signed the necessary enlistment documents, and was given a medical examination. I requested one month's leave of absence, so I could go home and put my affairs in order. This was granted.

On the train home from *Red Deer*, I met a Norwegian recruiting officer who did his best to talk me into enlisting. I listened to him for several minutes before telling him I'd already enlisted.

Christmas 1916 wasn't as pleasant as last year. Sister Evelyne came to visit, but she tended to take life far too seriously so that I missed John's good-natured hassling all the more.

I received a letter from him saying: *"I suppose Evelyne will be with you for Christmas. As I told you in my last, we are quarantined, but hope to have a good time—as far as eating at least. Being cooped up in here almost all the boys have taken to various forms of gambling for a diversion. I lost 1£/6 last night but intend to stop while I'm well off. I wish I could send you this $10 dollar bill which I brought over from Canada. It's no good to me. Well, I'll write again soon after Christmas, so wishing you all kinds of good luck— No, not luck but opportunities for the New Year. I remain your brother, John Edward."*

A month later, on January 19th, 1917, my leave was up. I had disposed of my assets, such as they were, and rented my house to a neighbour. Having spent the night sleeping in Manzer's shack, on the next quarter southwest of mine (land I eventually purchased), I got up bright and early. The snow was deep and the weather chilly, but I had no choice but to walk the thirteen miles to the small town of *Leslieville*. It was noon when, cold and hungry, I reached *Leslieville*. I found food and a warm bed at the Foreman Hotel and there I stayed the night.

At 5:30 the next morning, I took the horse-drawn mail stage bound for *Condor*, a railway station five miles southeast of *Leslieville*. Halfway there, the team spooked at the sight of an abandoned auto. Before the driver knew what was happening, the horses jumped to one side, the sleigh flipped over, and the driver, mailbags, and I were tossed into several feet of snow. It was still very dark. We couldn't see the horses, but we could hear them galloping wildly across the unfenced field. With a few muttered obscenities, the driver picked himself up and ran after the fast departing team and sleigh. What to do now? It was too cold to stand waiting, so I set off walking, following the ruts of a well-traveled trail heading east. I was half a mile from *Condor* when the mail stage flew passed me. Later, I learned the runaway horses had finally stopped when they encountered a four-foot snowdrift. I needn't have worried about missing the train. The mixed passenger freight train was two hours behind schedule and didn't crawl into *Red Deer*—a distance of forty miles—until noon.

After arriving at the station in *Red Deer*, I made my way to the Exhibition Grounds. However, before I'd actually had time to report for duty, I was met by a long-faced sentry named Hapgood who was slowly pacing back and forth. When I told him I'd enlisted, he shook his head sadly. "I'm sure sorry for you," he said in such a miserable tone, that I wondered if joining the army was such a good idea. Well, it was too late to worry my head about it. I was in the army now.

The 191st (the Battalion I'd been assigned to), was getting ready to move down to *Calgary*. No one paid much attention to me. Come to think of it, there were several more new recruits standing around with their hands in their pockets, feeling like misfits. We spent most of the evening listening to violin music rendered with patriotic zeal. The lyrics were sung by a man named Hill. I recall one of his selections was, 'We'll Never Let The Old Flag Fall.'

Early Sunday morning we went by troop-train to *Calgary* and we were happy to be moving. There were very few *Red Deer* folks at the station to see us off, and that was disappointing. We reached *Calgary* at noon and were detrained on a siding at the Victoria Barracks, at the north end of the Exhibition Grounds. I was assigned to "A" Company with three other new recruits. We were needed in "A" Company to fill vacancies caused by the rejection of four men who had to drop out for health reasons.

****

The Bigger Picture: The First World War began in 1914 and ended in 1918. It was the bloodiest conflict that had ever occurred up to that time. The Allied forces included France, Russia, Italy, USA, and Great Britain and her colonies, one of which was Canada. Their adversaries were Germany, Austria-Hungary and the Ottoman Empire. By 1917, the frontline trenches dividing the opposing forces zigzagged about 1,000 kilometres across Belgium and northern France.

In the summer of 1917, when William Lees arrived at the front, things were not going well for the Allies. Russia was in no position to supply troops; she was in the midst of her own revolution. Help from the United States was limited as her military was not well organized; and German U-boats were blocking the Allied supply chain. Into this challenging state of affairs, came Canadian soldiers whose exuberance, energy, and resiliency changed the course of the war.

****

CHAPTER THREE

Now life began anew—I was a soldier. For the first few days, a dozen of us new recruits were given elementary squad drill by a middle-aged, lance-corporal, who had spent two years in the Boer War. One helpful hint he gave us was to turn our socks inside out every time we put them on. This aired our socks and kept our feet drier. It was great advice for combating trench foot when we were on the front line later on.

Before the week was out, a dozen of us new fellows were paraded downtown for a further medical examination. After that, we were issued new Oliver equipment, consisting of a waist belt, an eighty-round cartridge pouch, bayonet frog, pint water bottle and carrier, knapsack, mess tins and canvas cover and a set of braces with shoulder yoke to carry the weight. Having received the necessities, I mailed my civilian clothes back to my sister who was now in *Edmonton*.

The meals at Victoria Barracks were quite good, far better than any meals we had after that. Regardless, some of the men grumbled: "Too much liver; not enough bacon," and so on. Some wanted coffee instead of the regular tea. Others groused because the stew (also known as mulligan), appeared too often. To put it mildly, many of the complaints were expressed in language hot enough to blister your ears.

There was also griping about Colonel Cruickshank who shipped leftover food to his farm for pig feed. Some said the colonel purposely ordered more food than necessary in order to fatten his pigs. On two occasions, a Texan by the name of Pearce and I were mess orderlies, so we heard every complaint under the sun.

About this time, our platoon had a pay parade—our first—and I received $6.20. After the pay parade, we had our first route march. The weather was bitterly cold, possibly the coldest day of the year. We were equipped with greatcoats, belts, and bayonets and marched to St. George's Island Park.

After lunch on Sunday, February 4th, 1917, I decided to go for a walk and set off alone, towards a distant ridge in the Manchester Subdivision. I wanted to get a good view of the mountains—and did. Presently, I was overtaken by a man in a car. He offered me a ride, saying he was going out to Sam Brogden's farm, five miles southwest of Midnapore to look at some cattle. Not wanting to miss a chance to see the country where I first worked when I came to Canada, I gladly accepted the ride.

On the walk back to *Calgary,* I was overtaken by a young Englishman on horseback. He was driving 20 head of horses into *Calgary* on the McLeod Trail. I accompanied him on foot for at least half an hour, walking and talking about the war and the Kaiser. Then, when another car came along, I was able to catch a ride back to the barracks. There were few cars on the roads in those days, so I counted myself lucky to get a ride the greater part of both ways.

By this time, we new recruits had settled down to the regular routine of the training camp with plenty of squad drill: slope arms, order arms, stand at ease. We soon began to feel like real soldiers. One day we had a bath parade to the YMCA followed by a route march. This involved the whole battalion marching to a point six miles southwest of what was then *Calgary's* city limits.

On route marches, uncomfortable boots and tight puttees (leg wraps to protect the legs from barbed wire or other sharp

24

objects), were often the cause of men falling out of line. The extended marches in Mewata Park soon became monotonous. However, when Sergeant Major Davidson was in charge, we had to look smart. The Sergeant Major had been in the Imperial Army in the South African War and stood for no nonsense. Any man who made a mistake promptly got a bawling out with such dry wit that on two occasions I couldn't keep a straight face. Of course, the Sergeant Major saw me grinning. Then I, too, got the full force of his biting sarcasm.

One feature of army life in the city was the downtown picket when we were marched to the police headquarters. There we were divided into two sections. One section of men would be paraded down the streets for two hours, then they would change over with the men who'd been resting. At midnight we returned to our barracks and had a lunch of tea, bread and jam, before retiring.

Once, I was assigned to serve as an orderly at an officers' banquet with two other recruits. Before noon, we had to set up two long tables and one short one, then lay them with table clothes, napkins and highly polished silverware. When the meal was ready, the officers filed into the mess hall in full uniform and ceremoniously took their places at the table, while we three orderlies acted as waiters. We orderlies had to watch our 'Ps and Qs during the meal, but after the officers retired, we gave ourselves of the best, before washing dishes and polishing silver.

One evening I was pleasantly surprised to run into John Waters at the barracks. He was the young well-educated Sarcee Indian I met earlier when I first came to Canada in 1912. Originally, his name had been "Head Above Water," a name the missionaries changed to John Waters. He asked after my brother, John, and I told him John was now overseas with the 196th Battalion.

On February 15th, 1917, a notice was pinned up in the mess hall. It was advertising for men to volunteer for an overseas draft. A few of the men had lame excuses for not wanting to go overseas. However, by allowing the men to suit themselves, the recruiting officers soon had more than the required number of volunteers. I was one of the first to volunteer, and after enduring another medical, I was among the two-hundred and fifty men chosen to go overseas. We marched in batches of sixty per day to the M.O. for vaccinations in the arm and inoculations in the chest. It was not the greatest experience a fellow could have. We were given the next day off to recuperate, a good idea since most of us were so sore we could barely stand up straight. This was repeated every four days until we were considered capable of throwing off any kind of foreign germs.

I looked forward to Sundays. After church parade, we were free to leave the barracks, and I took long walks over the hills to the west of the city. I never tired of seeing the miles of rolling foothills and snow-capped mountains. This was Alberta, my adopted home and I was always intrigued by the immense beauty of her varying landscapes.

On the first of March, a final one-and-a-half-day leave was granted. This, together with company drills in Mewata Park and longer route marches, was a good indication the long-awaited sea voyage was close at hand.

And so it was that at eight o'clock on March 10th, 1917, the first overseas draft of the 191st Battalion entrained at the CPR station. The battalion band was on hand along with a large crowd of friends and relatives. Among the folks waving goodbye was my sister, Evelyne. I'm sure we both had similar lumps in our throat as the train moved away from the station destined for *Halifax, Nova Scotia*.

When the waving and cheering subsided, my gaze went back to the mountains quickly disappearing in the west and I wondered if I'd ever see them again. As it turned out, it would be twenty-seven months before I was back in Alberta.

We made a half-hour stop at *Medicine Hat.* Although the streets were muddy, we troops were given a march through town. Back on the train, the townspeople handed us magazines and cigarettes, and then we were moving again. The train consisted of what was called "colonist cars," with tables set up between the seats during the day. In the evening, the seats reclined to form bunks, and each man was given two blankets to curl up in. During the night we passed through *Saskatchewan,* then stopped at *Brandon, Manitoba* where we marched up a muddy, slushy hillside to get the kinks out of our backs. At *Winnipeg,* we had the good fortune of seeing CPR engine #1 at the back of the station. We also had a good reception from the people of *Winnipeg.* The platform was crowded with well-wishers, handing edibles and magazines up to the men on the train. And a flock of young ladies was there, too, shaking as many hands as they could reach.

It was a cold, dismal day when we arrived in *Fort William.* Here, we were marched halfway to *Port Arthur* and back. On reaching *Schreiber*, we troops were given some physical exercises and drill. This took place right on the station platform. Again, in *Sudbury, Ontario,* we had a ten-minute march up and down the station platform. We then embarked and traveled along the Ottawa River for two hours. The sun was setting, and the scenery was magnificent in the waning sunlight, especially the beautiful, steep wooded banks on the *Quebec* side of the river.

We passed *Ottawa* sometime during the night, and at daybreak, the troop train arrived at a railway siding in *Montreal*. Later, we crossed the Victoria Bridge over the St. Lawrence River and had another short route march somewhere near the Chaudiere River. The Quebec Bridge had fallen into the river some months before, and the center span was still missing when we saw it. That night, after leaving *Quebec*, I woke from a restless sleep to find the train was moving backward. I could see there was a problem as we were supposed to be ascending a long hill. Obviously, the thirty coaches, loaded with troops, were too heavy for the engine to pull the grade. After two unsuccessful attempts, a booster engine came to our rescue and the steep incline was finally scaled with much fanfare. Shortly afterward we arrived in *Moncton* and were given a route march in the rain.

We reached *Halifax* on Saturday evening, March 15th, after traveling five days, more or less continuously. It had been a tiring trip, so the men slept in the next day.

I was up and around before most of the fellows. Nothing was happening, so I climbed on top of the coach to get a better view of the harbour. Then, since none of the officers were up yet to give orders, a Cree Indian named Makokis and I decided to walk down to the docks to where the cruiser, Niobe, was anchored. We climbed a wall to get to the ship, then after looking it over, we continued walking until we came to a guardhouse where a sergeant and some troops were on duty. Were we in trouble then! The sergeant was definitely not pleased to see us. He said we were lucky not to have been shot when we climbed over the wall. To make his point, he put us in the guardroom and sent for a corporal to come to get us.

Meanwhile, back at the train, some of the troops had been able to get hard liquor, and many of them had taken on far more than they could handle. A corporal, lately from the south of England, was in a state of delirium tremors, throwing everything he could lay his hands on at imaginary purple monkeys. Another drunken soldier was staggering through the coach, breaking one window after another, while a third was vomiting down the aisle. Further down the hall two separate brawls had broken out.

Needless to say, there was no point sticking around, so once again I went sightseeing with another recruit. This time we walked to the Old Fort and enjoyed a bit of history before returning to the train. It was evident we should have stayed away longer because when we boarded the train there was still no sign of law and order.

Late afternoon the following day, we were loaded onto a transport boat and moved slowly down the harbour. Then our transport lay at anchor while a second boat took on more men. We could see crowds of spectators on the shore. Now and then we could hear them shouting as the wind carried their voices over the water.

A man was standing on the skyline, signalling with flags. Our ship's signaller replied, and at six in the evening of March 28th, 1917, we joined a convoy consisting of six ships, and headed out to sea. Our battalion, the 191st, was traveling on *the* Saxonia, with the Lapland on our right side.

I stood, watching the coastline until it disappeared below the horizon, then went below deck. As you can imagine, being part of a convoy was a new experience for me and added to the excitement of being at sea.

The first day on the ocean was fine, warm and relatively uneventful; the subsequent day, March 31st, the weather was similar. I was on guard duty that day for two hours, standing beside an iron door with eight heavy, bolt-type locks on four sides. When shut, this door sealed off a watertight compartment. If the ship was torpedoed, orders were to shut the door, bolt it and get up on deck, immediately. That afternoon, the gunners on the Sutherland began practice shooting and smoke screening. At first, some of us thought the gunners were firing at a submarine. March 1917 was the month of the heaviest shipping losses in the entire war, so naturally there were a few tense moments until we realized it was only a practice drill.

One day a funnelled steamer was sighted on the northern horizon, so the cruiser, the Calgarian, cut over to intercept it. It turned out the steamer was an allied ship and the Calgarian soon returned to take her place in the convoy.

The men's quarters were crowded, rations were poor, but two fellows who had been on kitchen duty, pilfered some raw turnips and onions. We ate these with our rations along with the ship biscuits that were issued. "Iron rations" we called the biscuits because they were hard as rocks. They were dry, had a stale taste, and some had weevils in them. No doubt they'd been stored in the ship's hold for several months—if not years.

On the fourth day out it was windy. The sea had been lovely and calm on the previous days, but now the wind churned the sea into huge waves of dark rolling water. Most of the men were seasick, myself included. I didn't feel like eating, choosing instead to hang my head over the rail at various intervals throughout the day.

By the seventh day, the Saxonia—our troop transport—had fallen four miles behind the rest of the convoy. The other ships were now only distant specks on the horizon. Six patrol boats arrived the following day. Their job was to escort the convoy, and they circled the troop ships at high speeds. One of the patrol boats, #410, came within hailing distance of the Saxonia, so we were able to exchange greetings. That afternoon the convoy was split up. The Saxonia and Southerland sailed in a northerly direction, while the other ships angled west. Our ship's course was very erratic;

sometimes the Southerland appeared to our left, at other times to our right.

From this point on, bugles sounded at four o'clock every afternoon to summon an emergency lifeboat drill. These drills were necessary as German submarines were scouting the coastal waters around Britain. All troops and seamen were ordered to "fall in" beside their assigned lifeboat. This didn't always go as smoothly as it should have. On one occasion I found myself standing beside a single lifeboat with thirty-two other men. Had it been a genuine emergency, an overcrowding blunder like this would certainly have had fatal results. After that lifejackets had to be worn at all times.

On Good Friday, April 6th, 1917, land was sighted to the north, this being the south coast of Ireland. Land was continuously in sight for the remainder of the day. However, by dusk we watched the headlands slowly receding in the west. There was no tacking now; our course was set. Occasionally we passed between the coast and other troopships. The coast appeared to be about ten miles away and, as we moved parallel to land, we sighted large numbers of porpoises.

At seven o'clock the next morning we caught our first glimpse of the Welsh Mountains. Their summits were covered with snow, reminding me of the first range of mountains west of *Rocky Mountain House*. It was almost nine o'clock in the morning when the troopships anchored near the mouth of the *Mersey River*. A dense fog hovered over the water—no land was in sight—but I could see a few other ships anchored nearby. Evidently, we were being protected from enemy submarines by a ridge of sandbanks somewhere out there in the fog.

Our ship, the Saxonia, swung around with the tide, making a complete ninety-degree turn as it was anchored at one side only.

Over on the Southerland, Afro-American troops could be seen, and music from their band drifted over to us as we stood on the deck of the Saxonia. After a while the fog lifted slightly and then we were able to make out low-lying sand hills skirting the north side of the river, and *Brighton Tower* which was less than a mile away.

Two minesweepers were combing the water. These were rather ordinary-looking boats with a wire net slung between them to locate explosives dropped by German torpedoes. Sometime later, tugboats arrived, swinging wide to accommodate the minesweepers, then coming straight towards the Sutherland and Saxonia. Their job was to take us to *New Brighton*, so very soon we were transferred from the Sutherland to the tugboats and taken up the *Mersey River*. I was impressed by the miles of docks and the hundreds of masts of ships lining the river.

CHAPTER FOUR

On docking at *New Brighton*, we men were lined up, two deep, on the pier with our kit bags and marched a short distance to a railway platform where we were crowded into ancient railway carriages, ten men in each compartment. When we were settled as comfortably as possible, we were issued cold rations of bread and bully beef. This we ate as the train slowly shunted along, crossing under the river through a mile-long tunnel. By this time, darkness had fallen. Blinds on the coach window had to be lowered to avoid lights being seen by enemy aircraft.

Since there was nothing to see, I found myself dozing off. However, by the time we reached *Birmingham*, I was fully awake. So, with several other fellows, I got off the train and bought buns and tea in the station restaurant.

During the night we passed through *Oxford, Reading, Guildford,* and *Milford.* Then, just at daybreak, we arrived at *Witley* and here we detrained. It was April 8th, 1917, a cool, hazy Easter Sunday. We troops were then lined up in the station yard, opposite the Railway Hotel, and marched down a country lane. On either side, homes, gardens and woods appeared neat and clean. English sparrows and skylarks were singing just as they had when I left England five years before. The grass had the same lush greenness, and the English gardens were just as lovely as ever. How these scenes reminded me of walks with my parents, sisters and brother, John. It felt good to be in familiar territory, again. We marched two miles down a winding road, and as we approached *Liphook*, I was impressed by the fine-looking residences. The road crossed a small stream and cool air closed in on us as the mist rose from the water.

33

Very soon, we reached Bramshott Segregation Camp, an army camp where troops arriving from overseas were quarantined. This was a protective measure to prevent infectious diseases from spreading into England from abroad.

We troops spent the remainder of the day getting settled in bell tents, eight men to a tent. Later, I was sent to the cook-kitchen to serve as an orderly until noon. After that, I ate my meal with the rest of the troops. Lunch that day was soup. We lined up two or three times for refills, but the soup was watery and did nothing to quench our hunger. We began to think we were purposely being starved to see if any disease would break out among us.

Picture of army bell tents from William Lees's collection.

Snow was falling the next day, which didn't postpone a compulsory route march to the little village of Hammer. However, after the men complained long and hard about short rations, the officers took pity on us. The next day, we were given a choice: we could stay in camp or march to *Bramshott Chase (or Common)* in *Hampshire.*

Hoping to see something of the area, I chose the latter only to find the lanes around *Bramshott* were lined with five-foot earthen banks, topped with willow bushes. Needless to say, it was difficult to see much of anything. Another day we marched along a sunken road which was ten feet below the normal lay of the land. The topmost branches of very old trees towered above us. We were crossing a railway bridge, when suddenly an express train came barrelling down the tracks. We barely had time to clear the track when it flashed by, scaring the living daylights out of those of us in the rear.

In the following days, we had daily route marches to *Greyshott Common.* To get to the Common we took a yellow road across the valley and returned to camp via Portsmouth Road. Both roads were rough, so we were played-out by the end of the day.

In those days, airplanes were a rare sight, so that when an airplane passed over camp during supper hour one evening, all of the troops dashed out to see it. It seems strange to think we actually did that—now air traffic is commonplace.

One Sunday we had a medical inspection, not a great experience since we were lined up, naked, in unheated tents. It was freezing cold! None of us could keep our teeth from chattering. Not long after that, I was detailed to the kitchen with a couple of other men. Our job was to unload boxes of provisions. Since we'd run out of money to buy food at the canteen, we nicked some bread and sausages at the end of our shift. Later that night, the men in my tent fried the sausage on a Tommy-cooker. To hungry men, a sausage sandwich was a real treat. Another time, we made short work of the half mess-tin of honey that I brought back after a stint as Mess Orderly. When we were broke and hungry, which was most of the time, all we could think of was "food." I used to hang around the canteen hoping a friendly soldier would buy some eats and be generous enough to share them.

On one of the few afternoons the sun shone, we marched past *Hindhead* to *Beacon Hill.* At 895 feet above sea level, *Beacon Hill* is the highest point in the area. An interesting feature of this extraordinary hill is the London-Portsmouth road which runs in a semicircle around a deep depression at the foot of the hill. This is known locally as the Devil's Punch Bowl. There is also an incredible view of *London* from the top of Beacon Hill.

The farms in this area were not prosperous. On one farm, two men were ploughing a very small field with a walking-plough pulled by a single horse. The first man led the horse while the second man walked behind. I couldn't help thinking how different this was from farming in Canada where fields and machinery are much larger. Another day on the way back from a long march, a tractor frightened a horse that was pulling a lady in a two-wheeled trap. The horse jumped to the side, knocking Captain Jackson over and breaking his leg.

While we were at the camp at *Bramshott*, most of our time was spent marching, often in the rain. Then, as other battalions arrived in camp, such as the 210 Infantry Battalion from *Moose Jaw*, our men helped set up their tents. I personally took my turn on quarantine pickets to keep the new arrivals in line. I also served on 'water pickets' to make sure no water was wasted. Occasionally we had rifle practice, but it was generally believed that we were just putting in time since we weren't getting enough food for hard drills.

Payday was on April 26th, 1917 and I received an English pound. The next day, we were issued a six-day leave. This was much appreciated as it meant I could go by train to visit my relatives in *Lancashire*. But before leaving for the north, I spent a day in London enjoying the sights: walking across the Westminster Bridge, seeing the rows of factories and warehouses that lined the north side of the Thames, and Victoria embankment that lay to the south. It was a cold damp day, but I continued east along the embankment, until I passed Cleopatra's Needle and could see the distant Tower Bridge.

At seven o'clock in the morning of the 28th, I left London's Euston Station on a northbound train. My first stop was *Liverpool*. Leaving the train, I wandered over to the first eatery I could find, a scruffy-looking joint on a side street. All it offered was French-fries, bread, butter and tea. Since I was hungry enough to eat anything, I downed a plate of greasy fries and boarded a bus to *Southport*.

It had been five years since I lived in the county of Lancashire with its ancient dry-stone walls and dark hawthorn hedges. What good memories returned as I made my way to my former hometown. Although, it had been some time since any of my relatives lived in *Southport*, it still felt like home. While there, I had a barbershop shave. Then feeling well turned out, I took a tram to Botanic Gardens where I wandered aimlessly among huge beds of flowers. Later I sat on a park bench and watched swans gliding in a lazy stream while ducks and pigeons scrambled to catch the crumbs, I tossed to them.

Botanic Gardens, Southport, credit A. Gray

BATHING POOL, SOUTHPORT.

Southport Pier circa 1917: From William Lees's Postcard file

I also walked along the Promenade, the way I'd done as a teenager, then made my way to Southport's Pier. The oldest iron pier and second-longest in Great Britain, it spans a distance of 1,108 metres. In 1917, the Southport Pier Tramway carried passengers to the end of the pier, so I rode out and walked back.

On Marine Drive, I saw a blind man cranking a hand organ. This made me smile, when I realized he was the very same organ-grinder I'd seen on the day I left Southport, five years before. While in *Southport*, I also spent a day trekking through the sand hills and the smaller communes of *Hallsail, Ormskirk,* and *Shirdley Hill*, all familiar places, bringing to mind the carefree days of my youth.

On April 30, 1917, I took the ten o'clock train from *Southport* to *Manchester*, arriving in *Blackley* before noon to stay with Auntie Jennie. She was delighted to see me, having hosted Brother John only a short time before. She lived at 104 Old Road, near a large chemical factory which filled her house with evil-smelling fumes whenever the wind blew in her direction. Auntie Jennie's nephew, my cousin Harry, came by after dinner, so Harry and I walked to Heaton Park. On other days, Harry and I trudged to Queen's Park and Bogart Hole Clough. While in *Blackley*, I dropped in to see my aunt Sarah. She, too, rolled out the welcome mat, serving delicious cake fresh from the oven and soothing chilled wine. Before my leave was up, I also visited other relatives including three uncles who were working diligently in wartime garden allotments.

Soon it was time to return to army-life, so I took the train from *Southport* to *London*, arriving in the city as hungry as ever. At the platform, there were other 191st men. We had only enough time for a quick snack before our train left for camp. We'd hoped to get a bite to eat when we got to camp, but nothing doing! We had to wait until breakfast the following morning. After breakfast we had a sixteen-mile route march—loaded down with packs and rifles—to a military site at *Borden*. This was a practice march to see how fast we troops could be deployed in an emergency. The next day we were given time to rest, however the next week we trained in earnest. It was physical training in the mornings, followed by bayonet training, rifle instruction using dummy cartridges, visual training, and map reading. There was one instructor for every ten men.

Concert parties often came out from *London* to entertain the troops and were much appreciated. One Saturday Henry Lauder arrived, and what a treat that was. I was on fire picket with one other soldier at the time, but hearing that Lauder was at the next camp, I went over anyway. Between two and three thousand men had gathered to watch the show. I was lucky to hear Henry Lauder sing one of his own songs, "The Laddies Who Fought and Won." But before the show ended, the bugle blew and the Sergeant gave orders for the men of the 21st reserve (mine), to report to their billets. This was accompanied by groans as the men were lined up. Nevertheless, this was an emergency! All of us were given a shovel or a pick, loaded in transport trucks, and driven to a fire north of *Hindhead*. A strong wind was blowing, and a few civilians were futilely trying to put out a fire that had started in long grass and overgrown gorse. Our men quickly spread out across the hillside and the fire was soon extinguished.

When there was a pause between training, I enjoyed finding a buddy to go sight-seeing with. Hiking was always a welcome relief from camp life. Due to daily roll call when we answered, "Here" to our surnames, we got into the habit of calling each other by surnames only. (*First names of soldiers are seldom mentioned in this book.*)

One Sunday, a friend of mine, Private Tompkins (from my camp), and I walked five miles to *Haslemere* in Surrey. We had been told the great poet, Lord Alfred Tennyson, lived for a time in Aldworth Manor in *Haslemere*, and both Tompkins and I were anxious to see the manor for ourselves.

Clouds drifted in and it started to rain before we reached the town. We kept on in the drizzle and soon came to a privately owned museum where we were met by the curator, an elderly man wearing a Norfolk Suit with knee britches and long grey stockings. He told us he had travelled extensively in *Africa*, and we believed him. The museum cases were crammed full of African curios: spears, shields, headdresses, and necklaces made from alligator teeth. We caught a fleeting glance of Aldworth Manor, and then it was time to return to camp. I liked Private Tompkins. He was a great companion. (Sadly, he and I were together in the frontlines on January 8th, 1918, when he was killed by shrapnel).

On this particular day in May 1917, when Tompkins and I reported what we'd seen in *Haslemere*, it perked the interest of other fellows, so a week later, I returned to *Haslemere* with Turner, Peat, and Swabey. Turner and Peat dropped off at the museum and Swabey and I made our way to St. Christopher's Tearoom where we had a light lunch and played jumble puzzles for the rest of the afternoon.

Another time, a buddy named Eby and I scouted the area for different types of vegetation. Eby had been a horticulturist back home in Ontario and I was happy to help him set up his camera to photograph a variety of flowering plants.

During this time, my unit was moved into "B" Company. The evening we moved, three friends, Batemna, Easson, and Hollingshead, walked over from Witley Camp where they were billeted, and we talked and joked all evening. Shortly after this, "B" Company was taken out on "night patrol," from 9 pm to 12 pm. We were divided into two sections for a mock battle. My section was assigned to holding trenches like those in the front line. Then we sent out scouts to see where the other section (the designated enemy), was located. It happened to be the darkest night of the month, and both sides lost track of one another. So, nothing was accomplished. The next night a sham fight was arranged, and we were told the enemy was in bushes ahead of us. Orders were given: "Prepare to advance; Advance; Take cover," and then "Five rounds rapid-fire," and so on until we got into the bushes. This drill was also a failure because it was too dark to see where we were going.

By way of diversion we were engaged in filling sandbags and putting up barbed wire entanglements. During this time the discipline was lax, which suited me fine, but when the Duke of Connaught paid us (the 21st Reserve), a visit, it was back to formalities.

Sometime later, when taking part in the obstacle course, I sprained my left ankle. It was extremely painful and got me out of marching and squad drill for several days. Thankfully, before leaving England, the sprain mended enough to able to walk to *Petersfield* in Hampshire, a seven-hour roundtrip.

When we had pay parade, we were lined up outside the paymaster's office and paid in alphabetical order. The sergeant began by calling the names of soldiers whose surnames began with the letter "A", then "B" and so on. As their turn came up, the men presented their playbooks, had them stamped, and collected their pay in English pounds and shillings. After being paid, there was always a race to the canteen. Unfortunately, the men whose surnames began with letters at the end of the alphabet, such as Tompkins, Wilson, and Young, often found the canteen was sold out of necessities—cigarettes and cookies—before they got paid. Incidentally, while in the army, I developed the habit of smoking one cigarette after every meal, so I knew that going without a fag was a nail-biter.

We resumed our daily drills along with various menial tasks, and then in early June we had our first .303 rifle practice with live ammunition. Two days later, we were put through a gas chamber for the first time. For this, we used gas helmets and had a small box respirator. The gas chamber was underground and as the men went down the steps, single file, we passed under a wet blanket and into the gas. Other wet blankets covered the sides of the trench. On taking off our respirators we were surprised to find our brass buttons and buckles were badly tarnished. Of course, this meant more polishing, something I hated with a passion. When it came time for inspection, a soldier who made an especially good job of shining his boots and buttons was usually asked to step forward as an example for the rest of us to follow suit. We were also expected to shave everyday. Most of the time I got away with shaving every other day.

One Saturday, we were marched to Longmoor Ranges (Hampshire), eight miles away. The day was hot, dry, and dusty and the last two miles my old foot injury began to act up. I was in a good deal of pain when we finally reached our destination. Here we were billeted in bell tents, six men to a tent and rested the remainder of the day.

Although the next day was Sunday, there was no church parade. However, the colonel spoke to us, finishing up by telling us we'd be at this location for a week, and while we were here he advised us to visit an ancient Norman church in *Selborne*, Hampshire. By this time, my foot was feeling much better, so several others and I hiked the two miles over to *Selborne* through a lovely green wooded area. The rector of the church invited us inside, and we Canadians were impressed by what we saw. The church had been built sometime before 1200. Four tombstones were set in the floor, covered with ornamental brass which bore ancient inscriptions. Supports for the roof of the church were round stone columns, three feet in diameter. Magnificent paintings by a *Selborne* artist adorned the walls. We were told that various art collectors had offered astronomical sums of money for the paintings, yet not a single offer was accepted. We wrote our names in the visitor book. Then, after thanking the rector, we went to find food. After walking through *Empshott,* we came to *Liss* (Hampshire) where we ate supper in the open air. It was much like a picnic, an amiable get-together that drew us closer as a team.

In the days following, we put in a week of target practicing on the ranges. About twenty-five targets were set side by side. They were four feet square, and each target was double and worked on a swivel. Bullet holes were patched up on one side while the other side was being shot at. An attendant would signal the shot with a black and white disc on the end of a long pole, bull's-eye, inner ring, magpie, outer ring, or washout. There was a line of sandbags every hundred yards across the range, from 600 yards down to 100 yards, and we were given bull's-eye, group fire, rapid-fire, and silhouette tests. All went according to plans, but patching bullet holes while being fired at was a nerve-wracking business.

We were all very happy at the Longmoor Range. The weather was sunny and warm with beautiful sunsets and there was just enough rain at nights to keep the dust down. On the final day on the ranges, I was graded First Class Marksman with a score of 96 points. I recall the afternoon was very hot and we sweated buckets on our march back to the camp at *Bramshott*. The day after that, we had medical inspection—naked of course; then it was clothing parade followed by a route march. It was a difficult march in full marching order, and soon my old ankle injury pained me something fierce.

On Wednesday the 20th of June 1917, a reinforcement draft composed mostly of 191st Battalion (my outfit), was put on short notice. Something exciting was in the wind and we soon discovered what it was. Some of the 191st Battalion were going to France immediately. Names of the men selected to go were called out, and my name happened to be on the list. We were told to turn in our blankets, palliase (a bag that could be used as a mattress when filled with straw or other material), and rifles before marching to the railway siding at *Liphook* (Hampshire). Several hours later we were detrained at *Folkstone* in Kent on the southern coast. Here we were billeted in a row of empty mansions not far from the waterfront; the whole street having been taken over by the armed forces.

And so the time had come—the time most of us had been waiting for. We, who were previously in the 191st Battalion, were being placed in another unknown battalion and going to be shipped to the frontlines in France. We were considered well-trained. We had endured gruelling marches and tedious drills; we'd conquered difficult obstacle courses; we'd achieved high marks in bayonet and rifle practices with live ammunition. Most importantly we had developed comradely, a sense of being one of a proud army of Canadians. We imagined we were ready to fight for King and country, but did we suspect the terrible conditions we'd be fighting in? I think not! We were green as grass with no idea of what we'd signed up for. One thing for sure, we were about to find out.

****

The Bigger Picture: The Battle of Messines (June 7-14, 1917), was an attack by the British Second Army on the German front near the village of Messines in West Flanders, Belgium. During the battle the British detonated 19 mines, causing the largest non-nuclear explosions of all times. Yet, the British still struggled to hold their ground and were badly in need of Canadian assistance.

On June 26-29, In the middle of a heavy thunderstorm, the Allies kicked off a major attack, successfully driving German troops back. In this advance the 4th Canadian Division secured Eleu and most of Avion. Meanwhile the 3rd Canadian Division established a strong front on the Avion-Arleux Road.

****

CHAPTER FIVE

At 4 pm on June 21st, 1917, we were away. We still hadn't been told which battalion we were going to join. All we knew for sure was we were leaving England for France. We stood at dockside, waiting impatiently for other soldiers to be unloaded, before we could board a troopship. Some of the soldiers disembarking were going on leave, but most were wounded men. Seeing such a large contingent of soldiers on stretchers and columns of walking wounded, was very sobering. After leaving the harbour, the ship followed the coastline where the White Cliffs of Dover stretched for miles like great ivory wings. I craned my neck to catch a glimpse of the disappearing shoreline, but the deck was too crowded to see much.

Torpedo destroyers bobbed on either side of our ship. Their job was to guard the troop carrier in case of attack from enemy torpedoes below. Above us, a surveillance balloon scouted the water for enemy subs. For the next half-hour while navigating the English Channel, we weren't able to see land, and wouldn't until just before we reached the *Boulogne* harbour in the north of France. When we arrived at *Boulogne,* our ship then turned and backed alongside the pier where a small crowd of Frenchmen greeted us with outstretched hands and sober eyes. Their clothing was noticeably different from that worn in Canada or England. The French boys wore peaked caps and frocks, and the men wore baggy trousers.

By late afternoon, we (former members of the 191st Battalion), were lined up on the wharf and given full marching orders. Full marching orders meaning we carried a full kit bag and haversack, bayonet, rifle, entrenchment tool, greatcoat, mess tin, along with a web harness to which everything else was attached.

We then moved past the docks over a tidal creek and marched through the town of *Boulogne*. Several peddlers tagged along beside us, selling oranges and chocolates. After buying some of their wares, we discovered we'd been given French coins in change. This money was quite a novelty to Canadians. None of us had ever seen French coins before, so we passed them around for inspection. Later, we stopped to rest on a hill and encountered a different set of peddlers. They were selling watery 'vin blanc' for one franc a bottle. All too soon our rest period was over. We continued on for three more kilometres (about two miles, uphill). Finally, we reached St. Martins Rest Camp, and were billeted in very crowded huts and then given meal tickets for the cook kitchen and canteen.

At nine the next morning, we were joined by approximately one hundred New Zealand Red Cross men for a 30-kilo march. The French countryside was unlike anything I'd seen in Canada or Great Britain. Everything was different: cars, houses, clothing, and curious-looking government-operated railway stations. Our first rest stop that day was near a small stream that wound its way through the valley bottoms. In spite of the absence of fences, the landscape resembled a patchwork quilt with fields of green, yellow, and wide furrows of warm brown. Wayside crucifixes could be seen at every kilo. We noticed that civilians passing by the crucifixes never failed to cross themselves.

At noon we stopped at a rest camp, stacked our equipment, piled arms, and filed into long tents to eat. After lunch, when we got our marching orders, it was pouring rain, so we had to wrap our groundsheets around us to keep as dry as possible. We crossed a railroad track twice and passed through several small villages.

About this time, one of our men began to sing "There's A Long, Long Trail A Winding," and we all joined in.

After climbing a steep hill in the late afternoon, we were surprised to catch sight of the open sea. The day had been so overcast we were under the impression we were marching east when in actual fact we'd been traveling south along the coastline. As we marched on, the weather began to clear, and we soon realized we were approaching an estuary of a large river. This turned out to be the *Canche River* that runs through a curved belt of chalk downs before flowing into the English Channel. Strangely, it is no more than a thin trickle at low tide and a mile-wide flood at high tide.

Beyond the river, we saw a large army camp far in the distance. This camp, known to the soldiers as the 'bullring,' stretched more than two kilometres along the main road. Eventually, we arrived at the camp only to find the Canadian section was on a low hill at the far end. By the time we staggered to where we were billeted in tents, we were thoroughly exhausted. This 30 km stint was the hardest day's march we'd had so far, and my left foot was throbbing like a bad toothache.

The town of *Etaples* lay between the camp and the *Canche River*, but troops weren't allowed to go into town without a pass. Only two men per company were given passes. I wanted to see as much of the country as possible, so was disappointed when I didn't get either one of the coveted passes. Sentries were posted along the railway track (a busy artery from *Paris* to *Boulogne*), making it impossible to slip over to *Estaples* without being caught. Since hiking for pleasure was limited at this camp, any hike was memorable. I recall walking down an approved country lane one Sunday with a Montenegrin soldier by the name of Jugish. He drew my attention to deep ridges cut into the lower edges of fields. He said this was caused by ploughing in the same direction for hundreds of years, a method practiced in his country.

We soldiers of the former 191st Battalion trained at this camp for two weeks, while waiting to be called up as reinforcements for some unknown depleted battalion. During this time, we were issued with small box respirators and given further gas tests. We were marched to the bullring every day where we built reinforcements, cribbed trenches, filled sandbags, and sawed quantities of 2" X 4" and 2" X 6" lumber of different lengths. We practiced digging in with entrenching tools, a chore that had to be accomplished in five minutes or less while lying flat on our bellies and pushing dirt in front of us like rodents.

We also had lectures on judging distances as well as bayonet fighting. For the latter, we used dummies made of sticks that were arranged on frames. We were given two live bombs for grenade-throwing practice. Another day was spent in trenches. These trenches were constructed to the exact measurements of those in the frontline on which we'd soon be deployed. We were even taught to perform the German goose step as a disciplinary exercise. We not only resented this exercise, but openly scoffed at having to imitate the enemy.

Sunday, July 1st, 1917: This was Dominion Day (fifty years since the Canadian Confederation of 1867), so we Canadians were allowed to spend the afternoon racing, jumping, playing baseball and tug-of-war. Another thing (unique to Canadian troops) was each morning bugle calls started with the first four notes of O' Canada, to distinguish us from other units.

When we were at the 'bullring' one day, we had a visit from Queen Mary, and I was privileged to see her at a distance.

After we'd been at this camp for two weeks, we had several parades. The last one was a pay parade. This was the first time we were actually paid in French money. Afterward, the Camp Commandant spoke to us, telling us about the challenging conditions at the frontlines. No doubt he wanted to prepare us for the horrible state of affairs we'd soon be experiencing firsthand.

We of the former 191st were also told that our unit was an "Entrenching Battalion." This meant we were being held in readiness. When the need arose, we'd be attached to an infantry battalion to make up for casualties. (I think we already knew that.) We then got our marching orders and were given ration sacks. Next, we were loaded into French freight cars marked *40 homes ou 8 chevaux* (forty men or eight horses).

Shortly after our troop train shunted down the tracks, we came upon the town of *Montreuil*. Here we saw an ancient high-walled château on a hill to the south. This was the British Army Headquarters. The next place of importance was *Saint Pol,* a railway junction with a large freight yard. We were sidetracked at *Saint Pol* for an hour and this gave us time to eat our lunch of hardtack and bully beef. While we were eating some hungry-looking children discovered we had food and raced up, begging for something to eat, so we tossed them some cans of meat.

It was soon time to move on to the coal mining town of *Calonne* where our unit was billeted in a garret over a bakeshop. Whenever someone went upstairs, dust floated down to settle in the open bead-mixer, but the cook didn't seem to mind. The day had been cloudy and dull with short spells of rain, and a nearby river was in flood.

When a flight of over twenty planes flew overhead, the men eagerly raced out to see them. This was the first time we'd seen so many planes. It was also the first time we heard the distant rumble of gunfire. Before dark, I took a walk around town and was shocked to see how many houses had been destroyed by shellfire. Doors and windows had been blown out and some were missing roofs. Taking in the devastation, it was plain to see we were nearing the war zone.

The next morning at eight, we left *Calonne* with hordes of children running beside us, anxious to sell oranges and chocolates. Although our march led up a very steep hill, the kiddies climbed right along with us. When we stopped to catch our breath, I stepped out of line to buy chocolates from them. In the scramble to get back in line, I didn't get my packsack on properly. So, the march was incredibly uncomfortable, even painful, until we arrived at the next rest stop and I was able to balance the load.

I was marching beside a fellow by the name of Leiper from *Bolton, England,* who was born in Scotland and still carried a broad ancestral accent. He said he'd already been at the front, had been wounded, and was now heading back up the line for a second tour of duty. We passed through *Divion* but didn't stop. Later, Leiper pointed out *Bruay*, to the north, where he had spent the previous Christmas at a rest camp.

After leaving *Divion*, the road dropped into a long narrow valley. And then we came upon the small picturesque village of *Houdain* which lay along the lower side of a densely forested hill. Here we came to a halt, piled our arms, took off our equipment, and ate the lunch we'd packed with us. Then, at bugle call, we resumed our march on a dusty road. After passing a sign that read 16 kilos to Arras, we marched on, finally reaching our destination, *Gauchin-Légal*, at four in the afternoon. My platoon was billeted in a hut that had once been used by the French troops. There was no bedding of any kind—not even a forkful of straw to lay our weary heads on. Cracks in the wall allowed a cold wind to whistle through the hut, so we spent an extremely uncomfortable night.

We stayed a second night at *Gauchin-Légal*. Not wanting to spend another night in a draughty hut, several of us located a barn full of hay. We were ecstatic. Finally, we could roll up in sweet smelling hay and get a good night's sleep. However, that was not to be. The barn door faced the farmer's house and he spotted us. While we went back to get our equipment, he raced to the barn and locked the door. What a disappointment!

Yet I had no intention of catching pneumonia in a dilapidated shack. I watched the other fellows drag themselves back to the huts. Then I climbed into the rafters of the farmer's implement shed and bedded down in some flax bundles that were stored up there. The next morning when my buddies complained about their lack of sleep, I smugly told them about my comfy bed in the implement shed. At first, I thought they were going to hit me in the mouth, but they were too tired to scrap. They only shook their heads and one of them countered with, "You lucky son-of-a-gun! 'Wish we'd joined you."

After a very poor breakfast, we were on the march again, going to the top of a hill where an army water tank was sitting. Here we filled our water bottles with good clear water. On the previous march to *Gauchin-Légal* we'd found a well, but the water was unfit to drink. From this point, we marched along a perfectly straight road. Presently, after an hour of steady marching, we came to *Estrée-Gauchy* (northern France). At that time the town was only a small collection of farm homes and outbuildings which extended for about a kilo on either side of the road. We continued on, crossing over two rail lines. One was a metre-gauge line. The other, a two-foot gauge light railway, was strictly a military line laid down by the army engineers.

At noon we arrived at *Villers-au-Bois,* a small village that stirs up sad memories of my brother John. Yet, on this particular July day, I had no idea where John was, let alone that he was less than a kilo away.

On the day we marched into *Villers*, I was focussed on the quaint little town itself I found it to be much the same as *Estrée-Gauchy* in that it was a cluster of farm homes facing the main road. Behind the houses were cobble stone yards approximately 100 feet square, and beyond the paved yards were barnyards with manure piles and cesspools. The stench from these was quite strong, especially when the farmer decided to haul manure while we ate our noon rations.

At *Villers*, we were billeted in barns and other farm buildings where bunk beds were three-deep and fashioned from chicken wire. We had few complaints at this camp. We had our own camp kitchen and meals were slightly improved. For example, the daily onslaught of mulligan was finished off with a special treat of plum or apple jam. (Yes, we considered jam a treat.)

Villers-au-Bois is situated 11 kilometres northwest of *Arras*. From here we could see Vimy Ridge, the range of hills taken almost single-handedly by Canadian troops, on April 9th to April 12th, 1917. The French and British attempts to take Vimy had failed, but the Canadians' method of the 'creeping barrage' won the day. The Battle of Vimy Ridge was Canada's most celebrated military victory and occurred only two and a half months before I came on the scene. I discovered later my brother, John, fought in the frontlines of this historic battle.

William was billeted in a barn across the road from this home.
Picture taken of Gertrude and Jane Lees on a return trip in 1935

At *Villers*, we were only a kilometre behind the Allied observation balloons, so we could see them plainly. We could also
see German balloons which looked like tiny dots in the distance.
One afternoon, we saw an enemy plane heading for one of our balloons. The plane circled the balloon. Shots were fired; the balloon
burst into flames and disappeared in a trail of smoke. We could see
two observers floating down in their parachutes as the German
plane turned and headed back across the line. This was the first real
bit of warfare my unit had seen, so it was talked about for some
time. An anti-aircraft battery was located nearby and every now
and then we could hear the men firing at some unseen target. This
was yet another indication we were near the front lines.

While we waited to be sent to the front, we were kept busy with physical training and bayonet fighting. One afternoon we were ordered to make accommodations for 260 men using any materials we could salvage from the immediate area. So, we roamed the countryside, picking up anything that was movable like boards, poles, wire, and tin sheets. After the regular route marches, this scavenging expedition was considered a picnic and enjoyed by all. Sorry to say, the temporary shelter project was finished the next day, so it was back to more mundane tasks.

One Monday we were marched over to where the Forestry Corps had established a sawmill. Here logs were brought in on a tramway to be sawn into lumber. Forestry men did the sawing while we of the armed forces were divided into groups: one group loaded the small cars; another pushed the loaded cars to the mill, and another threw the slabs back after the logs were sawn. This lumber was all heavy duty to be used in the war effort as trench supports, gun emplacements, etc. We spent a week working at the sawmill. Every day, after breakfast we'd fall-in on the roadway where roll call was taken. Then, wearing our caps, tunics, trousers but no puttees (leg wraps), we'd march over muddy roads to the sawmill where jobs were alternated.

Far more men were on hand than were needed at the sawmill, so some of us devised ways to entertain ourselves until our turn came to be put to work. I remember how four other men and I shoved a truck up a long slope. Then we hopped on and coasted down from the top. The idea was to jump off at the bottom just before the truck left the rails and ploughed into a bank.

We often had free time on Sundays. And since I noticed twin towers over to the southwest, I decided to hike over and check them out. I'd been told these were the ruins of *Mont-Saint-Éloi Abbey* which was built in the 7th century. Having been heavily shelled in 1915, their height had been reduced from 53 meters to 44 meters and were all that was left of the once beautiful old abbey. I tried to climb up through the debris by way of a winding staircase, but the upper portion of the towers had been destroyed, so I couldn't reach the top. After climbing as high as possible, I cut my name in one of the stone walls and enjoyed the scenery. From the tower, there was a splendid view of the whole district. The surrounding topsoil appeared to be a reddish coloured clay. I could see *Lens* to the northeast and *Arras* to the southeast as well as a standard gauge railway leading to *Mont-St-Éloi Railway Station*. I could also make out the little village of *Ecoivres* as well as the *Scarpe River* which wound its way toward Arras. There were wooded areas to the south and southeast, but to the far east, the country had been heavily damaged by shell fire and had a bleak, bare, dusty appearance.

The next Sunday we weren't able to do anything constructive on account of heavy rain. But, after supper when the rain stopped, Private Wilkinson and I decided to hike to *Vimy ridge*. We found out after we returned that we men weren't allowed up on *Vimy*, but by then it was too late; we'd already been.

We walked to *Vimy Ridge* by way of *Carency* and just below the ridge we saw a battery of three of our own 5.9s, camouflaged to escape observation. One gun was firing several rounds at a distant enemy objective. There were signs of recent fighting on the ridge. In fact, the whole ridge was churned up into deep craters and shell holes. There was no vegetation of any kind to be seen, only broken dugouts, barbed wire, and sandbags.

SHELL CRATER - VIMY RIDGE

VIMY RIDGE

Pictures from William Lees's personal files, credit Doreen Thomsen

Burial parties hadn't taken out the dead. It gave us quite a jolt to see booted feet protruding from collapsed trenches. We came to an elaborately varnished cross on a twenty-foot-square plot, a memorial to officers and men of a Canadian Division who lost their lives in April in the *Battle of Vimy Ridge*.

We also saw smoke rising from factory chimneys on the eastern horizon, possibly in the large town of *Douai.* Eventually, we made our way back to camp. On returning to our billets we were told— in no uncertain terms—*Vimy Ridge* was definitely out of bounds.

The battlefield as seen by William Lees (1917-1919)

****

The Bigger Picture: The Battle of Vimy Ridge April 9ᵗʰ to 12ᵗʰ was part of the Battle of Arras. The fight for this ridge of high ground was the first occasion the four divisions of the Canadian Expeditionary Force had fought together. William Lees knew his kid brother had been transferred from the 196ᵗʰ Battalion to the 46ᵗʰ Battalion (South Saskatchewan), Canadian Expeditionary Force. The 46ᵗʰ battalion, otherwise named "The Suicide Battalion" (John Lees's battalion), played an important part of capturing Vimy Ridge at an extremely high cost, losing 1,433 men with 3,484 men wounded—a casualty rate of 91.5 percent in 27 months. As William surveyed Vimy Ridge he was not yet aware of John's whereabouts or the terrible struggles his kid brother had faced on this very same piece of ground.

****

The day after Private Wilkinson and I climbed up Vimy Ridge was a Monday, and we found ourselves behind a sawmill, learning how to make brush faggots used in road building. First the bush was slashed into 12-foot lengths and then bound with wire. These were fashioned into long bundles. The wire at both ends was made tight by using two poles to crush the bundles into tight bales.

By Tuesday all the lumber had been cut, so we were put to work tearing the sawmill down: removing the motor and ripping lumber from the shed. Next, we packed everything to *Château d'Acqand* where we set up the mill in another part of the woods. We made a rushed job of cleaning up the sawmill site because a nasty thunderstorm was bearing down on us. We barely finished when a heavy deluge forced us to take shelter.

On Wednesday morning, another fellow and I were detailed to take a team of horses and go for water to *Mont-Saint-Éloi* where a spring gushed from the foot of *Vimy Ridge*. The water from here was also pumped to soldiers up the line as well as to several nearby villages. After we returned with the water, we were sent back to *Mont-Saint-Éloi* with several other men to shovel coal.

The next day, a party from our Entrenchment Battalion—myself included—were sent to clean out trenches that had been shelled on the east side of the ridge. We wore metal helmets and carried gas masks. When we reached *Souches,* we were turned over to the Royal Engineers. The Sergeant warned us to keep low and proceed single file over the ridge. Three enemy guns were firing salvos, shelling a wooded area half a kilometre away. They shelled it furiously for a while. Then suddenly we were enveloped in an ominous silence—the kind of nervous stillness that comes before a storm.

We finally got to a deserted section of trench, where each man was given a pick and shovel and ordered to clean about ten feet of trench. There was water in the section of trench I was working in. This meant digging a ditch to let the water drain before I could begin cleaning-up. It was an exceptionally hot day, and a battery of our own 5.9s began shooting shells directly over our heads. We could hear the swish, swish as the shells whizzed by at close range. This alone was enough to give any man a case of nervous jitters, especially so, when a few of our men had already been wounded or killed by friendly fire.

The following day we returned to the same line of trenches where we found ourselves eating lunch opposite several dead enemy soldiers who'd been laid out in a dugout. Not a pleasant sight!

Later that afternoon, I investigated another flooded dugout and found a bundle of papers, including air photographs of the surrounding country. When I passed them on to our commander, he said these maps and photos had been taken by the enemy and would be most useful for future Allied planning.

CHAPTER SIX

What little mail we got—if we got it at all—was censored and slow to reach us. In a letter received from Brother John, he grumbled about not receiving the parcel Evelyne sent him for Christmas, 1916. He said, *"We get next to no mail. I never received the parcel you said you sent me, either. No need to worry—my pals shared the sweets they got for Christmas, so I made out well enough."*

With mail being irregular, I hadn't heard from John for some time and had been wondering where he was and how he was faring after his transfer to what was dubbed the 'Suicide Battalion.' Our father was also concerned about him and in a letter from *Onehunga* dated January 13, 1917, Dad wrote, *"I received yours telling of John's visit to Southport and Manchester. I certainly hope he will get through the war safely. He certainly has seen a lot of things."*

Some time later in a letter now yellow and tattered with age, John wrote, *"Last night a shell made a sizable hole in our trench, so my partner and I intend to cover it over and stay there tonight. They say, 'lightening never strikes twice in the same spot.' Hopefully, the same can be said of Heiny shells."*

John followed this up by adding, *"Several of the men I came over with have been killed and I wonder what is still to come. I think of you and the homestead often and if I make it through..."* (the page is torn.)

I'd been told John's battalion, the 46th (South Saskatchewan) CEF was located somewhere near *Château-de-la-Haie.* So one afternoon, when I was free—no parades or anything—I decided to walk over to where he was billeted. On the way, I met two 46th men and asked them if they knew John Lees. They said they did, before adding that John had been killed in action in May. They pointed to *Villers-au-Bois Cemetery* and suggested I search among the military graves there. This was only a few minutes walk in the direction I was going, so I was soon looking at a relatively new graveyard with mounds of dirt and very little grass. The largest part was taken up with French graves decorated with artificial flowers. Beyond the French section were British headstones, and farther still the Canadians section which contained about 30 graves. On each grave was a wooden cross marked with a tin strip bearing the name, serial number, and name of the fallen soldier. In the center of the graves was my brother's. He was 21 years old, a newly trained teacher with dreams of a bright future. Words alone can not describe my feeling of loss.

John

Duplicate

ATTESTATION PAPER.

No. 911406

Folio.

CANADIAN OVER-SEAS EXPEDITIONARY FORCE..

QUESTIONS TO BE PUT BEFORE ATTESTATION.

(ANSWERS.)

1. What is your surname?	Lees
1a. What are your Christian names?	John Edward.
1b. What is your present address?	Carlos Alta.
2. In what Town, Township or Parish, and in what Country were you born?	Southport Lancs, England
3. What is the name of your next-of-kin?	Thomas William Lees.
4. What is the address of your next-of-kin?	Onehunga New Zealand.
4a. What is the relationship of your next-of-kin?	Father
5. What is the date of your birth?	Nov 5 1895
6. What is your Trade or Calling?	Teacher
7. Are you married?	No
8. Are you willing to be vaccinated or re-vaccinated and inoculated?	yes
9. Do you now belong to the Active Militia?	No
10. Have you ever served in any Military Force? If so, state particulars of former Service.	No
11. Do you understand the nature and terms of your engagement?	yes
12. Are you willing to be attested to serve in the CANADIAN OVER-SEAS EXPEDITIONARY FORCE?	yes

DECLARATION TO BE MADE BY MAN ON ATTESTATION.

I, J E Lee , do solemnly declare that the above are answers made by me to the above questions and that they are true, and that I am willing to fulfil the engagements by me now made, and I hereby engage and agree to serve in the Canadian Over-Seas Expeditionary Force, and to be attached to any arm of the service therein, for the term of one year, or during the war now existing between Great Britain and Germany should that war last longer than one year, and for six months after the termination of that war provided His Majesty should so long require my services, or until legally discharged.

Date APR 7 - 1916   191   John E Lees (Signature of Recruit)

J A Sinclair (Signature of Witness)

OATH TO BE TAKEN BY MAN ON ATTESTATION.

I, John E G Lee , do make Oath, that I will be faithful and bear true Allegiance to His Majesty King George the Fifth, His Heirs and Successors, and that I will as in duty bound honestly and faithfully defend His Majesty, His Heirs and Successors, in Person, Crown and Dignity, against all enemies, and will observe and obey all orders of His Majesty, His Heirs and Successors, and of all the Generals and Officers set over me. So help me God.

Date APR 7 - 1916   191   John E Lees (Signature of Recruit)

J A Sinclair (Signature of Witness)

CERTIFICATE OF MAGISTRATE.

The Recruit above-named was cautioned by me that if he made any false answer to any of the above questions he would be liable to be punished as provided in the Army Act.

The above questions were then read to the Recruit in my presence.

I have taken care that he understands each question, and that his answer to each question has been duly entered as replied to, and the said Recruit has made and signed the declaration and taken the oath before me, at EDMONTON ALBERTA, this APR 7 - 1916 of APR 7 - 1916 191 .

Cecil E Rice (Signature of Justice)

M. F. W. 33.
6003...-4 -14.
H. Q. 1775-36-841

65

Description of *J. E. Lees* on Enlistment.

Apparent Age *22* years *7* months.
(To be determined according to the instructions given in the Regulations for Army Medical Services.)

Distinctive marks, and marks indicating congenital peculiarities or previous disease.

(Should the Medical Officer be of opinion that the recruit has served before, he will, unless the man acknowledges to any previous service, attach a slip to that effect, for the information of the Approving Officer).

Height .... *5* ft. *8* ins.

Chest measurement.
Girth when fully expanded .... *42* ins.
Range of expansion .... *5* ins.

Complexion .... *Light*

Eyes .... *Brown*

Hair .... *"*

Religious denominations.
Church of England .... *yes*
Presbyterian ....
Methodist ....
Baptist or Congregationalist ....
Roman Catholic ....
Jewish ....
Other denominations ....
(Denomination to be stated.)

CERTIFICATE OF MEDICAL EXAMINATION.

I have examined the above-named Recruit and find that he does not present any of the causes of rejection specified in the Regulations for Army Medical Services.

He can see at the required distance with either eye ; his heart and lungs are healthy ; he has the free use of his joints and limbs, and he declares that he is not subject to fits of any description.

I consider him* .... *fit* .... for the Canadian Over-Seas Expeditionary Force.

Date .... *April* .... 1916.

Place .... *Edmt* ....

.... *Medical Officer.*

*Insert here "fit" or "unfit."

NOTE.—Should the Medical Officer consider the Recruit unfit, he will fill in the foregoing Certificate only in the case of those who have been attested, and will briefly state below the cause of unfitness :—

....
....
....
....
....

CERTIFICATE OF OFFICER COMMANDING UNIT.

.... *J. E. Lees* .... having been finally approved and inspected by me this day, and his Name, Age, Date of Attestation, and every prescribed particular having been recorded, I certify that I am satisfied with the correctness of this Attestation.

.... CHAIRMAN .... (Signature of Officer)
COMMITTEE ON ORGANIZATION
196TH BATTALION

Date .... APR 1 4 1916 .... 191 .

Author's note:

From what my father told me, he did not know of his brother's death previous to his hike to Villers-au-Bois Cemetery—a hike that took place in mid July or the beginning of August 1917. Certainly, his father, Thomas Lees in Onehunga, New Zealand received a telegraph via way of NEW ZEALAND POST OFFICE TELEGRAPH on May 19th, 1917, saying, "Regret exceedingly inform you 911406 Private John Edward Lees 46 Bn Canadian killed on May 3rd."

Why did the news not reach my father in 2 ½ months? To hear of John's death by chance would certainly have been a shocking discovery.

In Memory of

Private

John Edward Lees

911406, 46th Bn., Canadian Infantry who died on 03 May 1917 Age 21

Brother of William Lees, of Carlos, Alberta. Native of Southport, Lancs, England. Educated at Stettler High School and Camrose Normal School.

Remembered with Honour
Villers Station Cemetery, Villers-Au-Bois

Commemorated in perpetuity by
the Commonwealth War Graves Commission

68

*Picture taken of the University Corps on the steps of
Camrose Normal School*

*Front row: (l -r) Pte John Edward Lees, Pte Pike,
Pte Linton, Pte Fawdry*

*Middle row: Pte M'Cool, Pte Baker, Pte Bagnall,
Pte Scott, Pte McIntyre*

*Back row: Pte Riley, Pte Barlow,
Sergeant Major Brison, Lieutenant McKenzie*

Pte Gudgeon, Pte Wilkie, Pte Sangster

Following the visit to my brother's grave, it rained steadily for several days. During this time, ten men including myself were chosen to conduct a rehearsal for a military funeral. It was slow march, reverse arms, and fire. Since this was not an actual burial, the graves were dug to a depth of three feet. It rained during the whole ceremony. Regardless, the chaplain read a few brief lines, then it was present arms and the bugler blew the last post. We then fired three rounds using blank cartridges. As I recall, one of the men got confused and fired only one round.

About this time, we were marched to *Château-de-La Haie.* In peacetime this château was a country residence but was now transformed into the Corps Headquarters. The estate consisted of several hundred acres of forest, and it was in this heavily treed area that the bow huts were erected to keep them hidden from enemy observation.

From William Lees's personal files

5   BATT. HEADQUARTERS
CHATEAN DE LA HAIE

The whole area was militarized with officers' homes, soldiers' billets, field guns, and even carrier pigeons. The St. Lawrence camp was also located there, a camp where troops returning from the frontlines could rest. The most appreciated amenities were showers, but the water was rationed. It was a sprinkle, then half a minute for soaping, another sprinkle, and then the water was turned off. Men then exchanged their clothes for clean fumigated shirts etc. Before we put the clean garments on, we had to give them a good shake to remove the dead lice.

Some mornings we'd have a squad drill, bayonet practice and occasionally we'd play football. The whole front was relatively quiet at this time with only an occasional burst of shellfire.

We were sent back to the old sawmill site one day to load fascines (bundles of brush used to shore up trenches or roadways). Another night we were sent up to *Givenchy* on the northeast slope of Vimy Ridge to manually carry timbers to the forward area for rebuilding dugouts and trenches. The first night out, the timbers didn't come, so we had to go back a second night to take the timbers from the dump to the gun replacements higher up on the ridge. We worked in total darkness as no lights were allowed. The only guide was a white tapeline which led through barbed wire entanglements. This tape wound along an old trench, through shell holes and mine craters. It took two men to carry one timber. Each of us made three trips up the ridge that night, struggling through an unforgiving maze with over two feet of mud lapping around our puttees. Periodically, we could see 'very lights' on the horizon. We knew these lights were being used at the front, so they gave us some sense of direction.

Returning from one of the night trips, some of us got a ride on a limber wagon that was taking a load of dead soldiers out to a burial ground. The lories were under fire as they picked up the bodies and body parts, so they piled the deceased into the wagon like so many cords of wood. There was no time for niceties along the front line—load the cadavers and get away from the shellfire as fast as possible. Seeing the dead treated in such a disrespectful manner would be enough to make a clergyman faint, but it had to be this way. Anyway, we were too tired to refuse a ride, so after one sad glance at the dead, we climbed on board and were dropped off at our bow tents.

Another night, we carried trench mats forward along Clucas Communication Trench, a trench that was originally built by the enemy. Germany troops had been routed from this trench a short time ago and were now shelling a coal mine near *Givenchy*—much too close for comfort.

One hot August afternoon, our unit (under full marching order), left *Villers-au-Bois* and went to *Ross Camp*. This camp consisted of a series of dugouts in a ravine which split the side of a hill known as the *Notre Dame de Lorette Ridge*. The dugouts were repulsive, makeshift affairs in an advanced state of disrepair. In places, they were roofed with rusty sheet iron. A steep bank behind the dugouts was the only protection we had from German observation balloons.

The second afternoon we were there, nothing appeared to be happening, so I climbed a nearby hill and discovered a patch of edible nuts. After eating my fill, I sat down and wrote a letter to my sister Evelyne. Although I could still hear gunfire, this hilly, tree-covered spot was serene with crickets chirping, and larks soaring overhead.

However, on August 20th, 1917, there was a heavy bombardment going on in the frontline area, but neither our Allies nor the enemy gained an inch of ground. In case the enemy broke through, we, in the reserve, concentrated on fixing trenches for defence of the ridge: digging them deeper, placing trench mats, and packing sandbags. It was dirty work.

Two other fellows and I were so filthy one morning, we grabbed our towels and headed for a shell hole behind the camp to take a bath. It was scarcely worth the effort. The water was freezing cold, despite the hot day, and the clear looking water turned dark brown after we stirred the mud up. Let's just say we came out as grubby as we went in.

The next day my platoon was given the task of taking up German trench mats, carrying them forward, and laying them down in new trenches. Our job was well underway when a high-ranking officer passed by and stopped us, saying the old trenches were still serviceable, so the mats were to be left in their original position. Such was army life when every officer had a different view of what needed to be done.

After six days we prepared to leave Ross Camp. By this time, we'd made our camp more liveable, so we were sorry to go. It was a nice spot even if the food was poor and in short supply. We returned to *Villers-au-Bois*, had a clothing parade and I received new boots, puttees, and socks at the Quartermaster's store. Some of the men deliberately tore holes in the knees of their pants and puttees in order to get new ones. The QM store was housed in a farmer's barn which had recently been damaged by shell fire. In the barnyard were a number of 16-inch, chalk cubes. They'd obviously been salvaged from shelled buildings. Some unknown soldiers had carved their battalion badges on eight of the cubes. Every badge was different, and all showed excellent workmanship.

After the clothing parade, we were marched to the Divisional School at *Château-de-la Haie.* Nothing was happening on the next Sunday, so Griffin and I walked over to *Gouy Servin,* a small farm village consisting of about a dozen houses and a few barns built of chalk blocks. After walking another kilometre, we came to *Servin* where we saw a large château, an army hut, a YMCA building, and a church with a spire that had been badly damaged by shellfire. As a brisk wind was gaining momentum, we didn't linger but headed back to camp. The following day we were divided into classes for instruction on the use of the Lewis gun. Other than that, all else appeared to be routine. Yet, there was a sense of expectancy in the air. Something was about to happen.

****

*The Bigger Picture: The Vickers machinegun was used exten-
sively by the Allied forces in the early part of the First World War.
However, the Lewis machinegun was smaller, only 28 lbs. Easier
to set up and light enough to be carried by hand, the Lewis machinegun was used by Canadians in the latter part of the war.
(William Lees used the Lewis machinegun.)*

The Lewis Machinegun

*August 15 and August 25, 1917, The Battle of Hill 70 was
the first major battle fought by Canadian troops under a Canadian Commander, Arthur Currie. The battle took place between
the Canadian Corps and four divisions of the German 6th Army,
on the outskirts of Lens, France. During this time, German forces
fired an estimated 15,000 to 20,000 shells of gas into Canadian
trenches. In early September, William Lees experienced a similar
poison gas attack by enemy forces. The Canadians with an army
of 100,000, suffered some 9,200 casualties in the ten days between 15th and 25th of August. Nevertheless, the battle is regarded
as an impressive victory for our Canadian troops.*

****

CHAPTER SEVEN

August 30th, 1917, the day before my twenty-fourth birthday, our unit was issued full marching orders and went about one half-mile to another camp in the woods of *Château-de-la-Haie*. Here we were divided between different companies, and I landed in the 13 Platoon, 'D' Company of the 50th Battalion (4th Division).

On Sunday, September 2nd, 1917, the 50th Battalion left the Château for the frontlines. I'd been in the armed forces for nine months from the end of December 1916 to September 1917. It had been months of manual labour: hauling logs, digging ditches, repairing trenches, assembling shelters along with exhaustive marches, and military training. At last, I was going over the top.

It was a hot day and we felt the full force of the sun. We had next to no time to catch our breath until we got to *Souchez*, which was late in the afternoon. After sunset, we proceeded single file via the Clucas trench, up the line to the support trenches. (we were ordered to walk 'single file' in order to cut the risks of large clusters of soldiers being killed in one explosion.) Clucas Trench began on the east side of *Vimy* and zigzagged across open country toward *Avion*. It was likely constructed by the Germans when they held the Ridge at an earlier time.

That night, the front was reasonably quiet with very little shellfire going on. However, the second night was different. We were sent as a work party along the line to the left. The night was pitch-black with the ground muddy and littered with broken trench hardware. It would have been easier to build a new trench instead of repairing this old one, but orders were orders. So, we carried on.

I was the lead man and was being extremely cautious, moving along the dark trench one wary step at a time, wondering what we were going to find when we turned the next corner. Suddenly, enemy guns opened fire. A flash of light lit up the trench and I saw a misty cloud descending. I yelled "*GAS!*" at the top of my lungs. And then I was fumbling with my gas mask with trembling fingers. This was my first serious brush with lethal danger. I have to admit I was afraid, but within a minute or two, I overcame the sensation and never again felt that same degree of panic.

The bombardment was a mixture of whiz-bangs and gas shells which continued for several minutes. So, the officer in charge passed the word down the line for us to pick up our tools and clear out. Unfortunately, my division had already suffered two deaths in that attack.

We hustled along, best we could, but it was very dark. Moments later we realized we were lost. There was nothing to do but backtrack until we reached the support trenches. The dugouts on this part of the line had been German and were shored up on the wrong side for our troops. Knowing we were exposed to the enemy, we couldn't have lights of any kind, otherwise we'd be observed by German balloons: no candles to find our way or cigarettes to calm our nerves.

Finally, we made it to the Red Trench where we stayed (as a work party), for four days, before being sent back to reserve trenches. The Red Trench lay between the *Arras* road and *Vimy* and was a series of dugouts, twenty steps deep and very cold and damp.

One day after sunset, we were taken up Beaver Trench on a work party, and here we stayed doing pick and shovel work until

1:00 am. We had taken all of our equipment (full marching order), so we were loaded down to the hilt. On getting to the road we marched four abreast toward *Gouy-Servin,* a distance of about 14 kilometres. We had begun marching in an orderly fashion, but we didn't end up that way. We were so tired our unit came straggling into camp, more like a mob of slum-bums than an orderly regiment of Canadian soldiers. In fact, many of the men didn't make it into camp at all but slept out on the road all night.

It was 5:00 am when I reached *Gouy-Servin.* It was just coming daylight and I was the seventh man in. After retrieving my mess tin, I headed for the cook kitchen for mulligan, potatoes, and tea, but I was in too much pain to eat much. As I puffed on my after-dinner cigarette, my shoulders throbbed, and my feet felt like I'd been walking on hot coals. The word 'tired' wasn't nearly strong enough for the exhaustion that had set in.

We rested the next day. The day after that, we had inspection by the Commanding General and the day after that we had inspection by the Brigadier General. The troops (myself included), were annoyed at having to spit and polish, then stand loaded down with heavy equipment while the big brass, who had no such worries, took their own sweet time chatting up a storm.

That evening there was a Divisional Concert Party at *Château-de-la-Haie*, a two-kilometre walk, but before leaving for the concert, three other men and I were assigned to clean out a ditch— town fatigue they called it. Consequently, we missed most of the entertainment. When the following Sunday rolled around, we had a church parade followed by a pay parade in which I received 15 francs. A few days later several men, including myself were detailed to dig latrines.

We left *Gouy-Servin* on a very hot day. We marched past *Carency* and *Ablain-St-Nazaire* and on to six new bow huts near *Souchez* where we were billeted. We liked this place very well and here we stayed for about a week.

Then something that seemed important at the time, occurred. We were marched back to *Château-de-la Haie* where we were shown a ground plan of a sector of the frontlines. An offensive was being planned with the objective being to drive the German troops out of Lens. The 50th Battalion's objective (near Avion), was marked out on the ground with white tape. We were to memorize our positions on the map, so when the time came, we would know exactly where we were going and what we were expected to do. However, this offensive did not materialize in 1917. For some unknown reason, the plans had to be put on hold until 1918.

Shortly after this, I was among a number of troops who were issued new gas masks. Following that, we marched to a rifle range that lay between *Villers-au-Bois* and *Château-de-la-Haie.* We were taken the long way around via *Bertonval Wood* near *Mont-St Eloi.* When we finally got to the rifle range, I was assigned to the butt party. There was one butt man to each target. At a signal to the man firing, it was my job as a butt man, to hold a disk (on the end a long rod), over the actual target. For example, if a bull's eye was required, I held the disk over the center of the large circle. If the man was firing at a moving target, then I moved the disk up and down or to the outer ring (a magpie). I don't mind saying, it took nerve to stand in front of a man firing at the disk I was holding. I only hoped he didn't sneeze. Before leaving for camp that day, we were given a cup of hot tea. It had been a very chilly day and we appreciated a hot drink.

The next day was September 25th, 1917 and I went with a work party to *Souchez.* The village had been severely damaged by recent shellfire, so the civilians had been evacuated. We dug ditches to drain water off the road where necessary. The same night our work party went up the *Lens-Arras* road to fill in shell holes and remove bricks which had fallen from damaged walls. We were working at a point where the Columbia Communication trench crossed the Lens-Arras road. This was between *Avion* and *La Collette,* a kilo closer to *Lens* than we were to *La Collette.* There was a narrow valley to the west with a railway embankment built of white chalk running down the middle of the valley. This embankment had been shelled quite heavily at a point where the Columbia Trench cut across the bank.

On September 26th, instead of having a formal parade after our noon meal, the Company Commander, Captain Frazer, addressed the troops. He was a short, thick-set Scotsman with a dark complexion who had risen up through the ranks the hard way. He told us what the immediate plans were for our Battalion, saying we were to take over a section of the *Avion* front, going by way of Clucas trench and on past *La Coulette.*

Later, while we were eating our regular mulligan, bread, and tea, an enemy fighter plane suddenly appeared and shot down one of our observation balloons located over *Meuville-St-Vaast.* It took a full minute before the balloon burst into flames and then there was only a thin column of smoke to mark the place where the balloon had been. Yet the 'Heiny" kept coming right over where we of the 50th were spread out eating our meal. Looking up, I could see the black German insignia under the plane's wings. Our machineguns were quickly set up. We were able to get off a few rounds, but as far as we knew both plane and pilot got away unscathed.

At dusk, our battalion set off for the march up the line. It had been very windy all afternoon, but the wind died down at sunset, leaving the sky a glorious mass of red, yellow, and gold as we marched over *Vimy Ridge*.

On the northwest side of the ridge, the engineers had built a new road in a terraced formation over four or five fields with a rise of eight or ten feet separating each field. This area had been so heavily trenched and shelled, it looked like large piles of sand and chalk, yet the engineers had managed to build an easy grade to the top.

After a strenuous climb carrying full gear, we were just sitting down to rest when we heard the hum and buzz of another enemy plane. The pilot was going after another balloon, the one over *Noulette*. He came in above the balloon, dived, and began shooting. About every tenth bullet was an incendiary one that lit up the sky showing the pilot where the balloon was located. The two observers who were in the balloon jumped, and when their parachutes opened, the German pilot made a quick turn and began firing at the men as they glided to the ground. We of the 50th were furious to see these poor vulnerable devils shot in midair and said so in no uncertain terms.

Just as we were using our strongest cuss words, we spotted three British planes coming out of the haze to the east. They circled, got on the enemy's tail, and shot him down. It appeared the enemy landed in a field above *Ablain St. Nazaire*, so the pilot may have survived. We of "D" Company had seen the whole affair against a night sky and talked about it for some time after.

We were in better spirits as we continued, even though we were still exposed to enemy shell fire. The road we were on had been recently constructed of 3" X 8" x 16-foot planks. And anyone on these new roads were easy targets, liable to be shot down at any time. This route took us through *Givenchy,* a badly bombed village.

We then cut across fields until we came to a road which passed the La Coulette Brewery and a brickyard. After that, it was straight up to the frontline location where we were to be on active duty.

I was one of six men to be placed at #5 post, a shallow trench. During the first night on duty, another post (#2 post, a little way down the line from me), was attacked by an enemy raiding party. Two Canadians were killed, and one was wounded. One of the dead was Private Lucas, a friend of mine. He and I had come over from Calgary together.

On the second night at the front, all was calm at first. I had been on the firing step when my partner traded places with me at 1:00 am. No sooner had I dozed off, than I was jolted out of my sleep by the sound of hand-grenade explosions and rifle fire. My partner shouted, "Come on! Come on!" We quickly headed down the trench toward #6 post with other men of our section. However, by the time we got to #6 post, we found the enemy raiders had been driven back to their own lines across No Man's Land. My partner and I returned to our post. You can be sure we both stayed awake the rest of the night.

On the third night out, I was on the firing step at #5 post, looking towards some bushes in No Man's Land. It was quite dark, but I thought I could see something moving from one bush to another. Sure enough, when I looked more closely there was a dull glitter followed by a dark figure moving across a gap in the bushes. I told my partner to call the corporal, while I kept watch. By the time the corporal arrived, I'd seen three more shadowy figures in the bushes. The corporal said none of our men were in that sector of No Man's Land, so what I'd seen had to be the enemy. We passed the word down the trenches not to throw any bombs until the corporal fired a shot at the leader. This would be the signal for the rest of us to start heaving grenades. Unfortunately, as we waited with our grenades at the ready, a bomb exploded near #4 post, whereupon we all started firing. At least one of the enemy was hit. We heard him shriek as well as others shouting out there. From where I crouched, I could see several dim figures fading away in the darkness. Two scouts were sent out to search for the wounded, but they found only a German rifle.

Of course, the corporal wanted to know who had thrown a bomb before he gave the signal, and Lenny at #4 post admitted he had. He said it appeared the enemy was getting within bombing distance of #5 post. However, our defence would have been more effective if Lenny had waited for the signal.

The next evening all was quiet, except for the rumble of distant gunfire. I remember squatting by my post, watching a beautiful golden sunset. I was thinking of the calm evenings I'd spent on the homestead and couldn't help wishing I was there.

By Sunday night, we knew the enemy was prowling around somewhere in No Man's Land. From all appearances it seemed they weren't anxious to venture near #4, #5 and #6 outposts again. As darkness approached, a dense fog rose in the east. It was too quiet, and we wondered what was going on over there.

We of the 50th were supposed to be relieved at 10 pm on October 1st. After a long wait, men began grumbling, but finally, two men arrived to relieve my partner and I at #5 post. We quietly told the newcomers what we knew about the trenches, how far the enemy was from #5 post (60 yards away), and what enemy activities we were aware of.

We then moved off with our section of men in single file, down the long communication trench back to the chalk pits of *Vimy Ridge,* fully aware that bombs were dropping all around us and each step could be our last. By this time, we were grubby and tired.

Walking in front of me was a rather delicate-looking fellow from the south of England. He was quiet and well-spoken, but exhausted. He couldn't keep up, so I carried his rifle while another fellow carried his packsack. I found out later, the frail little fellow was given a job as a librarian and an instructor of the French language down at the base. This was a much better fit for him.

It was 1:00 pm before we reached the chalk pits. Here the men of my section were crowded into a shallow dugout about 8 feet by10 feet. This was enclosed by a two-foot wall of sandbags with a roof of corrugated metal sheeting. The dugouts were lousy—that is to say, they were crawling with lice. As well there were rats darting over the sandbags, looking for food in a chorus of rusty squeaks. But, after wakeful days and nights in open trenches, we were glad to be undercover.

The next day saw us trying to clean up our quarters and make them comfortable enough for a proper night's sleep. However, just after sundown, we were sent out on a carrying party on a trail we called the 'Mule Track' which led to a badly shot-up civilian cemetery. While we waited for darkness, I took in the view that included all of the frontlines, from north of Hill 70 down to *Arras*. A crossroad nearby was known to the troops as 'Dead Horse Corner' and here the road branched off to *La Coulette*.

When it was dark enough to move on, we followed the road to *La Coulette* for over a kilometre, and at last, reached a narrow-gauge railway dump where army supplies had been dropped off. It was here that we picked up trench mats to be used in trenches farther up the line. While packing the mats, we moved in single file down a communication trench and through the cellars of a badly shot-up village. Then we headed up the line and deposited our loads in a trench at the front. After my partner and I dropped off our first load, we started back to get another load, but took a wrong turn in the ruins of the village and went at least a kilometre out of our way. Occasionally we could see flashes and very lights, but that didn't give us enough light to find our way coming or going. Eventually, we got back to the railway dump and were able to carry the rest of the trench mats to higher ground. Much later we returned to our dugouts, so tired we barely noticed our creepy companions—the ever-present rats and lice.

The next night we went on a pick and shovel party to a trench in the frontline, left of Clucas Trench. This had recently been shelled by enemy gunfire and was a terrible mess: pools of water, thick mud, and damaged cribbing. There were ruined buildings higher up, where we knew enemy snipers were hidden. This put us in a very dangerous position. We couldn't expose ourselves above the trenches, so we worked in a crouched position the whole night long.

No shells fell where our party was working that night or the night after. Yet we could hear a bombing raid farther down the line, as well as an occasional firing of our own big guns. Even with the lack of action, it was still two nights of miserable drudgery in heavy rain.

The rest of the battalion moved out the next day, leaving the corporal, four other men and me to stay back on sanitary fatigue. In other words, we had to clean up all the rubbish our companions left behind. This meant filling bags with trash to be packed down to burn in incinerators. It took us an hour and a half to get the job done. Then we six fixed dinner for ourselves. Our meal was what we called maconochi. It came in oval tins: meat, potatoes, vegetables and gravy, made palatable by heating the tins in boiling water. Immediately after this, we trash-collectors set out for the village of *Estree-Guachy*, about six kilometres to the rear. Each of us carried a rifle, 60 rounds of ammunition, our kit bag, a bayonet, entrenching tools, and a couple of bags of trash. We went by way of *Villers-au-Bois* and reached *Estree-Guachy* half an hour ahead of the rest of the battalion. They had kept to the road, going by *Berthonval Farm* and *Mont St. Eloi,* whereas we had cut across country. The result was we (who had the nasty clean-up job), were first in. So, we got the first choice of billets. *Estree-Guachy* was still occupied by civilians, and we chose a farmer's hay shed with three-tiered bunks made of chicken wire. As it rained so hard the next morning, the planned inspection was cancelled. Instead we had clothing parade and I received a new pair of pants.

In spite of the nasty weather, the 50th left *Estree-Guachy* that same afternoon, wrapped in groundsheets with our heads down against the wind and pelting rain. We marched downhill, through *Gauchin-Legal*, finally reaching *Château d' Olhain* where we were billeted in an old cowshed. The shed's tiled roof was intact, but large chunks of plaster had fallen out of the walls. It was anything but homey. I was wet and cold, but tired enough to sleep like a sloth in spite of the shed being overcrowded.

The rain continued through the night and into the next day, so we did nothing but stand around. There was one bright spot in the day; I received a parcel from home containing a sealed tin of Cadbury Chocolate. As the tin was the same size as our sealed rations (which were not to be opened except in emergencies), there was a chorus of, "Don't open it, Lees, or you'll be shot at dawn!" But their warnings turned to grins when I took the lid off the chocolate container and shared the contents.

We were lucky to be billeted near a small stream where we could wash-up and shave. Although cleanliness wasn't a problem at this camp, there was never enough food. Many of us lined up for seconds only to be told there was nothing left.

On the morning of October 11th, we of the 50th Battalion were on the move again. We were loaded onto old London busses. Twelve vehicles were needed to carry Company 'D'. We were none too cheerful as we were headed for the *Ypres Salient* and that salient had a very bad reputation.

We rattled along in the old busses, through *Houdain* and over the hills to *Bruay* traveling in a northerly direction through a gently rolling, wooded area. Along the way were several coal mining factories and small farms. We reached *Lillers* which was situated in a valley. Then up we went through high rolling hills and down to the flat *Flanders Plain*. After five hours on the busses, we arrived at a 'drop off' in the middle of nowhere. It was 2 pm. We were all cold, hungry, and suffering from cramps as we hadn't been able to stretch our legs on the bus. When leaving the bus, our first sight was of a dead horse that had been recently shot in the head after being wounded. Although this was an unpleasant sight, it was nothing compared to what was to come.

As soon as we'd retrieved our equipment from the busses, we were lined up and marched a kilo into *Guarbecque*, an undamaged town in the far north of France. At first, the officers in charge couldn't find our billets. We actually marched in a complete circle around the town before we found the right place. My section was billeted in a hay barn just outside of town. And the hay made a very satisfactory bed.

After we settled in, I took a walk around town. All of the houses in *Guarbecque* were painted or whitewashed, giving the town a bright, clean look. A long straight canal ran along the north side of town and was said to connect *La Bassée* with the town of *Aire*. The canal itself was more than 80 feet wide, much larger than those I'd seen in England. The barges in the canal looked to be about 20 feet wide by 100 feet long. Some were rigged out with masts and sails to take advantage of the wind. On either side of the canal were tall Lombardy poplars. The canal itself had been built with high banks to prevent flooding. At an intersection in the road, a swinging drawbridge stretched over the canal. Here an attendant operated control from a nearby cottage thus accommodating both road and canal traffic. While I was looking around, three French planes flew over and I couldn't help noticing how the markings on their wings differed from English planes.

The farmer who owned the barn I stayed in, told me he had two sons in the French army and two daughters and a son working in the nearby ammunition factory. We stayed at this farm the next day as well. My visit here may have been perfect had it not been for a certain inspection and parade. It was extremely difficult to clean up and polish our boots and buttons in a hay barn, so I decided to skip that detail. I told the sergeant I hadn't been warned in time to do any polishing. That excuse didn't tally with this sergeant who ordered me (and a few others), to go back and polish up, then return to the parade ground. He put us through a gruelling parade, and to add to our troubles it was raining.

The next day was October 13th, '17, the day the 50th left *Guarbecque*. It was full marching order (loaded down with equipment and gear), and before the day was over, we had marched 20 kilometres—a long weary march when we were packing that much weight. It was almost as long as the bus ride, two days before. We didn't pass through any towns in the morning, but around noon we came to a small place by the name of *Staples*. We didn't stop but continued on for another two hours until we were completely exhausted.

At a certain prearranged spot in the road, we were split into platoons, one platoon going in one direction, the next in another. The platoon I was with, continued along the main road. Some of the men were dropped off at a brewery for the night, while the remainder of us went farther down the road to be billeted in a barn. It was 2:30 in the afternoon before we had anything to eat. The rest of the day we were able to take it easy.

This farm was a short distance from the ancient town of *Cassel*. Perched on a high grassy hill, *Cassel* has existed since Roman times. With her whitewashed homes, she looked for all the world like a scene from a fairy tale. Four working windmills skirted the town, each having revolving canvas sails that were rolled up when not in use. The farm where my section was billeted was considered 'large' by French standards. The owner had a spacious house, several well kept outbuildings, and about thirty head of cattle. We were asked to refrain from smoking or lighting candles in the barn. That was understandable; he didn't want us to burn the place down. Madame, the farmer's wife, was very hospitable and gave us hot water for shaving.

A sixteen-year-old girl lived with the farmer and his wife. She was a refugee from the Ypres area. It was her job to milk seven cows. Three of the troops were only too happy to milk the cows for her, while I stood and watched.

When supper time came, we had to walk back to the brewery we'd passed on the way to the farm. There we had our regular fare of mulligan, rice, and tea. In the morning we were issued dry rations for the day: cheese, bacon, bread, and jam, too little to quench our hunger. The Imperial Army was stationed along the road to the brewery and had bulletins with the latest news pinned to a wagon. Real news! We Canadians were desperate for news. Hearing so little from the outside world was always a sore point with us. The Imperials also had a canteen and generously allowed us to buy cigarettes, chocolates, cookies, and jam.

October 14th was Sunday and another day of rest. I couldn't coax anyone to walk to *Cassel* with me, so I went alone. I followed a light railway track until I came to a fairly steep hill. In order to make the grade the track zigzag to the top. There was a footpath that was more direct, so I took the path to the top and soon came to a narrow, crowded street. Presently I found myself in the town center where I was immediately spotted by a military policeman (black armband with red M P letters). He made a beeline for me and asked to see my pass. Of course, I didn't have one.

"You'd better get right back to your unit!" he growled. "In any case, you're not dressed correctly."

I'd forgotten to put on my belt and bayonet which were the minimum dress code for a war zone soldier. Afterward, I learned *Cassel* was an army headquarter area and definitely out-of-bounds for us troops.

The next day was payday. I received 25 francs, but I had nowhere to spend it, so I sat down and wrote a letter to my sister, Evelyne, which I mailed on the 16th of October.

On several occasions, I noticed a dog-wheel attached to the side of a farmhouse in this northern region. The wheels were boarded up on the sides and were 7 inches in diameter and eight inches wide. A large dog would be placed in the wheel and trained to keep it moving. I was invited into a home in which a dog-wheel had been installed. So, I was able to see a shaft running from the dog-wheel outside to a butter churn inside the kitchen. It was quite the labour-saving device.

On the 17th of October, there was a Brigadier's Inspection, and we were warned beforehand to make an extra good job of cleaning and polishing our brasses. On the 18th we suffered through a long boring lecture given by Major Parry who rambled on about the 'Boch,' which was slang for the Germans. After this, we were taken on a route march to *Zuytpeene* and back. *Zuytpeene* is situated on the river *Peene* in the *Hauts-de-France*. The two most noteworthy sights along the way was a church with an extremely slender tower and members of the Army Service Corp making rope with a small hand machine.

That Saturday, Lieutenant Farmer (age about 55, tall, slim and mild-mannered), came to our platoon, pencil and notebook in hand. He was taking names of likely-looking recruits to form a separate unit. I couldn't help noticing that instead of ordering men to join, he was politely inviting men to volunteer. This impressed me, so that when he came to me, I said, "Yes," without hesitation.

****

The Bigger Picture: By October of 1917, British forces were exhausted, as were the decimated Australian and New Zealand (Anzac) troops. On October 30th, 20,000 Canadians began their assault in the Ypres sector. In a series of attacks from October 26 to November10th, 1917, the Canadians succeeded in capturing the ruins of Passchendaele, Belgium, during a violent thunderstorm. They advanced, inching from one shell crater to another, often waist deep in muddy water and exposed to constant shellfire. Suffering heavy casualties, Canadians overcame what seemed like impossible challenges to win the battle for Passchendaele.

****

CHAPTER EIGHT

All told, there were 12 men, three from each company, who vol-
unteered that day. Our duties would be carrying all food rations to
the four Companies of the Battalion during the drive on *Passchendaele.* We were given a briefing on exactly what our duties entailed,
then we gathered our full equipment and were now a separate unit
under Lieutenant Farmer.

After the briefing, we were issued with a tumpline each. A
tumpline is a strap which is attached to both ends of a heavy load.
By placing the center of the tumpline over the top of the head—not
the forehead—heavier loads can be carried as the weight is evenly
distributed down the neck and spine. (Tumplines were used extensively in the Canadian northwest.) Our tumplines were 10 feet long
leather straps, 2 inches wide in the centre, tapering to an inch both
ways. As it turned out many of our loads weren't shaped for tumpline use, so we still had to pack bulky, odd-shaped items in our
arms.

This new tumpline unit was then dispatched to the Ypres salient to get food rations to the frontline infantry. The rations were
brought forward in bags by rail or trucks from the Base to the railhead. Bags were then tied together in two's, slung over the backs
of mules and taken forward. As mules could not go closer than two
kilometres from the frontline, a rendezvous would be arranged with
the tumpliners who then carried the bags up the line. Six bags of
rations were the standard load for a mule. For tumpliners, like me,
it was four bags per man. Carrying four bags of rations was quite a

feat as we were also expected to carry our rifle, bayonet, gasmask, and kit.

On Sunday the 21st of October, we were loaded on a motor transport and driven to the Ypres Salient. We were loath to leave the farmer's accommodations as he had been good to us. And as previously stated, conditions in the Ypres Salient were known to be hellish. We took the road to the right of *Cassel Hill*, through *Steenvoorde* to *Poperinghe* which had been badly shelled. Once beautiful homes and the town's only church now lay in ruin.

Postcard William collected at Poperinghe and given to his sister.

POPERINGHE

Photo from William Lees's postcard collection. Through the Great War, Poperinghe was used by the British Army as a gateway to battle fields of the northern Ypres settlement. Much of the city was destroyed by war's end.

The farther we went, the greater were the signs of war with big guns sounding increasingly louder. As we sat cramped in the transport, I glanced at my companions. All looked shaken, and no one spoke. We didn't need to be told; this was the real McCoy—no sham battle here.

It was noon when we reached the area directly behind Ypres. Here we of the 50th were unloaded amid the deafening crash of enemy shells exploding in previously damaged buildings. Every time a shell hit, we could hear the initial bang, closely followed by the hideous screech of splintering wood and shattering glass. This one-of-a-kind noise is something I'll never forget.

A New Zealand outfit (with dusky Maoris among their ranks), was just coming off duty. They rushed past us, hell bent for leather, and piled into a transport. They weren't losing any time escaping the flying shells. On reaching Ypres' market square, word was passed back to spread out and go single file. We'd no sooner received our orders than a shell exploded around the next corner—bang, crash, and a whiff of acidic fumes filled the air.

Thirty seconds later a four-horse limber wagon with a driver riding horseback came galloping around the same corner. One horse was seriously wounded. It lost its footing and collapsed, causing a pile-up. Then two more horses appeared, their riders slumped in the saddle. We could see they were too shot up to survive. Someone called out, "You've got a good blighty!" But the wounded men were too far gone to take notice. (Blighty meant a wound serious enough to send a man back to a British hospital.)

We didn't stop. We had to keep moving through *Ypres*. Presently we passed the famous *Cloth Hall* which was seriously damaged by shellfire. Next, we came to the *Menin Gate*. Before the war, this had been the ornamental entrance to the city, now it was severely damaged like everything else in the vicinity. Directly below the main wall was a makeshift bridge over the canal; the original having been destroyed. We crossed on the bridge just as a brilliant red sun was setting, the color due to the smoke-filled air covering the city.

Cloth Hall, Ypres: Built in the 13ᵗʰ Century, Cloth Hall served as a main market for the Flemish city's prosperous cloth industry and was laid to ruin during artillery fire in WWI.

Photo credit: Canada Department of National Defence/Library Archives/PA-000314

Shortly after the sun disappeared, we were warned not to lose sight of the man ahead. After going another kilometre, we turned off the *Menin Road* and went through what had once been a grassy countryside, but at this time was a slough of mud and shell holes. We were now well into *Ypres Salient* and it appeared the enemy was directing shellfire at a crossroad in the main part of the city.

When we were in less danger, we stopped to eat the dry rations we carried with us. After we'd eaten, we set off again, this time toward the frontlines. A kilometre farther and we came to a road the enemy had shelled quite heavily. There was nothing left of the road, just wreckage: smashed trucks and ammunition wagons, splintered wood, bricks, dead horses and mules, and plenty of deep, gaping shell holes. Next, we came to a plank road which had been laid down after the original road had been destroyed. On either side of this were more dead animals. There were two big gun encampments nearby. The Germans were targeting these gun encampments, making this a very dangerous place to be. I recall a four-horse team speeding past. It was pulling a wagon, loaded with big guns.

At the next junction, we left the road and followed a duck walk named "K" track (or sometimes "II' track). The soil here was too water-logged for trenches. We were still walking single file, and now it was dark—pitch black. Shell holes filled with water were everywhere, some so deep men had drowned in them. In order to avoid them, we had to grope around with the toes of our boots, hoping to keep our feet under us and our packs from slipping.

Soon, we came to what had once been a road covered in at least four feet of unforgiving mud, and again there were unseen obstacles. Invariably, we'd stumble over these and let out an appropriate cuss word. Some distance away, a large bombardment was in progress on the left front. We couldn't distinguish if it was allied or enemy fire—likely both.

Sometime during the night, we arrived as a much-battered German "pillbox," only a half-mile from the present frontline. This pillbox was to be "D" Company's headquarters. Lieutenant Farmer told us to dig in as best we could since this chunk of 'hell' was to be our billets for awhile.

The Corporal., two other men, and I tried to fix up a six-foot shell hole to rest in. But the hole turned out to be too narrow for four men. As luck would have it, I went around the other side of a gun emplacement where Gilmore (from Lacombe), and another fellow were digging in. Since there were only two of them, they invited me to join them, which I did. After digging to a satisfactory level, we sat down to have a bite to eat: a biscuit and hardtack each, and we divided a can of bully-beef between us.

About this time, a tumpliner from "B" Company got hit by a shell fragment and needed assistance to get to a dressing station. So, the corporal. (the man I originally planned to share a dugout with) and I were detailed to take him out as a 'walking wounded.' Neither the corporal or I knew where the dressing station was, so it took us at least half an hour, wading around in muck, wire, and shell holes before we finally located it.

While we waited for the dressing station to take the wounded soldier in, the corporal and I had a lengthy conversation. He told me that he came overseas with the 50th Battalion two years before. He'd been wounded once, and spoke despondently, saying he didn't think he'd ever see Canada again. Unfortunately, he was correct.

I'd barely got back to my dugout when I received word a mule train had arrived at the ration dump a kilometre away, so off I went to get four sacks of rations with the occasional shell whizzing overhead. Each sack of food constituted a meal for one section of six to twelve men; the fewer men the more food each man got. After dropping the rations at Company Headquarters, I returned to my dugout where Lieutenant Farmer was making the rounds with rum rations. This was no more than a good swallow and the first rum ration I'd had. Usually, rum rations were given out around 4 am when our energy level was at its lowest.

In the meantime, the enemy began shelling in earnest, and when Gilmore returned with our rations, he said a bomb made a direct hit on the shell hole I'd moved out of the day before. My bunkmates, the corporal and his two companions had been killed instantly. I was stunned. Their sudden deaths were impossible to comprehend. Less than two hours ago, the Corporal and I had been visiting at the dressing station. I shook my head as the ghastly news sunk in. I was more than lucky. As the English poet, John Bradford, wrote, "There, but for the grace of God, go I."

I helped bury the corporal and his companions, side by side in shallow graves. After which, we set up identification markers to be used for later internment. We had no sooner finished burying our buddies than another tumpliner got hit in the face by a ball of shrapnel. This time, I wasn't asked to walk the injured man out out. One of his buddies did the honours. However, with the recent five losses, Lieutenant Farmer was in a bind and had to send word to Battalion Headquarters for replacements.

On the next trip out to the ration dump, we found the rations had not yet arrived by mule train. We kept walking and soon discovered the gunnysacks piled at the side of the road. Later we heard that one of the mules had been hit by shell fragments and had to be shot. Consequently, the rations were immediately unloaded, and the mules turned back. But you can appreciate how awkward these sacks were, especially when we had to carry them twice as far in mud that as often as not came up to our knees. It was a hell of a struggle! We decided to carry six sacks each to the usual drop, then four sacks each to Company headquarters. After dropping our first load, we still had to make another trip back to get the rest of the sacks. When we finished for the night, we were totally exhausted. Part of the strain was due to the non-stop shelling. If there was one good thing about thick gooey mud, it was that falling shells were sucked into the ground. They usually exploded and kicked up mud, but they didn't ricochet as they normally would on hard, dry ground.

We were supposed to wear our equipment at all times when carrying rations. However, our equipment (along with forty bags of rations), was far too bulky and heavy to manage. So, we defied orders, taking our gas masks and leaving the rest of our equipment in a dugout.

We'd been making these ration trips in the black of night, but a day later, Lieutenant Farmer let us make them in daylight. Struggling with heavy gunnysacks in mud in the dark was taking too much out of us. The lieutenant said, "Moving in the daylight is a 'calculated risk.' Enemy observation balloons are on the lookout for us."

We all knew it was a risky business; we could see enemy balloons with the naked eye. On our next trip down, the rations hadn't arrived yet, so we went over to a nearby pillbox to wait. It was here (about a week before), that British guns scored a direct hit on the strong point, smashing the roof and killing the German occupants. We observed about a half dozen enemy soldiers, or parts of then: legs, arms, and heads, under the debris, awaiting burial.

A small party of Imperial signallers were operating in this pillbox and were eating their lunch as we came up. Their lunch consisted of the basics—bully beef and hardtack—and they generously shared their limited fare with us tumpliners. We waited in the pillbox with the Imperials for some time. Every so often a burst of shrapnel exploded close enough to kick up dirt in our direction. When we felt enough time had elapsed, we doubled back to the supply dump, but no rations had arrived. So, we had to go back to Headquarters empty-handed and explain to our mates why they'd have to go hungry again.

Famished or not, our day's struggle wasn't finished by any means. We were called out to carry ammunition. It rained all night, so it was another sloppy job, again feeling our way by the toes of our boots, so to speak. The enemy was shelling the area around us quite heavily, cutting the darkness with blinding light and deafening explosions. We were each carrying a box of ammo, 10" X 10" X 16" which weighed all of 80 or 90 pounds. We carried the boxes high on our shoulders, resting the weight on the back of our necks. I tried using a tumpline, but it didn't work very well. After a short distance, we had to stop to rest. Believe me when I say it took a long time to move the ammunition half a kilometre to its destination. We dropped the first load, then back we went, making two more trips, wading through six inches of slop the whole way: slip, flounder and curse.

No sooner had we finished hauling the ammunition than we were switched over to packing hand grenades. These came in 6" X 6" X 20" boxes. We carried two boxes at a time and each of us made two trips up the line. Some machinegun outfits had entrenched themselves in shallow pits directly behind where we were carrying the ammunition. They were shooting high trajectory over the ridge, at a crossroad behind enemy lines. It was a nerve-racking business walking in front of active guns. Not surprisingly, that night one of our men was accidentally shot in the lower leg by friendly fire and had to be taken back down the line.

Still, we tumpliners were not done. We had one more trip to make, this time packing shovels in bundles of six. After this, we made our way back to our billets where Lieutenant Farmer doled out a more liberal rum ration. We were soaked to the bone, and everything in our dugouts ranged from damp to dripping wet. To make things worse no lights were allowed, so we were still staggering around in pitch darkness.

I spread my groundsheet in a corner, took off my boots, and put on new socks that came up with the rations. Then, using my greatcoat as a blanket, I curled up and slept, but not for long. Less than two hours later, just before daylight, we were called out again. This time we were sent after rations. No rations had come through the day before, so this was an emergency. Up to now, our Battalion had nothing to eat for almost 24 hours.

We stood shivering until all the tumplners were ready to go. Then back we went to the dump and were surprised to find the rations were already there. Hallelujah! On the way back, two high explosive shells landed directly behind us. Several more exploded on either side of us, yet there were no casualties among our party. As we hurried along, we came upon a dispatch rider whose horse had been wounded by shell fragments just moments before. The rider took out his revolver, shot the writhing animal, then proceeded on his way on foot.

The next day was Friday. We tumpliners were sent out—in the daylight—to pack ammunition forward, from where it had been stacked near a pillbox. We were warned to stay concealed in a cellar until we got the word to move. Lieutenant Farmer, himself, ignored the warnings, and walked to and froe as his duties required. While waiting in the cellar, I came across a three-page letter written by an English soldier. In it, he described his experiences, where he'd been and when he was going into the Ypres Salient. I've often wondered what happened to that particular soldier. Had he been wounded or killed in action? Was this his last letter home?

After a while, word came that it was time to move out. We collected our boxes of ammunition and reached the railway cutting on the *Ypres-Roulers* line, which is the line between *France* and *Belgium*. We then followed a 20-foot-deep, cut-line for a half a kilometre. The noise of shells exploding around us was horrendous—

and non-stop. There was no railway track left, just pieces of twisted rails scattered about. Soon we were climbing out of the cutline and cautiously making our way across the top of a low ridge. From this point, we could see *Passchendaele, Belgium,* both the church and the village. The city lay about one and a half kilometres northeast from where we stood. We could also see German soldiers walking around as there were no trenches here, due to the ground being waterlogged. The ridge we were walking on had been the frontline only a few hours before. Consequently, there were many dead soldiers, both Canadian and German, still lying where they'd fallen. We were not at liberty to move the dead unless ordered to do so. Like everything else in army life, each job was compartmentalised. Picking up bodies or body parts was assigned to burial squads.

We left the ammunition on the forward side of the ridge and made our way back through the railway cut line. About this time, we saw two wounded Scotsmen who had been in a pillbox all day because one of them was so badly wounded he couldn't walk out. The least injured of the two waved me down, "Can you help us?" he asked. "I can't get my mate out alone." So, I helped them to the dressing station which was a fair distance away.

The next day the 50th went over the top. It was another short objective of about 250 yards. Of course, there was more heavy shellfire from the enemy. Another tumpliner was wounded, not a 'bad blighty,' so he was able to walk out on his own. Later in the day we were sent up the line with a sack of Tommy-cookers. These were made by army personnel back at the base and consisted of a tin of hardened grease with a piece of gunnysack for a wick. They came in handy in the trenches to boil water for tea. Tea, hardtack, bully beef, and a small jam ration was the usual meal in the trenches.

In the trenches, photo from William Lees' collection

Around midnight on Saturday, we got orders to "Stand to!" with full equipment and fixed bayonets. We were manning the second line of defence in the event the new frontline was broken by an enemy counterattack. We were told to dig ourselves in as best we could and await developments. All the while explosives were falling around us. The noise was deafening and the flashes from explosions were blinding.

After spending most of the night digging, sitting, and standing in a complete blackout, Lieutenant Farmer came along the line to tell us to go back to the billets, but we were not to take off our equipment. If the enemy broke through the lines, we'd be called back immediately. So, we did as we were told. We ducked and dodged our way through the narrow trenches with more than a little trepidation. Even in the dark, enemy guns appeared to be zeroing in on our every movement. Finally, we found our billets, such as they were, crawled in, and tried to rest until daybreak.

Sunday morning and the 50th Battalion were told we'd be relieved the following evening. Nine days at the front seemed like an eternity and having to wait another twelve hours taxed our nerves to the limit, especially when we were under attack. Yet, we held our ground, counting each minute until we'd be relieved. Sorry to say, not all of us would leave. Five minutes before we moved out, another one of our tumpliners was killed.

Ten days before there were twelve of us making up the original tumpline unit. Now only four of us remained to answer the roll call—myself and three others. The other eight men were either wounded or killed outright. Once again, I'd beaten the odds. My guardian angel was certainly working overtime.

The 3rd Division of another battalion now relieved the 50th. On moving out, we were required to carry salvage along with our full marching order equipment. I had to carry a damaged machinegun, a cumbersome lump of steel when added to an already heavy load. Thankfully one of my buddies took a turn packing it, and this was greatly appreciated. An officer at the head of our crew was supposed to be leading us out, but he lost his way. He stopped and sent word back for Lieutenant Farmer to go to the front of the line. After a lengthy discussion, the lieutenant ordered our party to about-face and we went in the opposite direction. We were still lost. The night was blacker than the devil, so when the men at the front of the line came to an abrupt halt, those behind bumped into the fellow ahead. This had a domino effect, bringing a few men to their knees in a series of muffled snarls and curses.

Once again, we turned around—heavy loads and all—and very soon we were back at the starting point. This time we kept going, inching past shell holes and getting hung up in wire entanglements until we were completely fatigued. At one point we came across a dead Canadian soldier lying on the duck walk. Obviously, he'd attempted to walk out alone after being wounded, but hadn't made it.

Finally, in desperation, my section of men stopped at a pillbox which was already occupied by troops. There was a makeshift lean-to against one of the pillbox walls. Another fellow and I climbed into that. It was such a tight fit, neither of us could rest comfortably. The ground was damp and the wind cold. All we could do was shiver and pray for morning to come. At daybreak, we were hungry, but our rations hadn't made it up the line. All we had was a rum ration compliments of Lieutenant Farmer when he rounded us up to make our escape from exploding bombs. We started out along the "K" track, then walked about two more kilos until we came to some farm building. We stayed in the farmer's field the rest of the day, scattered around in shallow dugouts, hoping we were stopping for the night. However, we were called up again.

With Lieutenant Farmer leading the way, we went for rations. The men quite liked the lieutenant. He was one of us, always willing to go the extra mile for us—and with us. On this march, he carried a water bottle filled with rum and gave each of us a nose cap. When we got to the ration dump, the rations weren't there, so we kept walking until we located them at the side of a very narrow, rutted road.

One of the tumpliners, a Canadian Métis named Barnett, claimed he'd been hit by shrapnel and was given permission to walk down the line. That left us shorthanded. So, another fellow and I were given all of "B" Company's rations to deliver up the line. Considering the heavy packs we were carrying; the mud and mess we had to plough through with shells flying thick and fast, it was a true miracle that we made it to the company headquarters, arriving there just as the sergeant was doling out rum rations. It was plain the sergeant didn't expect us to reach the top in one piece. He was so pleased, he praised us for delivering the rations "under fire," and gave us a double quota of rum.

After delivering "B" Company's rations, my partner and I still had to carry "D" Company's rations forward. Once again, we struggled through thick mud and debris with shells flying overhead, and once again we were given another hearty shot of rum. The problem was, after downing that much liquor, I couldn't walk a straight line. I had to get back to my billets by way of the twisty, uneven "K" track, and I found it physically impossible, so I sat down on the duck walk until I sobered up. Fortunately, enemy snipers hadn't spotted me, and I was able to return to my unit unscathed.

****

The Bigger Picture: It was extremely dangerous to lose one's footings on the duck walk. These narrow plank boardwalks wound around shell holes filled with thick gooey mud. Many soldiers had slipped into the unforgiving mire and died there. One story told of several soldiers who were heading to the front line when they came across a poor devil in a shell hole bogged in the mud past his knees. In spite of four men trying to extract the victim, they simply couldn't do it and were ordered to move on. Two days later the same men passed that way and found the unfortunate man was still there. Only his head was visible, and he was raving mad. (reference: Reagan 1992)

****

CHAPTER NINE

The evening after my predicament on the duck walk, I began looking for a dugout to spend the night in. In the end, I settled for sharing a shell hole with three others. We salvaged anything we could lay our hands on: boards, poles, bricks, and a large piece of tin. We had barely got our quarters patched up and were warming up cans of bully beef for supper when we got word we had to move to the rear. We felt no remorse. The shell hole was an ugly piece of work, so we gladly grabbed our equipment and set off with the rest of our division. We passed the big guns and made our way to the *Menin Road*, where a first aid station was located. Due to the heavy bombardment all afternoon, there were many walking wounded. Some leaned against a wall, others sat bleeding in the grass—all waiting their turn to get assistance. As we marched by, an ambulance loaded with more blood-soaked uniforms arrived. Farther along we saw dead soldiers, too many to count, lying where they'd fallen. The whole gruesome scenario was worse than the most horrible nightmare I'd ever had.

We continued on, past buildings that had been badly bombed, and presently came to a YMCA Canteen. Here men were dishing out hot tea into pre-used milk containers, and bully-beef tins. They were also giving out free cookies. No one could appreciate these more than we weary soldiers who had endured so much in the past few days.

From this point on, we straggled along in one's and two's with no attempt at marching in an orderly fashion. We were thoroughly exhausted. It was still dark when we came to a man standing at the roadside, directing us to billets and a cook kitchen.

As it turned out, only a few of us made it back to the 50th Battalion headquarters that night. I was one of those who did. I tossed my equipment in a bell tent, took out my mess kit, and headed for the cook kitchen. I was one of the first to reach the kitchen where after another shot of rum, the cook filled my mess tin with mashed potatoes, boiled beef, and rice. There was also pickles, bread, butter, tea, and rice pudding.

After eating as much as I could, I was issued two blankets and was soon fast asleep in a bell tent. I never remember feeling so utterly played-out as I did that night. My back ached so badly I was bent over like an old man. It had rained all week and we'd remained in wet clothing the whole time we were at the front. It had been a true test of endurance. Yet, there was no sleeping in the next morning. The bell tents had been erected after dark and had to be taken down before daylight. If tents were left standing after sunup, they'd be observed by enemy balloons. The tents had to come down!

The next day was Tuesday, October 30th, and we continued our march away from the front. As I recall, we marched past a civilian cemetery where marble headstones had been smashed by shellfire. Once again, we wound through the side streets of *Ypres*, but this time we took a different route and avoided *Cloth Hall*.

On one street, some Imperials were cooking a meal. I noticed they were serving tea, so I dashed over and was given a tin full of tea and two pockets full of raisins. I drank the tea in one gulp and shared the raisins with the fellows who were marching next to me. We finally arrived at the railhead and discovered this was the very same place where lorries had dropped us off ten days before. Half an hour later, a train backed into a siding. It consisted of very old French carriages that ran on three pairs of wheels. We crowded into its wooden seats with one thought in mind. That was to get as far away from *Ypres* as possible. After twelve kilos, we got orders to detrain and march three kilos south, toward *Dickebusch*. Here we were billeted in regular army camp huts, and I received a parcel from Sister Evelyne and a letter addressed to my brother. Since John had been killed the previous May, his letter was redirected to me.

After depositing our equipment most of us went in search of a YMCA canteen. Yes, we were as hungry as ever.

A parade was scheduled for November 1st. So, the previous day was spent polishing brasses. Then on the first, we were paraded down a muddy road to get our gas masks tested. On route, we were able to see British observation balloons about three kilos away. At four in the afternoon we were told to fall in—full marching orders—in front of the "Y" hut. While waiting, a few of the fellows and I ran to the nearby canteen where we could get potatoes, bully beef, hot rolls, and tea, all for ten francs. The next thing we knew, the troops were marching off without us. We wolfed down as much of our meal as possible, then ran to get our place in the column. At *Vlamertinghe,* we were put on a very crowded train; ten men and their equipment to a compartment. Standing room only.

After a two-hour trip, we reached *Caëstre* (still in France), at eight in the evening. We were detrained in *Caëstre* and marched through piles of stacked lumber, past a sugar refinery, and on to an encampment of bell tents. Here we got settled for the night with ten men to a tent. As it turned out, we were at this camp for a week. I didn't mind staying put for a week. I needed the rest and so did my companions.

Caëstre was very different from *Flanders*. All the fields in the area were level and grassy. The main road was topped with crushed rock and well-graded, yet there were neither ditches nor hedges. One afternoon, I went downtown by way of the sugar factory and I recall the sickly-sweet smell it gave off. I crossed a plank bridge, then walked down a winding path leading to main street. I browsed through some shops but had no money to spend. Another day we had church parade, the first religious function in many weeks. Then, after the church service, another soldier and I walked to *Caëstre* and looked in at every shop. Neither of us had money, so we were only able to look at embroidered cushions and postcards.

The following day, November 5th, we had Corps Inspection by the Brigadier. Our company was ordered to turn out every item of our equipment onto groundsheets for kit inspection.

Photo credit: William Lees's collection

After inspection, we troops were put through a march-past and dismissed for the day. I used my free time to write a letter to my sister.

We tumpliners (along with the new recruits who replaced the casualties), were still together as a unit and were taken out as a group for PT before breakfast the next day. Discipline was very lax. When we were called out, we went dressed in whatever we'd casually pulled on for the day. Some of us wore puttees, some didn't. And instead of orders, the sergeant asked us what we'd like to do. Having had so much rain, the ground was still very muddy. We chose to walk down the railway track and back. We'd just completed our lap when we heard the bugle call from the cookhouse. Each company had its own cookhouse, and there was always a scramble to see who'd get there first. Then we'd wolf down our grub as fast as we could, hoping we'd be in time to get seconds.

November 7th was another cold, cloudy day. It was payday, and after signing our name in the page ledger, we were given cash in francs. Immediately we set off for the shops, where I bought chocolates and cookies as well as postcards of *Ypres* and *Poperinghe* (known as 'Pop' to us soldiers, and later spelled *Poperinge*). The little village lies eight miles due west of *Ypres*. While at this camp at *Caëstre,* leather jerkins were issued to the troops. Some were lined with fur and some with cloth. They were worn over our tunics and came halfway down to our knees.

The day after the clothing parade, we were taken out on a route march with our battalion band leading the way. We went north of *Eecke*, before passing a drab little village of old wooden houses and barns. (I don't recall its name.)

It rained again for the next couple of days, so there was really nothing to do, except dig ditches around our tents to keep them from flooding. All in all, the time we spent at *Caëstre* was considered extremely pleasant compared to what we'd endured on the frontline.

At four am on the twelfth of November, we were sent back to *Ypres*, with full marching orders. This time we went by train and stopped for the night at some crude, makeshift billets opposite a dressing station. A canteen was near the billets where we could get free tea, but we had to pay for biscuits (cookies).

Work parties were organized. Half the company would work the night shift, the other half worked the dayshift. I was put on day-shift. Although men on dayshift could see what we were doing in the daylight, we were in more danger of being spotted by the enemy. So, the next morning my unit went out to the "H" line, where we were detailed to fill in shell holes and dig drainage ditches. Then, after three and a half hours of pick and shovel work, we returned to billets.

The ridge we were working on was the same one we'd been on ten days earlier, when we'd struggled to carry eighty-five-pound boxes of ammunition, and crates of hand grenades to be used by soldiers manning the front trenches. We had done this under shell fire and in four to six inches of mud. Since then, the enemy had been beaten back, and *Passchendaele Ridge* had been taken by the allies. At this point in time, the enemy was about four to five kilos away from where we were now. Engineers were here, constructing a new road to *Passchendaele*, and marking the route with one-inch, white tape.

The next day, we hauled timbers for gun placements on flat bottomed trucks that ran on a 20-gauge rail line. The timbers had been salvaged by a previous work party and piled along the track to be used again. We were tasked with loading the 3 X 8 timbers onto railcars and taking them to a point near *Zion Corner*. Five men were assigned to each load. We made three trips each, loading and unloading timbers and transporting them to the new location. We didn't take rifles and bayonets along, but as a precaution we took gasmasks.

Although this work was much preferred over the life-and-death struggles, we'd had ten days earlier, we weren't out of danger by any means. The rumble of big guns was incredibly loud and threatening. There was a large concentration of British and Canadian guns being fired, and the Germans were shelling a road directly ahead of us. We were also close to an ammunition dump which had been blown up shortly before we arrived. On every side, we were confronted by churned up ground, remains of motor lorries and limber wagons, as well as dead mules, horses and remnants of men. In fact, the heavy bombardment never stopped. And as we worked, we saw a motor lorry take a direct hit.

We were sent out to the same location the next day. This time we took a variety of material a kilo and a half to *Zion Corner*: spools of barbed wire, bundles of iron stakes, sheets of corrugated iron, and more timbres. We each made two trips back and forth. On one of the trips, a burst of German shell fire exploded directly behind us, giving us an incentive to 'hurry harder.'

After getting back to the billets at 3 pm, we were taking it easy when we became aware of a squadron of German fighter planes high in the sky. They were escorting a big 'Gotha' bomber. The 'Heiny' was dropping bombs—about six—on the *Menin Road Dressing Center*. Not very humane, when the pilot could clearly see the red cross painted on the dressing center's roof. Later we heard the only injury inflicted in that particular bombing raid was to a man who cut himself while making a dash for cover.

The next morning, November 16th, we marched through *Ypres* to *Dickebusche* (both places are in France), and were billeted in some army huts just outside of *Dickebusche*. Quite possibly the huts had been set up by troops from either France or Belgium. They were definitely not English or Canadian. Each man was issued one blanket. As there were no cots, we slept on the floor. For the benefit of our troops a YMCA had been set up and a concert was performed that evening. However, the concert was so crowded, I couldn't get in edgewise, so had to rely on others to tell me about it.

On Sunday, November 18th, we were transported back to *Ca-ëtre* where my section was billeted in a farmhouse near a large British railway depot. There were dozens of steam locomotives on the sidings. As a result, there was lots of thick, black smoke which at times stung the eyes and made breathing difficult. Here we stayed two nights. While at this place, we tumpliners were put back in our respective platoons because the 50th Battalion was leaving the *Ypres* sector to go where we were most needed. In our spare time, while waiting to go forward again, we played circle ball and football. It felt good to laugh and joke in friendly competition. Any distraction that helped put the impending trench warfare out of our minds was a blessing.

On November 20th we packed up and were marched down a narrow lane to a bussing area where a long queue of very old English, double-decker busses were parked, waiting for us to climb aboard. These were dull grey with old advertisements showing through a poor paint job. I failed to get a seat in the top section, and since the lower windows were boarded up, I couldn't see a thing for the entire trip. We were unloaded near a town named *Merville,* and then marched another one and a half kilos, where the platoons were split up and billeted on different farms. On the farm where I stayed, the buildings looked comparatively new and were constructed of brick with red-tiled roofs. There was a ditch running around the back of the farm. The farmer said we could wash and shave in the ditch, but only if we went a good way down the road. We were not to wash up near the house as the ditch provided their only drinking water. We stayed at this farm overnight, then the next day we marched in easy stages to *Busnes* where the men of my section were billeted in a farmhouse overnight.

The next morning, with drums keeping us in step, the Battalion Band led us on a fourteen-kilometre march. With all the weight I was carrying, my shoulders soon became sore, so when we stopped to rest, I unfastened my pack from my equipment and then carried it by the straps the rest of the way to our destination which was the large city of *Bruay-la-Buissière*. It had been a hard, tiresome 14-kilo march, up steep grades and down the other side. Everyone of us complained of aching backs.

Number thirteen and fourteen platoons (mine was the thirteenth), were billeted in an old three-story brick building on *Rue-Marche Street*, in the city of *Bruay*. French civilians occupied the first two floors, so we took over the garret. The windows were set in the slope of the roof —three windows on each side—with two chimneys in the middle. A row of men bedded down on either side of the room with another row down the center. No beds, just the plank floor. It was very cramped, and everything was covered with dust. The company kitchen was located on the corner of the opposite block, so we had to leave our billets to eat our meals.

While we were here, we were never short of food. On market days, the *Place d'armes* in *Bruay* was filled with stalls where vegetables, apples, and oranges were sold much cheaper than you could buy them in a shop.

117

The previous day's march had been excruciating. So, the next day, we were allowed to sleep in. Later in the day, we marched to the market square where our trusty colonel was on hand to tell us what was planned for the coming weeks. He told us, enemy permitting, we'd be billeted here in *Bruay* for the next month. He also said he'd go easy on us. We'd have light daily drills, and he'd do his best to give us a good time. For our part, he expected us to behave at all times, especially when we went into town. We were not to get into scraps with the civilians. After the colonel's lecture, we were given our Christmas pay of 70 francs, a month ahead of time.

On November 24th, we took our towels and went to the *Bruay Colliers* on a bath parade. It was an excellent bathhouse with shower cubicles down each side and a double row of lockers down the center. What a blessing! After plodding through mud, day after day, to be able to bathe was a godsend.

CHAPTER TEN

The month that followed was most enjoyable. We had light activities as promised, which gave me plenty of time to attend several concerts and movies at the local theatre. Afternoon matinees were generally attended by French children who yelled out the words printed on the screen, making the silent movies anything but silent. My pals and I also went for walks around the countryside to places like *Rue des Escaliers*. Another time, we lined up for haircuts given by the company barber. What a disappointment! The barber was a novice and made a mess of our hair, but still had the nerve to charge a franc per haircut.

On November 29th, machinegun classes were held. They were designed to give all ranks a working knowledge of the Lewis machinegun. We were marched two and a half miles east of town to an area of brush and sandpits. Here we were given Lewis machinegun practice. Every sixth cartridge was taken out of the cartridge pan, so the gun would fire in bursts of five, signalling the next man's turn. We spent three days at these firing pits. Every day, we were accompanied (both ways) by the Battalion Bugle Band. At any time of day, a good many allied planes could be seen practicing aeronautic exercises.

A French refugee family from *La Bassée*, northern France, operated a little restaurant near our billets. The mother was a plump, middle-aged woman with a rosy complexion. She kept the eatery spotlessly clean. She said she hoped the war would end soon. Her eldest son was serving with the French army at Verdun, and her second son would be of military age in a few weeks. Then, he too would be called into service. She was very worried about her young sons serving in an army that had lost thousands of men in a single day.

At the restaurant, a popular meal with the troops was chips (French fries), two fried eggs, bread, butter, and coffee. This was so much better than the watery mulligan we were routinely fed— almost every day. One night the father came home from the colliers where he worked. He took several pieces of coal from under his sweater and put them in the coal bin. Turning, he grinned at us and remarked, "Tres bon, eh?" He spoke English and told us the population of *Bruay* had tripled from 20,000 to 60,000 due to refugees escaping the war zone. This was more than the area could accommodate, so many folks went to bed cold and hungry. "Families must be clever to survive," he said, nodding at the coalscuttle.

To be sure there were indications of hungry children in *Bruay*. Little ones often prowled around the camp kitchen, begging for food. Older children came to the rifle range, selling apples and cakes until the sergeant shooed them away. Chasing the children away annoyed the troops. We not only wished to buy snacks, but these children were polite, and we enjoyed their laughter. Thinking back, the sergeant was within his rights; a rifle range really wasn't a safe place for children to play.

At the rifle range, there were 12 targets. These allowed 12 men at a time to go over the course. We'd fire five shots at 600 yards, five shots at 400 yards, and five shots at 200 yards. For three more days we had machinegun practice, using Lewis guns. After that, we had one day of bombing, an informal exercise in the use of hand grenades and rifle grenades. For this, we went out in small parties to an old gravel pit. Shortly after, we were taken to gas huts, where our gas masks were tested in authentic gas chambers. I was always thankful when my mask passed inspection. I often wondered what would happen if it didn't.

Another day, "D" Company went to the ranges for instruction in open-formation attack methods and were shown different signals to be used when under fire.

On December 11th, the troops were given the opportunity to vote on the issue of conscription in Canada. The colonel emphasized the need for conscription, sighting how the British had made great gains in *Cambrai* and *Bourlon Woods*, only to lose two-thirds of their gains in a German counter-attack—all because the British didn't have enough men. The allies also suffered heavy casualties in both cities. "Men aren't volunteering in large enough numbers. We must have more soldiers. Conscription is the only way for us to win this war," the colonel told us.

The month we spent in *Bruay* passed far too quickly. On December 19th at 9 am, our Battalion was lined up in "column of route" with full marching orders. It was a cold morning with a raw wind. To top it off, a light snow had fallen during the night and our leather boots acted more like skis than proper footwear. What with slipping and sliding, we had a devil of a time keeping our heavy packs centred on our backs. We went past the airdrome, down the hill, and by *Houdain Church*. Needless to say, we were extremely tired when we reached St. Lawrence Camp at *Château-de-la-Haie*. Here we were billeted in bow huts for the next three days.

December 20th, 21st, 22nd, we were taken out for drills every morning. One day we went on a butt party to the ranges that were very near *Villers-au-Bois Station Cemetery* where my brother was buried. It was extremely cold in the rifle butts and the men were served hot tea after the practice.

My name came up for guard duty in front of the Battalion Headquarters, from 9 pm, Dec. 23rd to 9 am, Dec 24th. I was happy to get guard duty over before Christmas. There was a beautiful moon shining that night, and my watch passed without incidents.

Our billets in the bow tents were equally cold. Each hut was decked out with a clumsy-looking stove made by an amateur blacksmith. To all intents and purposes, it was useless; we had no wood or coal to burn. So, in the afternoon of the 24th, thirty hut-mates and I scoured the countryside for firewood. We set out in all directions. Some men tore down an abandoned building; some retrieved logs from a caved-in dugout and others picked up branches, sticks, and poles. That night we had heat.

On Christmas Eve, the battalion band visited the various camps surrounding *Château-de-Haie*. At each camp the band played Christmas carols. Then on Christmas Day, 1917, the morning dawned misty and cold, gradually warming up in the afternoon. There was a volunteer church parade at the Cinema Hall which most of the troops (including me), attended. Although the service began without music, a piano was brought in while the padre was reading the scriptures. Aided by the piano, we sang Christmas carols until noon, loudly and with great gusto.

We had the usual mulligan for lunch, followed at 4:30 pm by a proper Christmas dinner in each hut. Tables were set up for the occasion and battalion officers served the meal with more food than we had seen in many months.

There were two bottles of Basses Pale Ale for each man to compliment roast pork, dressing, applesauce, potatoes, and cabbage. There were peaches, cakes, shortbreads, mince pies, oranges, an assortment of nuts, and genuine Christmas puddings smothered in brandy sauce. What a feast we had, with every man eating and drinking all he wanted. Later Lieutenant Knowles, who had been attached to the 13th platoon since his return from *Passchendaele*, came around with two bottles of whiskey and gave each man a shot.

The following day the colonel took us out on a ten-kilometre route-march which he said was to walk off the effects of our Christmas indulgence. Towards evening, I walked over to the estaminet (café) with a soldier named Coggins from *Nova Scotia*, and another fellow whose name and background I've forgotten. On Dec. 27th (in both the morning and evening), I was on duty with another butt party, after which I went to an American wild west movie.

Shortly before 'lights out,' the next night we were sitting talking in our hut, when two of our men, Lenny and Latimer, came hobbling in. They'd taken a beating from some of the 2nd Division men, who they said had ganged up on them at the estaminet. "They knocked us down and jumped on us," the so-called victims claimed.

On hearing this, another soldier—a hot-head—hopped to his feet. "Come on! Let's go clean up on 'em," he said, meaning the troops in the 2nd Division. About half of the men in our hut followed the ringleader. As luck would have it, they happened to run into Lieutenant Knowles who was returning from duty at the Battalion Headquarters. He stopped them in their tracks and had them explain what they were up to. Lenny and Latimer said the incident began when some of the 2nd Division men called them "bomb-proofers." (Bomb-proofer was the term used for cowards who hid from bombs.) But since the lieutenant could see the complainants were inebriated, he discounted their story. In fact, the lieutenant sided with their adversaries saying, "The 2nd Division have been given more than their share of tough trips up the line." He then ordered the rebels back to their huts.

If fighting was what some of our men wanted, they were in for more than they bargained for. On the 29th of December, our battalion was marched out to the narrow-gauge railway. Here we were loaded into open boxcars for our next tour up the line. The rail line went through *Souches* and a rail yard called *Lorette Spur*. Then on we went to *Givenchy*. The later town had been repeatedly shelled and was mostly in ruins. A new railway track had been laid down over the rubble. We were within two miles of *Avion*, when we finally stopped and were billeted in a long support trench, known as *Balsam Trench*.

We spent three days in "supports" going out on work parties each night after dark, cleaning trenches, and packing trench mats.

Canadian soldiers laying trench mats
Photo Credit: William Rider/Rider/Canada.
Dept. of National Defence/Library and Archives Canada/
PA-002156

On the last night of the old year, I was on 'gas-guard' in front of one of the dugouts. Although it was a starlit night, there was no moon when the old year departed, and the new year came in. I was alone, with lots of time to think about the past twelve months, while at the same time wondering what the next twelve months would bring.

About 4 am the sergeant came down the trenches with rum rations for all on duty. By this time in the morning, we were usually cold, tired, and disheartened, so the rum ration cheered us up and was considered a necessity.

After dark on January 1st, 1918, we were moved forward out of Balsam Trench for frontline duty. On the way up, we had to scramble across ground that was being shelled by German machineguns. The enemy was firing almost non-stop, hoping to catch us unaware. We'd see blinding flashes, hear the whiz of shells followed by ear-splitting explosions. We'd flop to our bellies and lie low until the burst was over. This occurred three times before we reached cover. From here we continued along a section of Columbia Trench, reaching a line to the left of *Avion*, directly opposite *Lens*. We stayed up at this line for three days, my unit occupying about 30 feet of a frontline trench known as #4 outpost. There was a shell hole a short distance out in front. This was used after dark as a listening post. Two men would creep out to this post during the night. Before daybreak, they'd creep back to our own frontline trenches.

Four of our men were located at every frontline post. Two men kept watch while two rested. One of the men keeping watch stayed on the firing step, while the other sat or squatted close by. One man would constantly be looking into the periscope and reporting any enemy movement on the slagheap across No Man's Land. Even the slightest movement had to be reported.

125

A partly demolished house could be seen on the enemy side of No Man's Land, and once in a while a German soldier could be seen making a dash across debris in a room without walls. Sometimes there would be an unidentified shadow—a movement too quick for the eye to catch. Although the sector seemed quiet, the enemy wasn't far away. There was a slag heap to our left known as the *Green Crassier*. This was held by the Germans. They had a number of short-range trench mortars (guns) called minenwerfers (or slang: Minnie wafers), that launched the deadly bombs we called 'Moaning Minnies.' These guns were located across the *Green Crassier*. There were several enemy snipers out there, too. No soldier would knowingly show his head above the trench during daylight.

Several times a party of signallers came along the trench, repairing or laying down insulated wires of various colors. At other times we'd have a top-ranking officer come out on a tour of inspection. Invariably, these officers were always more friendly when conducting inspection in the trenches than they were on the parade ground.

On one of these days, myself and three others went for rations and brought back steaming hot cans of tea. To our dismay the first men to be served took a big sip, sputtered, and spit the tea on the ground. We soon learned why. The cans had been used to carry coal oil and hadn't been cleaned properly.

Early on the fourth night, the 50th were relieved by another battalion of the 4th Division, so we were moved back to the *La Collette Brewery* and billeted deep down in wine cellars. Again, the bunks were three deep and made of chicken wire. The cellars were unventilated, hot, and stuffy. Since we got so little sleep on the front line, we tolerated the conditions and slept as best we could.

We spent six days at *La Collette*, in the billets during the day and on work parties at night. The vaults were lit by candles, which added to the stuffiness. Men were not supposed to go outside during daylight hours in case they'd be spotted by enemy observation balloons. Regardless, the odd man would sneak out for a cigarette in the open air, putting us all at risk.

The company cook kitchens were located in one corner of the cellar, enveloped in smoke most of the time. There was a water pipe system bringing drinking water to the forward area from the west side of *Vimy Ridge* near *Souchez*. The water system was occasionally put out of commission due to shellfire. At such times, water was brought in by bucket, and I took my turn packing water for the cook—always in the dark.

One night I went on a work party along the *Lens-Arras Road* to where the Columbia Trench intersected it. We had wheelbarrows, picks, and shovels to fill in shell holes with bricks and chalk blocks. One hundred yards away was a newly built railway embankment constructed entirely of chalk. The long white streak of chalk could be seen quite plainly, even when nights were moonless. These work assignments were much preferred to frontline duty when our movements were seriously restricted. They usually lasted about four hours. Then word would be passed down the line to quit and we'd make our own way back to billets.

When we were returning to the Clucas Trench one night, the Germans commenced shelling the trench with whiz-bangs. Shells exploded on every side, directly in front and behind us for ten minutes or more. It was only by the grace of God that we had no casualties that night.

However, on January 6th, Private Tompkins, the friend who accompanied me to Hastlemere in the rain, was killed by shrapnel while he was on guard duty in front of the entrance to the brewery vault. This was the headquarter entrance. Another man with Tompkins was seriously wounded.

News of Tompkins' death was a bitter pill to swallow. And then two days later, on the night of January 8th, I was on guard duty at the very same entrance. It wasn't good to imagine what happened to Tompkins when I had to replace him, not when the shell holes I saw brought to mind recent snippets of conversation—the shared jokes and laughter that would never to be repeated. His memory kept me on high alert as shells continued to fall in the nearby woods, but none came close to the brewery entrance. Once more, I was among the fortunate few.

On January 9th, I was assigned to a work party, carrying full equipment beyond the Clucas Trench. On coming back to the dug outs later, we had to cross the road to *La Collette*. It was pitch black and we had a terrible time finding our way, stumbling onto shell holes, over barb wire, and great heaps of rubbish. The dugouts we occupied had been made by German troops. They were connected by a three-foot square passage which we crept through, dragging our equipment behind us. Then the passage ended abruptly at a point where another dugout had caved in. Eventually, we found our way out in a series of backtracking—all by guess and by golly in the black of night.

On the bright side, on January 10, a fellow from Edmonton and I both received packages from home: more cookies and candy, which we gladly shared with our trench mates. That night after dark, we moved up the line via Columbia Trench to the same sector we occupied the last time we were at the front. My unit was stationed at #1 post. And Private Coggins and his partner were stationed in No Man's Land at the listening post. They had instructions not to fire at anything, but to report back via way of a scout who would be sent out at various intervals. On toward morning, the enemy started bombarding the frontline with shells from a minenwerfer. This was only a short distance to the right of where my partner at I were at #1 post.

The 'Moaning Minnies' used in the minenwerfer were perhaps the deadliest bombs on the battlefield. The shells were large 18-inch balls filled with 200 pounds of ammonia nitrate-carbon and had a fuse on the outer edge. Each ball was attached to a heavy rod about 14 feet long and 1¼ inches thick. The rod held the balls in the gun while being fired. In the dark, we could hear them coming—a single pop—followed by the streak of a brilliant fuse that burned its way across the sky. We'd throw ourselves face down in the mud and listen to the moaning of the handle as it rotated around the bomb. Then came an explosion so great we fairly bounced with the concussion. If a man was within fifty yards of the blast, the concussion alone could kill him. On this occasion, most of the shells fell in low, swampy ground. However, two or three came so close to us at #1 post, they scared the living daylights out of us. I think it's safe to say the allied troops dreaded the shells from a minenwerfer more than any other bombs.

Next day, Lieutenant Knowles made a personal inspection, checking our rifles and every piece of our equipment. We strongly objected to his orders to clean our equipment to parade ground standards, especially when we were struggling to keep our footings in muddy trenches. Some of us didn't get it done.

CHAPTER ELEVEN

Our next Battalion cook kitchen was located a half kilometre to the rear in a dugout in a sunken road. Sunken roads were extremely dangerous places to be around, but we had to cross to them. The enemy would often shell these roads when things appeared to be quiet, hoping to catch us off guard.

Despite intermittent rain, the enemy continued to send shells our way. So, towards morning the Stokes Gun Brigade were given orders to retaliate and opened with a barrage. The Stokes gun was a British made invention. It had a steel barrel about 3 to 4 feet long and was 4 inches in diameter. It had a fixed firing pin in the lower end and a supporting rod in the center. The thick solid base was braced in the ground. It could be fired from our trenches, with its trajectory corrected by a simple periscope. After setting the gun for the range required, a shell was slid down the muzzle, hitting the firing pin and in a flash, the shell was away.

Several Stokes guns fired at once, and we knew they had caused some casualties. We could hear several shouts and groans. Apparently, the enemy abandoned one of their wounded men. For a long time, his cries for help could be heard in No Man's Land. Sometime before daylight, the barrage was lifted and several of our men were sent out to bring the wounded German in. He was still alive, but I never found out whether he lived or died.

It was raining steadily when I was relieved at the firing step. Intending to get out of the rain and have some rest, I crawled into a funk hole. This hole was two feet above the floor of the trench and was approximately five feet long by two feet deep, just wide enough for two thin men to lie side by side. Well, I had just settled down when I felt particles of dirt falling on my face. I pushed

131

myself out and jumped to one side just as the massive dirt roof collapsed, burying my rifle and equipment. If all that soil had fallen on top of me, I would certainly have been smothered. Another close call; another lucky escape! With rain still falling, one of my buddies helped me dig out my rifle and equipment before I went looking for another waterlogged funk hole to rest in.

After dark the next night, the men of the 50th were relieved and went back to the British dugouts via way of the Red Trench. The British dugouts were at least 20 feet deep, much deeper than any dugouts we'd been billeted in before. There were three stairways and each stairway had thirty steps. The interior of the dugouts was merely a long passageway with chicken wire bunks on either side. We were considered much safer here. The dugouts were too deep to be destroyed by the big guns and were out of range of the minenwerfers. They were also too draughty to be stuffy. Although the ventilation was much improved, these dugouts were unbearably cold and damp. And while I had my head turned, some sneaky beggar made off with my good quality greatcoat that was issued to me in Calgary. In its place, I found a very thin Imperial greatcoat on my bunk which did nothing to keep me from the freezing cold.

This was midwinter. For six nights I went from the Red Trench on work parties without a warm coat to wear. One night we had completed our work before 2 am, our designated time to go back to our billets. Five minutes before two, the Germans began shelling the trench we were in. The officer in charge, Lieutenant Knowles, happened to be with us. He was a stickler for rules and insisted we stay put until two o'clock on the button. Shells continued to fall—crash, bang with the smell of explosives and blinding light. Yet we couldn't move a muscle until the hands on the lieutenant's watch pointed to two o'clock. Nervous? You bet! Lucky for us there were no casualties as a result of his unreasonable dog-gedness to protocol.

On January 18, under full marching orders, we went up the line to clean a section of trench that was severely damaged by enemy fire. It was a dreadful mess and awfully hard to clean as most of the trench had been completely destroyed. After working on this for several hours, we started on a 14-kilo hike back to *St. Lawrence Camp*.

We arrived at a YMCA canteen at *Souches Corner*, and here we waited for motor lorries to take us the rest of the way to *Château-de-la-Haie*. But the lorries never came. First one man and then another set off on foot. Presently the rest of our outfit walked out. Much, much later we straggled into *St. Lawrence Camp* in penny numbers.

January 19th, 1918: We spent the morning cleaning up as we were filthy after our spell in the muddy, rat and lice infested trenches. Later that day, we had a pay parade and a clothing parade. I got new pants and new puttees, but no Canadian greatcoat to replace the one that was stolen. The weather was bitterly cold. Without a decent winter coat, I was chilled to the bone.

On the 21st, there were rifle grenade classes held in the woods on a hill above Ablain-St-Nazaire. We had an experienced instructor, and the rifle grenade we used was a Mills bomb with a short rod attached for inserting it into a rifle barrel. The rods were hard on the riffling barrel, so we practiced with rifles that were too old to be used in battle. We spent two days attending these classes and also did some Mills grenade bombing by hand.

On the second day, another fellow and I were placed on either side of the range's danger zone to warn others away while the bombing was in progress.

Of course, the nights were cold, and the wind blew incessantly. It was midwinter, for land sakes! How I cussed that thin Imperial coat! Yet, it would be two more weeks before I exchanged the thin coat for a good quality Canadian greatcoat.

William Lees wearing a top-quality, Canadian greatcoat,

sorely missed in the winter of 1918

On the 23rd, we went to *Maisnil Bouche* for rifle practice. The ground was wet and far too sloppy to kneel and shoot. Later the same day we went to the other side of the Château grounds for gas inspection. We were tested by going through an actual gas chamber—an experience to test not only the gas masks, but the strongest nerves.

In the following days, we were kept busy practicing with rifle grenades and some German 'potato-mashers'. There was also another German bomb demonstrated. This was a grenade shot from a Granatenwerfer. We weren't overly impressed by this one. In fact, we all laughed when the shell landed in the mud with a gentle plop. That being said, if correctly deployed, the Granatenwerfer shells were deadly. These grenades (referred to as pigeons because of their unique warbling sound), sent small bursts of explosives over a large area, thus causing a greater number of casualties.

Later in the week, after the lectures on bombs ended, I was put on sanitary fatigue, mostly cleaning ditches around the huts, etc. Then on January 27th, we had a church parade at the Irving Theatre before being marched to the bombing fields for demonstrations on flares. This, so we would be familiar with various signals used on the frontline. The first flare misfired and came spinning towards us causing everyone to scatter like a swarm of flies. One type of rocket would burst into three red lights, one above the other. Another would explode into a thousand coloured lights. Yet, another was bright yellow and used to light up No Man's Land. Soon a heavy mist crept in, so the rest of the demonstration had to be called off.

January 30th, 1918: Having had a ten-day break from the frontlines it was time to go back. So, after the noon meal our battalion was called out in full marching order for frontline duty. We went via *Albain St. Nazaire*, *Carency* and *Souches*, and about 4 pm we halted at the *Alberta Camp*, a series of bow huts along the road.

Here we stayed until dark, then started toward the front by light railway on a work party to *Angres*. It was another moonless, pitch-black night. We couldn't see anything or anyone as we carried rolls of barbed wire forward. This we attached to iron stakes which had to be carried and pounded in place, again the work was done without lights. As there was no one supervising the job, a few of the men got mulish and sat down. I went along with the majority and kept working. Eventually, the mission was accomplished, and we walked back to camp.

The next night I went out with a work party beyond *Lievin* to a trench constructed by German troops. Part of it had been covered over with poles, earth, and sod. It was our job to clean it out and make new firing steps.

At that time the front was fairly quiet. For the next ten days, we stayed at *Alberta Camp*, and went on work parties, always traveling forward by light railway. A trainload of soldiers was about eight wagons full, packed in tight, standing room only. Most often we were put off the train at *Australia Siding*, near a coal mine. Sometimes we'd build new trenches; sometimes we'd re-vet old ones. We always stopped for an hour at noon to eat our rations. There was only one sack of rations per platoon. Jam was always in short supply. As I said before, there was only enough food to wet the appetite.

There was a canteen at Alberta Camp where (if a man had money), he could buy chocolate bars, small packets of cookies and sometimes cigarettes. Once in a long while the canteen might carry the Overseas Daily Mail; not that it reported much news. It was only four small sheets of paper.

We had another gas mask parade, and I got a new gas mask complete with a new satchel as my box-type container was rusting through. Later on, I noticed a man by the name of Roberts from *Southern Alberta*. He was walking around with what looked like my old satchel, so I stopped to talk to him. Sure enough, he'd been given my rusty satchel with a new mask inside. Roberts told me he was a Mormon and had three wives, one in Montana and two in Alberta. I had no reason to discredit the story.

February 10th,1918, We left Alberta Camp and moved forward to billets on Rue Papin Street in *Liévin*. This street was a quarter of a kilometre long with a coal mine at one end and open fields at the other. We were billeted in abandoned mineworkers' homes. The houses were joined, making two long rows on either side of the street. By coincidence, #13 platoon was billeted in house #13— lucky thirteen. The buildings in this area had extensive damage from shellfire. About half of the roofs had been blown in and ground floor rooms were littered with fallen masonry. Yet, the arched cellars were intact and provided safe billets. These cellars below ground made a continuous room divided by brick walls every 20 feet. German soldiers had punched holes in the walls for no apparent reason.

From here, my platoon was assigned to work parties, first going to *Crocodile Trench* to shovel wreckage and scrape trench mats. It was mid-afternoon when we returned to our billets, so some of us went salvaging through damaged buildings. The civilians had all been evacuated, but their homes were fully furnished and weren't completely destroyed. My partner and I came to a room with a cabinet under a pile of rubble. In it were some beautiful satin quilts. There was also a nice-looking mattress, so between the two of us, we packed the quilts and mattress back to our quarters. My partner kept the quilts while I took the mattress which was far more comfortable than sleeping on a brick floor. The next day after repairing trenches, we were put to work, like so many ants in an anthill, salvaging anything of value from the ruins.

The same night about 5 pm, we were sent along a railway line in the direction of *Lens*. The roar of battle never stopped with enemy shells exploding a short distance ahead. We made a wide detour hoping to avoid a direct hit. We finally reached a trench where we set to work in heavy, wet soil. It was another bleak night with zero visibility. I could hear my colleagues working on either side of me but couldn't see them. We were scarcely aware of what we were doing, just feeling around with pick and shovel, digging as best we could until word was passed down the line to quit and follow the man ahead back to the billets.

The next night, I was with another work party, this time to the far-right section of *Crocodile Trench*. We made three trips each carrying loads of trench mats from the end of the railway to where they were needed upfront. It was a tricky business. The closer we got to the front-line trenches, the more likely we were to be targeted. We never knew if we'd been seen in the flashes from very lights or not. When we finished packing mats, we were directed to a temporary "Y" canteen located lower down in the remnants of a shelled building. Here we were served hot tea. This area had recently been occupied by German troops. All around was evidence of the struggle to rout them out: an unbelievable sight of huge craters and equally huge mounds of soil, laced with fragments of boards and metal. Yet the ghastliest sight was the remains of several enemy soldiers partly buried in rubble.

The ruins of a stark looking coalmine were close by, so some of us went over for a closer look. What a mess! One area was completely destroyed: twisted girders, broken mine shafts, and fragments of mine cars. Presently, we came to an engine room that was still intact. In the middle of the room a 6 X 8-foot table held a plaster of Paris model of the entire area which showed every rise and depression, every house and public building, as well as railways and roads. It was a genuine work of art, and by the looks of things had once been covered with glass. No doubt this model was extremely useful for the German army when they occupied this area.

The next night, we returned to the same railway terminal to unload gun emplacements and trench building material. We were reasonably safe here as we were out of sight of the German observation balloons.

Friday, Feb 15th,1918: The weather was frosty and clear when the 50th Battalion was moved up the line to *Aloof Trench* for a four-day tour of duty. *Aloof Trench* was partly on *Hill 70*, which was badly torn up, and there was almost a kilometre of low ground between the Canadians and the Imperial outposts. We were located on one side of the salient, so at night we could see flares and 'very lights' in every direction.

My platoon (#13) was billeted where a building had been razed to ground level. The Germans had roofed the rubble over, making it into a pillbox-type structure. Some trenches had caved in completely, so my second night there was spent deepening trenches. After that, my section took our turn carrying rations from *Liévin* to the men in the front trenches. The pack mules routinely dropped rations off somewhere in *Liévin*. It was up to us to find the ration dump, then fan out and carry the rations to the front.

I also took several turns as a gas guard. After that, it was back to packing rations again. One night, I went with Lieutenant Knowles and another man to take rations to various outposts. This entailed going along *Aloof Trench*, crossing a railway cutting, then to the last listening post which was across the open space of No Man's Land.

On getting back to my dugout, I was hoping to get some rest, however the enemy opened fire. This was another near escape for me because one of the first shells exploded in the same spot where Lieutenant Knowles and I had been standing only a minute before. The next shells exploded a few yards from our dugout. Suddenly, we recognized the sound that phosgene gas shells make when they're fired. We grabbed our masks, put them on, and kept them on the rest of the night. There were breaks in the shelling, but none long enough to clear the air.

A more vigorous enemy attack was expected before day-break. Because of this, my unit was sent to man the frontline trenches, to 'stand to' about ten feet apart. The attack didn't come immediately, but when it did it was a heavy barrage and mostly to our left. This kept up until dawn. We thought any minute we'd get orders to counter-attack, but the orders never came, so we simply held our positions. When the shelling appeared to die down, we opened our breakfast rations and were hit by the stench of poison gas. It wasn't only the bread; all our rations were ruined. We couldn't eat a single thing, and it was several hours before the next rations came up the line.

On February 19th, 1918: the men of the 50th were relieved at dusk and walked out under full marching order to the crossroads near *Liévin*. Here we waited for limbers which were supposed to carry our packsacks and a large number of empty cans we had to take with us. These same cans were used, over and over, to carry hot tea to men at the front. On this particular day, we waited for over three hours without taking off our equipment, but no limbers came. There was nothing for it but to start hoofing it—heavy loads and all—to *Lens Junction*. Once at the junction we waited again.

And for quite some time. Finally, an empty narrow-gauge train came along and took us to *Gouy-Servins Château*. Here we stopped, tired and hungry, but thankful to be away from those dreaded front-line trenches for ten days.

Gouy-Servins Château was a stately building: three stories high with an imposing tower centered on top of the building. It was about 150 years old and built of stone. A long tree-lined driveway led to the château. After passing through a gate under an ornamental arch, we entered the courtyard, estimated to be about 120 X 480 feet. On either side of the courtyard were brick barns and outbuildings. These were to be our billets, while rooms in the château were reserved for officers.

The following days were spent cleaning and polishing our equipment and rifles. Then on February 21st at 3:30 pm, we left the château and marched to *Hersin-Coupigny,* in the Lens district where our ten-day rest period would begin. Considering the back-breaking work we'd accomplished under fire, ten days to recuperate were none too long.

While resting, we were at liberty to go for walks to see the country. Between the château and *Hersin-Coupigny* there is a humpback ridge, one of the highest in northern France that ends at *Notre Dame de Lorette* where the world's largest French military cemetery is located.

One of the saddest things to discover (in any military cemetery of that era), are the number of soldiers who deserted, disobeyed orders, or broke under pressure. Consequently, these poor devils were dishonoured and put to death as an example to their comrades. To be shot at dawn was no idle threat. As Lord Tennyson so aptly put it, "It's not to reason why; it's just to do or die." Such was the life of a World War One soldier.

*Notre Dame de Lorette, site of the largest
military cemetery in France*

Picture from Wm. Lees' collection

Lorette Spur is the high point just to the north of *Vimy Ridge.*
Farther north yet was mining country, and to the south was agricul-
tural land: green fields and tree-lined lanes—spectacular scenery.
The town of *Lorette* situated in the *Gier River Valley* had sustained
some bombing yet was still inhabited by the original residents.
Those brave people had simply moved from homes that had been
completely destroyed to buildings with less damage.

Our days at Hersin-Coupigny were filled with humdrum
events. We had a clothing parade one day, but I didn't profit from
it. However, on pay parade, I received 25 francs. One evening after

church parade, my friend Private Swabey and I walked over to the YMCA.

The "Y" was a great place to buy snacks and converse with other soldiers. Another evening, I wandered uptown with Private Swabey and coming to a shelled building we went on a salvage mission. Although the roof had been blown in, the rooms were furnished. While Swabey collected ornaments and fretwork, I took a few picture postcards to add to my growing assortment.

Although we were supposed to be resting, we had regular machinegun classes. I didn't complain as I found them interesting. We also went to the gun range, taking turns firing a 'burst' of six shots. Every sixth round was taken out of the spiral pan, so the gun would stop firing after the sixth shot. By rotating the crank-handle and pressing the trigger, the next burst fired. This was done while lying face down. Even so, you got the full effect of the vibration at each blast, yet the spread of shots was no larger than the size of a saucer. The usual two man-guard was assigned to stand on the railway embankment to keep civilians away from the danger zone and I took my turn at that.

On the evening of February 28th, Swabey and I went for another walk, starting off through fields where barbed wire entanglements had been set down in the middle of growing crops. This was done in readiness for a possible enemy breakthrough.

Swabey was a good conversationalist and an interesting fellow to listen to. As we walked, he told me how he'd worked on a construction job on *Vancouver Island,* laying a pipeline from a reservoir in the hills behind *Nanaimo, B.C.* He spoke of the material they used and the difficulty of getting the necessary equipment into such wild terrain. Our hike took us to the top of a steep hill, possibly one of the highest hills in France. From there, we had a splendid view of a broad valley and several distant towns. We could see a busy industrial district east of *Lens* which was still held by German troops. We stood there for some time, imagining what the enemy might be planning to do next.

March 3rd,1918, was a Sunday and our ten-day rest period was over. It was time to leave *Hersin-Coupigny* to go back to the front. It was cold and dreary when we packed our kitbags and marched in the rain to *Casblain-Châtelain*. arriving there at 2:30 pm.

Casblain-Châtelain was a pleasant farming and light industrial village with two streets and a railroad. An old waterwheel, dating back to 1623, sat on a tributary of the *Clarence River* and was still being used to grind wheat into flour. Also, *St. Vaast Church* was built there in the fifteenth century and the ruins of a nearby castle dated back to the 11th century, attesting to the fact the area has been inhabited by productive citizens for many centuries.

We were billeted in a 20' X 30'garret of an old building. It had holes in the floor and was dusty, but compared to the frontline trenches, we didn't think it was all that bad, especially when it was filled with troops who by now seemed like family.

While at Camblain-Châtelain, from March 3rd to the 12th, we were worked hard and had very little spare time. The day after we got there, we were marched to a field near the top of a hill. It was a long, hard climb. We were craving a cigarette break. But oh no; we immediately had PT composed of every drill in the book. Needless to say, there was a good deal of grumbling. The next day we marched four kilometres to *Auchel* for 'bath parade.' Down the long, straight street we went, carrying our towels. When we got to the bath, a good many civilian miners were taking showers on one side of the building while we showered on the other. Later, that same afternoon, we were marched up the same high hill for more drills and more muttered oaths.

On March 7th, we were taken higher up the hill to where it was more open. Here we practiced attacking under cover of a smokescreen. We threw smoke bombs, one every ten feet, but the wind turned and blew the smoke back in our faces. Nothing would do but we had to keep trying until we got it right.

Our rations here consisted of watery hash, a little dry bread, and very weak tea. When payday came, a bunch of us went to a local establishment for a decent meal. I had eggs and French-fried potatoes, coffee, and vin-rouge. Never had anything tasted so good!

French children began coming to the cook kitchen at mealtimes. Instead of begging for food, they brought us cans of mulligan. No doubt their parents sent them, knowing how little we were getting to eat. The mulligan was free, but some children were selling pancakes that were delicious and still warm from the frying pan. A few of them carried the Paris edition of the Daily Mail which was well received.

Next, we were given intensive rifle practice. For this, we had to go 3 ½ kilometres to *Pernes-en-Artois* where we were given five clips with 25 rounds per man to be fired at one shooting. *Artois* is an old French province with *Arras* being the chief town. We congregated at an old stone church that sat at the edge of a stream. Here we lay in the shade to wait our turn at the ranges. Since we spent the whole day on the ranges, the cook kitchen came along with us.

When getting back to our billets, my section was put on guard duty. My post was in front of a schoolyard. I was supposed to be on guard from 10 pm to midnight—two hours. As luck would have it, there was a time change. Midnight came an hour early, so I was off duty in an hour.

Seven o'clock in the morning of March 12th, our Battalion left *Camblain-Chatelaine* under full marching orders. We passed through *Divion, Houdain, Rebreuve, Guachin-Legal,* and down a long straight road to *Estree-Gauchy*—fourteen kilometres in all. Here we were billeted in a barnyard overnight. In the morning, we started out again via *Maisnil-Bouche* to *St. Lawrence Camp* in the *Château-de-la-Haie* area. While there, another fellow and I walked over to *Viller-au-Bois Cemetery,* to my brother's grave which I hadn't visited since the previous June.

We left *St. Lawrence Camp* the next day at 1:30 pm and marched through *Aix-Noulette*, a badly damaged and partially deserted village near the frontline. From there we marched on to *Cite-Calonne*, arriving there at 4 pm. *Cite-Colonne* had been a community of brick houses built around a busy coal mine. However, it too had been deserted as over thirty percent of the town had been destroyed. Windows were smashed and roofs were blown in. We were billeted in cellars under these buildings and told not to walk outside in the daylight.

The same night we were sent out on a work party. We went via rail to *Cite-St. Pierre*, a town near *Lens*. (Lens was still in enemy hands.) Our job that night was to deepen a five-foot deep trench. The night was so dark we couldn't see a thing; still, we kept digging until just before daylight.

The next day a few of my pals and I moved out of the musty cellar, reasoning we'd sleep better in fresh air. We set to work finding wood to construct bunks for ourselves. Next, we cleared what had been a tiled kitchen floor, shovelling bricks, glass and splintered wood to one side, and building our bunks behind these piles of debris.

While we were stationed in this area, the officers took every opportunity to have demonstrations: rifle grenade classes and the like. They obviously felt they needed to keep us busy every minute of the day. When a load of rough lumber came up by train, we were put to work unloading lumber and carrying it to damaged buildings (out of sight of observation balloons). This was a nice change from working in trenches.

We would like to have stayed longer at this camp. The front was relatively quiet. We'd cleaned up the area around our billets and improved our sleeping arrangements. Regardless, after three days in *Cite-St. Pierre*, we were on the move again. One company was marching about a kilometre ahead of us. Our destination was *Canada Camp*, near *Château-de-la-Haie*. It was a sunny day and our highly polished brasses fairly flashed in the sun, making us easy targets for snipers, yet as far as I know there were no casualties.

The road ahead was steep, and we were loaded down with full equipment, yet we weren't allowed to rest until we reached the top of a big hill. When word came to fall out, we simply dropped in our tracks and rested our heads on our packsacks. We didn't have enough strength to loosen our equipment.

We were at *Canada Camp* for five days, from March 18th to March 23rd. It rained so hard the first day, we had an indoor parade with the troops being lined up in Nissan huts. In the evening we had a pay parade, also in the huts. (These Nissen huts, first used in WW1, were temporary corrugated steel shelters in the shape of a half-circle, similar to a Quonset.)

The day after we went to the rifle range, near *Villers-au-Bois Station Cemetery*, south of where my brother is buried. My section was shooting in the morning and in the afternoon, I took another turn at the rifle butts. Later in the day we had a lecture on tanks in the Irving Theater.

On Saturday we marched along a muddy trail towards *Mines-de-Gouy-Servin* for tank-training. Four tanks sat in an open field and we were instructed to keep 100 yards behind the tanks when advancing abreast, four feet apart, in open formation. During the demonstration, the tanks simulated 'strafing' along enemy trenches, while we (the infantry), would lie low until the tanks went forward again. We practiced this all afternoon, going back and forth on the one-kilometre field.

When it came time to eat, we all piled on the tanks and rode to the cook kitchen. We ate, marched back to camp, were shown a movie and then we got the bad news.

CHAPTER TWELVE

At first, we thought it was ridiculous to have a YMCA officer round us up only to read a brief bulletin. But the contents made our hearts stop.

This is what the bulletin reported, "After a short, intense bombardment, the German army has advanced 12 miles on the 50-mile front near *Peronne*." The officer also said *Albert* (pronounced Albare), 20 miles south of *Arras*, had been taken by the enemy. This was gut-wrenching news, and it gave us plenty to talk about as we made our way back to our billets. We could hear a big bombardment going on all that night straight east of our camp: a steady continuous pounding with intermittent bright flashes across the sky. Later we heard this was a gas bombardment by the Allied artillery, designed to relieve pressure on the area the Germans had broken through.

In the next few days, we had no official news, but plenty of rumours floated around the camp. Some said the Germans were still advancing; some said the allies had taken back the lost ground. We didn't know what to think, but on March 23rd, after an inspection parade, we left Canada Camp at 4 pm, just as the sun was setting. Our battalion was loaded on two trains, then on we went, passing through *Gouy-Servin*, *Coupigny, Aiz-Noulette, Calonne*, and on to *Loos* (about 3 kilos from *Lens*). *Loos* was partly situated on *Hill 70*. This is where the new draft of men who passed my outfit at *Etaples* (eight months before), had seen intense fighting, and suffered heavy casualties.

After we were unloaded, we marched through what had been the village of *Loos*—now a picture of desolation. The oncoming night cast dark shadows over an already bleak landscape. Streets were all but erased by fallen buildings, so that we had only a narrow, zigzagging path to follow.

Minutes later *Loos* was behind us, and we found ourselves in the 'reserve line' trenches—all chalk and mud. The reserve line, meaning we were waiting to spell off the men who were actively manning the frontline. And there we waited in dugouts until dawn when we found we could see both allied and enemy observation balloons but couldn't actually see the frontline. We felt the warmth of the sun as it rose higher in the sky, but the ground was still very muddy from the previous rain.

In the interim between gunfire, we could hear larks singing, and that was a welcome sound. However, a trench motor unit was very close to my dugout. Their intermittent boom, booming, not only silenced the birds, but kept us on our toes. A week before one of our men stepped in front of a similar gun and was accidentally shot to death by our own artillery fire. These guns were kept low, often in the mouth of an old German dugout and (until fired), were covered in a light-weight coconut matting. Being anywhere near a trench motor unit was dangerous because the guns automatically provoked enemy retaliation.

The next day it was our turn to move up the line to relieve the other half of our battalion. We exchanged places with them, and they became our support. The German-built dugouts were in good condition. Some of us left our equipment in a dugout, only to be told we weren't allowed in the dugouts. We were ordered to pick up our equipment and remain in 'battle order' in the front trenches at all times.

On the second night, one of our men stationed at the next firing step said he thought he could see something or someone moving down an enemy trench directly in front of us. So, he and I climbed out of the 'bay' and got down in a shell hole in No Man's Land to get a better look. During the night, a sergeant came out to check on us, but we had nothing to report and as daylight approached, we returned to our own 'frontline trench'.

We stayed on frontline duty for five days and nights. It was unusually quiet, in fact so quiet we knew the enemy had some devious plans in the works. On our final night, we got more rain and weren't relieved until midnight. We walked back to *Loos* in single file, expecting any minute for all hell to break out, but we were in luck. This time all of our unit escaped unharmed. Some of the men went to the cellars, but my buddies and I went to our open-air sleeping quarters which were located in some poor devil's ruined kitchen. We threw our equipment on the tiled floor, ducked under our makeshift roof. Then, still wet, shivering and hungry we slept fitfully until dawn.

The next day there were still no rations and our stomachs were rumbling. One of our men knocked on the door of an occupied house and asked for food, whereupon a civilian woman set to work cooking chips and eggs for us. We had barely started to eat, when Lieutenant Knowles came up, saying the trains were waiting to take us back to *Villers-au-Bois*.

The French lady watched in surprise as the men hastily abandoned their breakfast and headed for the train. However, Private Swabey and I ignored the train and kept eating. It was not until we saw the train leaving without us, that we made a dash for it. Breathlessly we scrambled aboard with no time to spare.

We stopped for a lunch break in a row of bow huts and stayed there until 5 pm. Then we were marched to *Mont-St. Eloi* where we spent the night in some old French army huts. After a full marching order inspection in the morning, we left *Mont-St. Eloi* and marched seven kilometres to *Roclincourt* where we were billeted for the next five days in bow huts. Because *Roclincourt* had seen massive shelling, the inhabitants had left town. Every structure had been damaged beyond repair. There were three-story brick buildings facing the square. They were a pathetic sight with walls missing, roofs smashed in, and all the window blown out. From here we could see in every direction—and what a nightmarish sight it was. In the past two years, the countryside and its ancient towns had been blown to bits. We stood shaking our heads in disbelief. How could this possibly happen in a civilized world?

Rain was pelting down when we arrived, so we endured another night trying to sleep in soggy clothing. The next day was March 31st, Easter Sunday. The sun was shining, but it was still quite chilly. We marched two kilometres to a church parade in an army church hut. Along the way, we saw many different army units: a medical hut, a cycling corps, a balloon outfit, and huts for dispatch riders. Army lorries continually dropped off supplies. Occasionally we'd see a fresh battalion moving forward, and once in awhile bedraggled enemy prisoners-of-war being escorted out.

Easter Monday broke with sunshine and a blue sky. When we were lined up for supper, one of the men in the rear spotted a small patch of smoke rising above the horizon to the south. We soon realized one of our observation balloons had been shot down. As we stared at the smoke, we made out eight more balloons and a 'Heinie' plane heading straight toward the first balloon. Next, we saw a spray of incendiary bullets and the balloon burst into flames. The plane made a tight circle and lined up on the next balloon, the one closest to where we were standing. So, we had a ringside seat as the enemy swept in to shoot again. Apparently, the occupants of the balloon saw the plane coming and baled out. Still, the plane kept going along the line of balloons, shooting down three more before he headed back behind the German line. As one of our men said, "I bet that pilot gets an iron cross for this when he goes back!"

Our morale was sinking. To many of us, it seemed like we were losing the war right then and there.

Before daybreak the next day, we went to the outskirts of *Arras* to put up barbed wire entanglements in case the enemy broke through our lines and made it this far. At that time, the possibility of German troops advancing was quite real. We needed to do everything within our power to save *Arras*. (Germany never did take *Arras*.)

There were quite a few army huts in the vicinity. In preparation for a possible enemy advance, we stripped the huts of anything of value. Then we put up all the barb wire available and waited for more orders. In subsequent afternoons, I went north with a pick and shovel party along the *Lens-Arras road*. Our job was to deepen old trenches used in 1916 and 1917. Again, we were making the trenches ready in case the allies were forced to retreat and fight for this ground. There was a certain degree of irony in these preparations. This whole weed-infested area had already been a battleground in '16 and '17, and here we were fixing it up in 1918, so it could be destroyed all over again. However, these preparations had to be made. At this point in the war, things were looking pretty grim for the Allies.

The following morning, we marched about five kilometres (full marching orders), towards the frontline to a point halfway between *Roclincourt* and *Bailleul*. Here most of the 50th Battalion spread out across open country and took up positions in old dugouts. My platoon was detailed farther west than the others and occupied huts about two to three kilos from the German frontline. There was a German cemetery near the huts with ornamental grave markers painted in bright colors. They were in stark contrast to the very plain British and Canadian grave markers. These brightly festooned enemy graves were another physiological blow that made us doubt our ability to win the war.

The *Arras-Cambrai road* was lined with a row of dead trees that had been laid to waste by shell fire. Over the trees we could see shells bursting in the air. On the third morning we were in this area, the Germans shot a lone salvo of four shells into our encampment. One exploded in front of a dugout where five men were standing. Two of the men were killed instantly. The other three were seriously wounded. Although I've forgotten his name, one of the men killed had just returned to his dugout after chatting with me. He told me he was from Montreal, Canada. A strikingly handsome, confident, and well-spoken fellow who would have made a dandy officer—had he lived.

My platoon went on three separate work parties very close to *Oppy Wood*, each night digging new trenches. Then on the night of April 9th, the Battalion moved forward to an area between the railway and the frontline. This area had barely been shelled, making it easier to move around. Here we were stationed in dugouts in an old German trench.

Now the German and Allied frontlines were only a half kilo apart, and it was our section's turn to carry rations forward to a prearranged spot which in this case happened to be a certain tree stump. Directions to the stump had been marked with white tape. This should have kept us from getting lost, but it didn't. On the first night out it was cloudy, too dark to see the white tape. Loaded down with sacks of rations, we staggered about blindly. Several times we headed in the wrong directions. It was only when the sky lit up with 'very lights' that we had any idea of where we were going. Finally, after a lot of grumbling, we located the evasive stump and dropped the rations at its base.

Each morning before daylight we were sent out to do some salvaging. This reclamation project was thought to be the brain-child of Major Perry, a ruddy-faced, good-natured Imperial man. We'd pick up anything useful such as abandoned ammunition belts, ammunition boxes, and rifles. At various times my buddies and I roamed around No Man's Land in the dark—not the safest place to hunt for useful items—but we were rewarded with several chunks of scrap iron. During the day, we packed all the salvaged items back to Battalion Headquarters.

Another day, skinny little Private Griffiths and I, decided to sneak over to the YMCA canteen which was about two kilos be-hind our dugouts. We were well aware going to the 'Y' was not sanctioned, but we had a few francs that needed to be spent. On the way down to the 'Y' the enemy opened up with several salvos that landed way too close for comfort. One shell took down the wall of a brick house directly behind us. That got us moving. We raced over to the "Y", bought chocolate bars and cigarettes and got to heck out of there. Not surprisingly, the big brass hadn't missed us. And since we knew our pals would cover for us if they did, we brought back enough goodies to share all 'round.

Three men and I took a stretcher case out one day. It seemed the man on the stretcher was a young lieutenant who had recently joined the battalion after spending a year in various officer training schools. This had been his first trip up the line. The night before this particular lieutenant was on duty, the 50th scouting party were gathering information, when they ran into the enemy doing the same thing. In the confusion there has been some bomb-throwing and casualties on both sides. The young officer hadn't been on that mission, but he'd heard of it. So, the next night this young inexperienced lieutenant was trembling in his boots when he was ordered to lead the scouting party. There hadn't been any grenade throwing that evening. He didn't appear to be injured; yet for some unknown reason, he remained unconscious all the way to the dressing station. He was six-foot tall and weighed over 200 pounds. He made quite a load, especially since Private Griffiths, who was one of the stretcher-bearers, weighed no more than 110 pounds. (We jokingly said Griffiths was safe from enemy snipers. He was so thin they'd never be able to hit him.) Needless to say, little Griffiths got winded and we had to stop to rest at least twenty times on our way out.

A few days later, I was returning from taking salvage to Battalion Headquarters, and came across my old buddy, Private Swabey. I hadn't seen him since February when we went salvaging together at *Hersin-Coupigny*. Now, he was sitting on a groundsheet in front of his dugout cleaning a Lewis gun. The groundsheet was covered with parts. He smiled up and said, "I'm with the machinegun section of "D" Company now."

"A machine-gunner, eh?"

"Yep," Swabey replied. "It's not such a bad placement. I like it better than being gun fodder in the bloody infantry."

Talking to Swabey got me to thinking. Maybe I'd be better off as a machine-gunner. That is to say, if the opportunity presented itself, maybe I should take it.

And the chance came sooner than I expected.

On April 15th, 1918, Sergeant Maconochie came to our battalion. He was from the highlands of Scotland. Since Gaelic was his native language, he was difficult to understand. He'd been sent to make a list of suitable men to join a new machinegun corp. This corps, when fully operational, would provide a machinegun battalion for each Canadian Division on the line. The sergeant was choosing 12 men from each company, four from each platoon. On coming to the 13th platoon, he didn't ask any questions, he just wrote down four names and mine was one of them. Having recently spoken to Private Swabey, I wasn't about to protest. I didn't know it at the time, but I'd be going for machinegun training immediately. It would be three and a half months before I'd be back on the frontline.

Now, I'm not downplaying the role we were assigned to as machine-gunners. We had an extremely dangerous role to play in trench warfare. In the event the allies were forced to retreat, we machine-gunners would be ordered to hold our positions to allow our main body of troops to escape. As machine-gunners, we were well aware of the risks. If the enemy was advancing, we would be required to remain at our guns until we were killed or captured.

Fifty men were being sent to machinegun training school. And after preliminaries, all fifty of us were marched to *Neuville-Saint-Vaast*, a small farming village four miles north of *Arras*. The buildings in this town were mostly constructed of chalk blocks and had been bombed to pieces. (44,833 WWI soldiers were buried in the German War Cemetery at *Neuville-Saint-Vaast*.)

We waited here until April 17th when we were on the move again, this time marching through *Mont-St. Eloi,* and past *Villers-au-Bois*, then downhill to *Verdrel Woods* where we stayed for a week, waiting for the machinegun school to be organized farther west.

To stay in this restful countryside was a blessing no words can describe. We were so drained by the constant rain of shells that everything away from that hideous bloodbath had a bright new look. We were free to stroll down country lanes lined with living trees: tall green elms, oaks, and sycamores, and our only parades were to the cookhouse door. This was wonderful! A breath of life replacing the dead and dying!

Food was still in short supply. So, one day Private Frazer and I walked two kilos to *Barlin* for a square meal consisting of three fried eggs, fried spuds, bread and coffee—all for only two francs and fifty centimes.

While at *Verdrel Woods*, we brushed off a site for boxing matches. The first match was between two new machinegun recruits. One wore the regulation kilt of a Canadian Scottish Regiment (although he didn't have an ounce of Scottish blood in him). His opponent was a little French Canadian dressed in black, who said, "Back home I lived on eggnogs when I was training to be a boxer" What a show they put on! We laughed and cheered until we were hoarse.

From *Verdrel Woods,* we went to *Camblain-le-Abbe*, a beautiful village in a wooded area complete with an ancient church, and a very old flour mill that had a working water wheel. We didn't stop long here but went back to *Mont-St. Eloi* where we were billeted in huts for eight more days.

After coming off guard duty one day, I saw about eighty enemy prisoners in dull grey uniforms. Some of them wore tin helmets, some were bare headed; a few were still wearing greatcoats, but to a man they were the picture of doom and gloom. Maybe we were winning the war, after all!

On the first of May, our route march was through *Villers-au-Bois*. This was the last time I passed my brother's grave as a soldier in uniform.

Eventually, we were set up near the picturesque town of *Guisy* in bell tents with wooden floors. Machinegun classes didn't start until the middle of May. Until then, we were employed in various manual tasks: levelling the ground for bow tents, erecting huts, carrying building material, sections of floors, and corrugated sheets of iron for roofing. We also went on route marches, which were made pleasant by good-natured officers. I recall one march was made towards *Guisy* on a scorching hot day. After an hour, a halt was called for the customary "five-minute-rest-per-hour." However, in the heat of the day, the officer in charge didn't order the men to 'fall in' until it was time to get back to camp for supper—over an hour later.

Monday May 13th, 1918, the machinegun classes finally got underway. We had a sergeant-instructor for every eight men, this being a full machinegun crew. The formal parade was dispensed with. At bugle call, men simply fell into the left of their instructor. Then we were lined up at six-pace intervals, one in front of each other. After that, we'd march to the storage shed to get our machineguns. If the weather was fine, we'd march down a country lane to a large open field and sit in the shade, well-spaced so as not to disturb one another. When it rained, classes were held in bow tents.

The first week was taken up with stripping the Lewis gun and learning the names of parts and their function. My instructor was a likable man, knew his job, was friendly, and level-headed. He suggested that notebooks would be helpful, so I bought a notebook at a little shop in *Aubin-Saint-Vaast* and carried it with me to every class. During the second week, each of us had to take the gun

159

apart, clean it and put it back together. We also took notes on stoppages and how to remedy them. Then we learned what procedures and actions to take when firing. The third week, we had gun drill and an intensive review of the course. Each officer was in charge of eight classes. The men in these classes were then lined up on the parade ground. At the command, "Mount gun," each #1 picked up the gun; each #2 picked up the tripod and each #3 took a box of ammunition, then we raced forward, and set up the gun as quickly as possible. Numbers 4, 5, and 6 remained standing with spare ammunition.

The next command was "Load gun," with the sergeant standing by to see his orders were carried out satisfactorily. At this stage only dummy ammunition was being used. After this drill was completed to the sergeant's satisfaction, he'd give the command #1 fall out. Number one would then be presumed to be a casualty and number two would take the fallen man's position. And so it went until each of us had taken a turn at every position. The next command was "Dismount the gun." We'd then take the gun apart, run back six paces with it, and the drill would start all over again. As each man took over the gun, he'd repeat the order given by the officer— yelling the order so all could hear.

In days to come we had firing practice with live ammunition, firing at targets in front of a bank of clay. Every 7th round in the cartridge belt would be taken out, so that the gun would fire in bursts of six, signalling the end of a man's turn. As each man took his turn, he'd sit in the firing position, roll the crank handle over, fire and retire to the end of the line.

It was now mid-summer and days were longer and warmer. More hours of daylight gave us more time for classes and drills, and still left us about two hours of free time before the 9:30 pm roll call. After the day's classes, many of the soldiers would be sitting or lying in the grass, reading, studying notes or just smoking. A few of the men would go down to the *Canche River* to swim—not the best idea as the river could be unpredictable. Two men drowned in the *Canche* while I was stationed in the *Aubin-Saint Vaast* area.

When I had free time, I preferred to round up a like-minded fellow and set out to see the country. On May 21st, I walked to *Hesdin* with Private McNeil who was in my gun section. In civilian life, McNeil was a truck driver for Burns and Company in *Cranbrook*, B.C. The day we went to *Hesdin*, we were both broke, so couldn't buy a thing. But three days later when we got paid, we hiked back, and each purchased a bottle of champagne. After drinking one bottle on the way back, McNeil insisted I open the second. If I didn't, he was going back for another bottle. Consequently, only a small portion of the second bottle reached camp to be shared with Private Tempest, a well-educated Welshman from our section. Mc Neil was always ready for adventure, and we went on many more excursions together, rain or shine. Sometimes we'd go to *Hesdin*. At other times, we'd go on long hikes just to see what was on the other side of a hill. On two different occasions, I walked to the small farming community of *Lambus*. On the way I met a young French lad named Emil Mignot who was working on his father's farm. The first time he was pasturing a cow on the end of a lead rope as there were no fences. The second time he was stooking wheat. I enjoyed visiting with him, mostly by sign language. He knew a little about Canada, was anxious to come to Canada one day, and I promised to write to him when I got home.

When last I was in *Hesdin*, I noticed a photographer's shop operated by M. Singier. So, I stopped in to have a picture taken on May 29th. As there was no provision for cleaning myself up, I washed my hands and face in a rain puddle outdoors.

The following picture was the results. I wasn't pleased with the picture. Having recently been on frontline duty, it was obvious I was suffering from frontline stress.

May 29, 1918: William showing signs of exhaustion
Picture taken by Photographie Artistique Singier,
6 Rue des Nobles, Marche au Beurre, Hesdin, France
Credit, daughter Doreen (Lees) Thomsen

When the machinegun school was well established, we had time to put up a 30' X 60' drill shed and cover it with corrugated tin. My section got the job of digging shallow drain ditches around it. About this time one of the big brass got the notion we should scrub our web equipment. Nothing would do but we had to go down to the river to do the cleaning, And, of all things, use nail brushes and hairbrushes to complete the job. Another time eight men, including me, had to paint a building with hot tar.

On July 6th, 1918, drills and classes stopped for Sports Day and all the roads leading to the event were crowded with incoming troops. Even a few Americans joined in the celebrations. In the midst of ball games, foot races and boxing, several aeroplanes gave a fantastic aeronautic demonstration.

On the 25th of July, we had a personal clean-up. First, we took off all our clothes, except our greatcoats which we wore. Other garments were tied in bundles and then fumigated by dumping the bundles into a large tank of disinfectant. This was done under steam pressure. The clothing came out slightly damp with the brass buttons badly tarnished. To do a thorough job of sanitation that afternoon, we had to scrub the floors in every hut. Of course, after the thorough cleanup, we had to put a shine on tarnished buttons.

Polishing buttons was not something I enjoyed; it was an especially tedious job after a chlorine treatment. Partly due to having to shine buttons, I was late for 'parade' the next morning. As punishment, myself and three others were given an hour of pack drill. The sergeant came to our tent, called out our names, and gave the order. "Fall in on the parade ground, full packs and equipment! Immediately!"

163

Once at the parade ground (loaded down with all of our equipment), it was, "Slope arms. Right turn. Quick march!" Then after 20 paces the order was, "About turn. Quick march, 40 paces." Alternately, it would be, "About turn, Left wheel, About turn, Two deep." A time or two, one of us would get confused, collide with the man in front, and there'd be a devil of a pile-up. We were given a minute's rest after the first half hour, then the same drill, time and time again until the hour was up. We certainly got a workout, and it wasn't much fun. Naturally, I didn't go walking that afternoon.

Later on in the training program, a "map reading" class was added. This was a subject I'd excelled in at my school in England, so I thoroughly enjoyed this segment of the program. Other than that it was the usual machinegun classes, work parties and parades, but certainly nothing we couldn't handle. However, by the beginning of August, we knew we'd be leaving for the frontlines, and I think it's safe to say none of us were looking forward to trench warfare, again. We had been at *Aubin-Saint Vaast* for three months and three days. The good times had come to an end.

On August 6th, 1918, a whole trainload of machine-gunners were consigned to twenty French railway wagons—the kind intended for 40 hommes et 8 chevaux (40 men and eight horses). As the train slowly pulled away, I took a last look at the green countryside, realizing how different everything would be from here on in.

After going through *Hesdin* and *Saint-Pol*, the scenery was new to me. We passed *Frévent* and *Canaples* and into the *Somme Valley* where the *River Somme* was about 80 feet wide. The river was 30 miles from the sea and very muddy. *Picquigny* turned out to be our immediate destination. Here we were detrained at 4 pm and marched through town which (at the time), had a population of approximately 4,000.

Picquigny, built on the Somme River, was navigable by barges with a series of small docks to accommodate them. A few Canadian soldiers were already walking down the streets. However, we machine-gunners marched on, up the hill behind the town, then on to open fields where a number of bell tents had been erected. There were not nearly enough tents to accommodate us, but we crowded in anyway, 20 men to each tent. Neither was there enough food to go around, so we late-comers went hungry. Some of us decided to go in search of a "Y", but when we found one, the only things left to buy were a few packages of broken cookies. They were sold out of everything else. Little wonder as the main road was crowded with British, Canadian, Australian, and American soldiers. We didn't know it at the time, but all this traffic was part of the final preparation for the big, allied drive, scheduled to take place near *Amiens,* on August 8th.

****

The Bigger Picture: The Battle of Amiens, was the first phase of the hundred-day offensive by the Allies which ultimately led to the end of World War I. Allied forces, comprised of British, Australian, and Canadian troops advanced over 11 kilometres (7miles) on the first day. This led German Erich Ludendorff to say, that August 8th, 1918 (the first day of the battle), was "The Black Day of the German Army. For Canada, it came at a cost of 1,036 killed, 2,803 injured, and 29 taken prisoner.

****

CHAPTER THIRTEEN

From where we were camped, we had a good view of *Amiens*. We could see the cathedral tower rising 350 feet above the rest of the town which lay in a haze of smoke. An occasional burst of shells would explode somewhere beyond the town, followed by an ominous rumble.

The next day we had to get lunch at the quartermaster's store. This was located very close to *Picquingny Castle* and the *Somme River Bridge*. Soup and bread were the meal of the day. Several other men and I took our rations to the bridge to eat them there. As I sat on a girder, I couldn't help eying up the castle. How could I get into the castle and have a look around? I'd been told it was built in 1066 and had a long and very interesting history. So, after supper the same day, I convinced Private Bradley (a soldier from the 191st Battalion), to go to the castle with me. I'd met Bradley six months earlier when I was in the 191st.

Soon he and I were roaming around the outside of the castle, looking for a way to get in. One ten-foot wall sloped inward. We tried climbing it, got partway up, and then lost our footing. Several other walls defeated us just as easily. We were about to give up when we discovered a wall with sufficient finger and toe holds to slither up. This we did, and then wandered aimlessly around until we came to a flat stone courtyard. Here we ran into a problem. A dozen French soldiers were having a conversation on the far side of a low wall. They didn't appear to see us, so we quietly slipped into a passage that led to the main part of the castle.

167

We explored several dark, musty rooms and alcoves, peered through arrow slits that served as windows. When it came time to leave, we were met with several locked doors, and presently came to a massive gate overlooking the river bridge where I'd eaten lunch earlier in the day. This gate was fashioned with dangerous looking spikes as well as great iron locks. It was no use trying to climb that gate. We began to question whether we'd ever get out. Eventually, we found our way to the familiar courtyard. However, this time we were spotted by the French soldiers. Although they were yelling at us in French, we didn't need a translator. They were out to get us!

We raced back to where we'd come in and dived over the wall, pleased as Punch with our escape. Our arms and legs may have been bruised, but we'd got what we wanted: a self-guided tour of the famous *Picquingny Castle*.

August 8th: After supper Private McNeil and I walked downtown where we saw a whole trainload of wounded soldiers go by, six coaches marked with the Red Cross insignia. The setting sun was throwing a stream of light through the train's windows, showing a mass of faceless men with sunken eyes and heads wrapped in bandages. McNeil and I looked at one another. We were thinking the same thing. This could be us in a few days. We knew beyond a doubt, we'd be shipped back to the frontlines very shortly. What condition would we come back?

Sure enough, after dinner the next day, August 9th, we were marched through *Picquingny* to the railway tracks where a troop train was waiting to take us forward. Limber wagons had been loaded on the train's flatcars, and we scrambled into the nearest wagon and waited. But when the train showed no signs of moving, a bunch of us hopped down and ran over to the "Y" to buy snacks. By the time I got to the canteen, there were twenty men lined up in front of me. So, I waited impatiently. When I was the fourth man up, someone yelled, "The train's leaving!"

After waiting in a queue this long, I wasn't about to leave empty-handed. When the fellows ahead of me ran for the train, I stayed put and bought four packets of cookies and a handful of chocolate bars. Then I, too, took off at a gallop. The train which had been moving at a snail pace, was now gathering steam with three of us shoppers tearing down the tracks after it. The other two fellows quickly gave up, but I kept running flat out. I was within four feet of the caboose and my buddies were cheering me on. One of the men threw a hand out to pull me up, but the train outran me. I just couldn't make it.

Well, what to do now? I sat down on the track, panting, until the other two fellows caught up with me. Then together we walked to a railway crossing farther up the line and waited for another train to come along. The next train didn't stop. It was moving at about 8 miles an hour, as fast as an ordinary person could run. We immediately saw one boxcar with an open door, so we made a beeline for that and jumped in. This train was operated by the British Army Service Corps and was destined for *Amiens*.

We were in luck. When this train stopped, we could see the other train—the one we were supposed to be on—up ahead. However, before I got to my section, the elusive train started up again, so I hopped into the nearest carriage and travelled to *Saleaux Station* where all the troops were unloaded. I quickly found my platoon and blended in before I was missed by the big brass.

Late in the afternoon we were assembled in a 'column o' route' and marched fourteen kilometres to *Boves*, a farming village—nine kilometres in daylight and five after dark. The area was a conglomerate of woods and open fields, very picturesque in the daytime. It hadn't been shelled heavily, but the inhabitants had fled, taking their furnishings with them. So, there were plenty of empty houses for the troops to occupy. Rations were scarce, so the next morning a few of us went to search for a "Y" to supplement our scanty meal. However, the village of *Boves* had been under German occupation two days before, so the canteen hadn't had time to move up yet.

Later that morning, we noticed a great cloud of dust approaching. No rain had fallen in this area for some time, so the road was dry and dusty. Presently, we saw about one thousand German prisoners-of-war being herded along by allied mounted cavalry. The prisoners were walking four abreast and the column seemed endless. They were a sorry looking lot, in all styles of dress: caps and tin hats; some bare headed; most had leather trench boots. And to a man, they all wore the same expression of discouragement and fatigue. I had never imagined, let alone seen so many prisoners. My first thought was one of elation. If there were this many prisoners, maybe, just maybe, we were actually winning the war.

As the prisoners drew alongside, they stopped to rest. Seeing that we were carrying water bottles, the nearest pointed to the bottles and used sign language to ask for a drink. Most of us gladly obliged. While the bottles were being handed around, one of our own men showed his disapproval by shouting, "Aw, shoot the b…..s!" Other machine-gunners took this opportunity to search the prisoners' pockets for souvenirs. This was approved by the officers. If we were to win the war the big brass wanted us to not only hate the enemy, but to show them disrespect.

In the afternoon, twenty of us machine-gunners set out for Battalion Headquarters. As we marched along, we came to some British gun emplacements in a wooded area. These had been firing the day before but were now silent. Beyond these woods to the east, were rolling hills and a good many neglected fields of ripe grain. Farther along, we came to a partly demolished brewery. Here we stopped to rest and were surprised to find six dead enemy soldiers, lying in a row, partially covered in blankets.

Shortly after we resumed our march, a motor lorry came along, and we were able to get a lift for the next two kilometres. After being dropped off at the side of the road, we hiked a short distance across a field to Divisional Headquarters, arriving there just as the sun was setting.

Once at headquarters, we were turned over to the 2nd Battalion Canadian Machinegun Corps and the appropriate entries were made in our pay books. After eating the remainder of our rations, our section was sent forward to join our newly designated company. The night was cloudless, starlit, and the road narrow. At one point in a bend of the road, we came across some recently shot enemy soldiers, a half dozen, still lying where they fell. There was a large German gun close by. It was sitting under a bank, camouflaged. Before abandoning the gun, the enemy had spiked it by exploding a charge in its muzzle, reasoning that a spiked gun couldn't be used against them.

We passed through the small village named *Cayeaux* and stopped to rest in an opening among the trees. We could hear a plane coming in from the east. It turned out to be a German bomber which we could see when searchlights lit up the sky. The plane droned on, louder, and louder. When it was almost directly overhead, the 'Heiny' dumped his load. The explosion was deafening. We saw the brilliant flash, felt the shockwaves, but thankfully no casualties were reported.

Another one and a half kilos and we came to *Caix*, in *Luce River Valley*. The tiny village had been in enemy hands the day before. There were signs of intense artillery fire. And the buildings—what was left of them—were still smouldering. We wandered around hoping to find the unit we'd been assigned to. No luck! We had tramped over twenty kilometres that day and were extremely footsore. So, we entered the ruins of a brick house, threw down our packs, slumped down beside them, and slept until daybreak.

Sunday August 11th: Getting up in the morning, meant standing from a sitting position. I got to my feet and since the other men were sleeping, I took myself for a walk around what must have been a very pretty little town before the bombing. A mist had settled at ground-level. Above the mist, I could see a church tower, so I went to investigate.

The church had suffered very little damage, and since the door was open, I went in and climbed the circular stairway to the top of the tower. Due to the mist, I was only able to see the immediate area around *Caix*. What an appalling sight, nothing but devastation on every hand. The town had been behind British lines until March 1918, when the German had driven the British out. Now, it was back in the hands of our Allies.

On getting back to the pile of bricks, I found the other men were moving around, some yawning and stretching to get the cricks out of their necks. Others were shaving. At 8:30 am, we were mustered together, then marched a short distance to some chalk pits north of *Caix*. The chalk pits had been dug into an overhanging fifty-foot cliff. To one side of the cliff was a fairly level half-acre pad. Here we waited for rations to arrive. None came until noon when a cook kitchen showed up to ladle out a very meagre portion of watery mulligan.

As it happened, our section of the Canada Machine Gun Corps was reserves. We were not yet needed on the new frontline that was only two kilometres east of us. That afternoon, we moved farther west, behind some trees. As soon as it got dark, serious enemy bombing started up. We quickly realized this bombing was going to be a regular nightly occurrence while we were in this area—darkness and explosions, in that order.

We could hear the droning of German planes and searchlights threw light on the planes as they came toward us. They'd zoom over, dump their loads and just as swiftly fly back behind enemy lines. After the deafening crash of explosives, there'd be the rattle of allied machinegun fire, then a period of nervous silence.

There was a shallow trench that veered off about thirty feet from where we were hunkered down in the trees. No doubt it was used by enemy machine-gunners before the Canadian advance. We decided to deepen this with our trench tools and occupy it ourselves. Private McNeil deepened a man-size hole in his section, and I occupied an already deep hole next to him. We were fortunate the weather was sunny while we were there because we had no roof to shelter under. For much of that week, we troops slept with nothing under us but groundsheets, and nothing over us but greatcoats and the stars.

On August 15th, an Australian Cavalry unit was camped about thirty yards from our trenches and suffered a direct hit during the night. When daylight came, several of us went over to survey the damage. What a gruesome sight! Three Australians and twenty horses had been killed, and there were bits of flesh and bone scattered all over the place. Because this was close to the trenches we were occupying, we decided it was time to move farther back—which we did.

Another day we had a bath parade in German-made bath-houses. They had cement floors and decent showers, quite an improvement on the makeshift arrangements we were accustomed to.

For the next three days we did odd jobs: packed water in Dixie pots from a well a kilo away for the cooks to use in their mobile cook kitchen. We also cleaned limbers which wasn't in our line of work. But the job had to be done, and someone had to do it. When we were confronted with a dirty job, we did it cheerfully— or else. The army officers referred to this manual labour as character building, and I believe they were correct.

While out walking that day, I was to witness another allied observation balloon being shot down by an enemy plane. Never a good sight!

Rumours had it the enemy was on the run, and we hoped this were true. Toward sunset on August 17th, we got "full marching order" and started out to join the rest of our Battalion who were closer to the front. For some reason, we got on the wrong road and began going in circles. We came to a halt, stood around for several minutes while the sergeant got his bearings. Then off we marched again until we came to a narrow valley with several springs flowing from the ground. This happened to be the headwaters of the *Luce River*. We spent the night on the banks of the river in shallow dugouts.

The next day, Sunday, August 18th, 1918, at muster roll, I was assigned to #1 section, "J" Battery, #3 Company. This was my final transfer, and I would stay in this same section, battery and company until I was discharged from the army ten months later.

THE OFFICER COMMANDING,

OFFICERS, N.C.Os., & MEN

of the

2ND BN. C.M.G.C.

extend to you

the

SEASON'S GREETINGS

through

William Lees

The Field.   26ᵗʰ NOV. 1918.

ROLL OF OFFICERS

BATTALION HEADQUARTERS.

Officer Commanding, Lt.-Col. E. W. Sansom
2nd I/Command, Major Alex Graham

Adjt. Capt. G. N. Douglas.   Q.M. Hon. Lt. E. B. Underwood, M.C., D.C.M.
Asst. Adjt. Lt. S. G. Fildes

Signal O. Lt. S. E. Sacks, M.C.   Asst. Q.M. Lieut. A. P. Williams
M.O. Capt. J. A. Stewart (CAMC)
Paymaster Lieut. W. A. Fowler (CAPC)
Chaplain Capt. E. F. Johnston (C.C.F.)

No. 1 COMPANY.

O.C. Major J. Basevi, D.S.O.   T.O. Lt. L. A. Carrier

"A" BATTERY	"B" BATTERY
Capt. L. F. White, M.C.	Capt. H. A. Creighton
Lieut. R. M. McKenzie	Lieut. W. A. Carr
Lieut. J. H. Garlick	Lieut. G. E. K. Bingham
Lieut. L. A. Cuff	

"C" BATTERY	"D" BATTERY
Capt. G. Hobson, M.C., M.M.	Capt. G. E. Harley
Lieut. W. Beatty	Lieut. W. G. Welsford
Lieut. A. C. Smith	Lieut. D. Urquhart

No. 2 COMPANY.

Officer Commanding, Major J. E. McCorkell
Transport Officer, Lieut. W. A. Brown

"E" BATTERY	"F" BATTERY
Capt. J. Stonehewer	Capt. J. A. Ramsay
Lieut. D. S. Jackson	Lieut. F. Layton
Lieut. L. G. Howard	Lieut. G. A. Urquhart
Lieut. F. R. Bolton	Lieut. D. J. Hutchings
	Lieut. I. F. Price

"G" BATTERY	"H" BATTERY
Lieut. L. Withrow	Lieut. C. W. Blair
Lieut. A. H. Cameron	Lieut. K. S. Stover
Lieut. C. H. Colwell	Lieut. W. R. Cox
Lieut. L. Richards	

No. 3 COMPANY.

Officer Commanding, Major J. A. McCamus, M.C.
Transport Officer, Lieut. P. S. Wilson

"J" BATTERY	"K" BATTERY
Capt. H. S. Salisbury, M.C.	Lieut. T. H. Dudley, M.C.
Lieut. G. Marshall	Lieut. D. H. Ross
Lieut. H. A. Scott	Lieut. J. Ketchum
Lieut. G. Comstock	Lieut. W. E. Millsap

"L" BATTERY	"M" BATTERY
Lieut. A. B. White	Capt. E. J. K. Norris
Lieut. J. G. Garneau	Lieut. I. G. McLaren, M.C.
Lieut. A. F. Mahaffy	Lieut. H. M. Sibbald
	Lieut. G. Jack, M.M.
	Lieut. H. de B. Anderson

On August 19ᵗʰ, there was a pay parade (I received 20 francs). Just before dark, another company of troops arrived to relieve us and we (machine-gunners), received orders to move back. Under-cover of darkness, we marched through *Caix, Cayeaux,* and *Hangard* to the road going from *Roye* to *Amiens*. At this time *Amiens* was a hotspot with the enemy putting every effort into taking the city. We followed the road to *Amiens* for two kilometres then turned into a forested area, the *Bois Gentelles*, where we stayed overnight. It was now midnight; and we had no bedding, just groundsheets and greatcoats.

175

We rested until 3 pm and then set off again, making our next stop just outside of *Longueau,* five kilos from the city of *Amiens.* We were amazed to see the vast number of German machineguns and artillery the enemy had left behind. Several machineguns looked like Vickers-Maxim but were four times as large. After seeing this huge accumulation of enemy guns, one of our men remarked with a big grin, "This *really* looks like we're winning the war!"

We still had no idea where we were going, but we resumed our travels partly by train, partly by lorries, partly by long tedious marching, and finally we came to *Moncheaux.* At this stop, Private McNeil and I had time to walk a kilo and a half to *Buneville* to buy snacks. The weather had warmed up considerably, so McNeil and I broke the rules by taking off our tunics and carrying them over our shoulders. It was very peaceful, with farmers haying, birds singing and not a single sound of guns firing.

On August 20th at 3 pm, we left *Moncheaux* and marched to *Petit Huvin* where we waited for a train. While waiting we were able to fill our water bottles at an unusual type of well that had a coiled spring apparatus bringing water to the surface. And then we were on our way by train via *Saint Pol* and detrained near *Maroeuil.* This small town was northwest of *Arras.* From here, the big guns could be heard quite clearly. Two loud detonations occurred at close range as we began our forward march. We soon learned we'd be going up the line from *Dainville.* Part of the battery had already set out after dark, but the men I was with had not received orders to advance.

While waiting, I wrote to my sister Evelyne, wondering if this might be my last letter home. From here on, we'd be in the thick of war. A well-organized, all-out Allied push had been planned, and we thought we were prepared for what was coming—as prepared as we could be for such a fierce winner-take-all battle.

Finally, just before dark, we got orders to get ready to move out. We were under full marching order plus each of us carried a box of machinegun ammunition. After five kilometres of marching, we reached *Achicourt*. The little town had been badly shelled and was still occupied by a few civilians.

We didn't stop here but kept marching. Soon it was totally dark, and it began to rain. For a time, we slogged along through the drizzle with mud lapping at out puttees. Now the sound of big guns pounding away was deafening, and we knew we were closing in on the frontline. We came to another village where we rejoined the part of our battery that left the day before us.

We late-comers found our billets: a bombed house patched up with scavenged boards, planks, and tin sheets. Eight of us took over an eight by twelve room that had only two walls standing. The missing walls and roof were enclosed with scraps of wood and tin to make a ham-fisted shelter. We were soaked to the bone. About two in the morning, rations were brought around, and they included a healthy rum ration. This was followed by the news that we were due to go over the top at 4 am.

After lining up in the rain, we started marching along a road through open country. We were under full marching order and spelled off carrying machineguns as well as ammunition. At times, when the sky lit up with an explosion, we could see spikes of bombed trees poking up along the roadway. Eventually, we found a trench. Slipping and sliding, we followed that until at last we reached the frontline trenches where an infantry battalion was hunkered down, waiting for zero hour—four a.m.

We were past being excited, just cold and shivering in the pelting rain. Still, we crouched low, hearing only occasional gun-fire. After what seemed like a lifetime, four o'clock finally came. Very suddenly every gun in the country opened fire, a heavy barrage that lasted several minutes. Then somebody yelled, "They're away!"

CHAPTER FOURTEEN

August 21, 1918: We knew the infantry had their orders to advance over the top. A minute after they plunged ahead, we got the word to go. We jumped out of the trenches and raced forward. Being dark it was hard to know which way to go, but orders were to keep advancing—to close up behind the infantry. The troops behind us would 'mop up', round up prisoners, and give aid to the wounded.

Shells were exploding around us. A shell slapped into the mud between me and the man ahead. It was a dud. Had it exploded both of us would have been killed instantly. We kept going. We came to a concrete strong point. Two of the enemy were manning a machinegun. No doubt they had just come out of their dugout when the infantry ran by. We grabbed our rifles, dropped to the ground and fired several rounds at them. As we crawled close to the strong box, we saw the two Germans slumped beside their machinegun—dead. We also saw several heads poke up from the trench—enemy soldiers. Having abandoned their machinegun, they were holding their hands above their heads. Immediately, the mop-up crew arrived to surround and disarm them.

A tiny streak of daylight was slowly lighting the eastern sky. The rain had stopped, but the mist was rising. The second wave of Canadian infantry came abreast. Two of them threw hand grenades down the entrance of a strong-point dugout. Suddenly, a Canadian tank loomed out of the mist. It cut across in front of us, on its way to destroy enemy machinegun nests, known to be placed at intervals along a secondary trench.

We pushed ahead, hurrying as hard as we could in a muddy mess churned up by heavy shelling. It was hard slogging with our rifles, bayonets and equipment; #1, carrying the gun; #2, the tripod, the other four men each carrying a box of ammunition.

Presently, we came to another trench. This one had been heavily pounded. Here we got orders to halt, set up the machinegun, and await further developments. The infantry was a short distance ahead. They also halted as they had reached their first objective.

While we were setting up our gun, several prisoner-of-war straggled by accompanied by two Canadian lieutenants. One of the lieutenants had been wounded and wasn't able to walk farther. The uninjured officer had bandaged his friend's head and shoulders and was attempting to make the prisoners understand they had to carry the wounded man out. Having worked himself into a rage, we half expected the lieutenant to strike one of the prisoners before he got his message across. In due course, the unwilling stretcher-bearers were subjugated, and the procession disappeared in the mist.

About this time, two more men walked up to us. They were from a tank that had just been razed by shellfire. One of them, a blond young man, had a gaping wound below his left shoulder. He asked if anyone could give him a field dressing, so I cut the sleeve off his tunic, clamped my own field dressing on him, and bandaged him up. Before he set off down the line, he gave me an army-service, field revolver and ammo to use with it. He told me the revolver had belonged to his tank commander who had been killed earlier that morning when their tank was put out of commission.

We were supposed to be in the vicinity of *Monchy-le-Preux*, but due to the heavy smoke, we couldn't see the place. The heavy gunfire had let up somewhat, so we stayed here with the machineguns at the ready for three hours. At noon the mist and smoke rose, and we could see *Monchy-le-Preux*. The town was still held by the enemy who were taking a real pounding from British guns.

We finally received orders to go ahead. After moving a short distance, we came to an old German communication trench with funk holes covered by corrugated iron sheeting. We were ordered to stop here until further notice. While waiting, I found a new pair of woollen socks. They were dry and I put them on straight away.

At 6 pm, orders were received for our section to move another kilometre forward, until we were opposite *Monchy-le-Preux*. This we did. Two others and I were in an open shell hole. It was very windy, so we crept out hoping to find enough salvage material to make a cover for ourselves. We found a few small scraps of wood, certainly not enough to keep the wind at bay. As a result, we spent a miserably cold night, waiting and watching for our next order.

At last morning came, and after daylight we could clearly see *Monchy-le-Preux*. A hill to the south of the town was being subjected to another severe shelling from British guns. However, we didn't move forward until 10 am, going across open ground until we came to a low chalk ridge. We could see piles of white chalk. This had been excavated by the German troops in order to construct their communication trench. This trench zigzagged over the ridge and was deep and well built with trench mats along the bottom. We moved through this trench a short distance. Then a temporary halt was ordered due to German shelling immediately in front of us. Here we stayed for half an hour, wondering what to expect. A walking-wounded staggered by and stopped only long enough to say, "It's a hell of a place, up there."

We soon got orders to advance in single file. We were to leave 10 feet between ourselves and the man in front of us—in order to lessen casualties under fire. We turned down a shallow trench, right into an area that was currently being shelled by the enemy. Three infantrymen had just been hit. Two were already dead, the third had his face shot away, but he was still groaning most pitifully. Although it was a distressing sight we couldn't stop. We had to follow orders and keep moving as quickly as possible.

After some time, we stopped to rest at a point where the trench took a ninety-degree bend. Here an entire enemy machinegun section had been wiped out. I was becoming hardened to the sight of death and felt in the pockets of one of the dead. I found some picture postcards and kept them to add to my collection. I also found a metal matchbox holder with a "Big Bertha" gun engraved on it. In retrospect, robbing the dead seems like a heartless thing to do, but when we'd been indoctrinated to believe these young Germans were to be hated, taking from an enemy didn't seem immoral. And after all, one of them killed my brother.

Presently, we went ahead again and came to what had been a tree-lined stream. Now, the trees were twisted and split, and the ground so badly shelled we could barely see where the original watercourse had been. We waded through shell holes, then climbed a steep slope and found ourselves in a sandpit. We stopped here, while one of our men was ordered to crawl on his belly, look over the ridge and observe what was happening in the next valley.

While we waited for his return, I took off my gasmask to adjust it, set it down, and forgot to pick it up. The scout soon crept back, saying we'd have to go back about 100 yards and take a different route. So, we started off, backtracking and had gone some distance when I realized, I'd left my gasmask behind. I hurried back, found it, then raced to catch the others who were taking a break in another sandpit. The Germans had lined this dugout with planks. It appeared they had occupied the dugouts the night before.

Two other men and I went down into the dugout and found nothing more than a few pieces of broken equipment. We came back up just as some prisoners of war were passing by. They, too, were held up by our machine-gunners who went through pockets but found little in the way of souvenirs.

Just as we began moving ahead, we heard an enemy bomber coming. We made a dash for cover, not knowing whether the pilot spotted us or not, but the bomb he released exploded less than 100 yards away, so it's my guess he did. We were now past *Monchy le Preux,* yet still not as far forward as we should be.

It was 3 pm before we came to another sandpit with improvised shelters. We spent the night at this spot. However, the shelters could be observed from the enemy's side of the valley, and any movement we made could be seen with the naked eye. Most of the men (myself included), dug into the slope of the sandpit with our entrenching tools, and made a shelter to lie down in. We were exhausted. We weren't supposed to doze off, but some, including me, did anyway. As the sun sank below the top of the sandpit, a cold wind arose, and I woke up shivering and hungry. We were all famished; we'd had nothing to eat since early morning.

Just before dark, Private Hughes and I were detailed to go out to meet the ration wagons. We cut across to the *Arras-Cambrai* road where a stone bridge had once spanned the *Cojeul River.* The original bridge had been blown up and now engineers were repairing it with timbers. We walked a little farther and waited at a crossroad beside a building that was eighty percent demolished. While we waited, four stretcher bearers appeared, carrying a wounded man. As they stopped to rest, some POWs came along and were immediately detailed to carry the stretcher. Hughes and I waited until after dark, but when no rations showed up, we went back to the sandpit. An hour later we returned to the crossroad, waited, and waited, but no rations came. So, our platoon went hungry until rations came up just before dawn the next day—our first food in twenty-four hours.

Shelling through the night was intermittent. Nevertheless, one of the machine-gunners from another section took a piece of shrapnel in his leg and got permission to walk out. It was very early in the morning, when the enemy turned their guns on our immediate area. No doubt they knew where we were as shells came at us, fast and furious. Several of the men left their shallow funk holes in a hurry as shells exploded at a rate of one per minute. Three shells hit a few yards from the fellows who stayed in the funk holes, but they escaped unharmed.

The shells were being fired from the enemy's light field guns across the valley—guns that we could plainly see. With prolonged shelling, we wanted to get out of the line of fire, but we had to wait for orders. Finally, orders to move came at noon and we crept forward literally ducking shells as we went. All this area was part of the old Hindenburg Line, a line that had been occupied by German troops since the beginning of the war. At one time, the *Sensee River* ran through the valley below, but it had been shelled so badly no trace of the river was left. Another German defence system of trenches, dugouts and strong points were called the *Queant-Drocourt Switch* and extended to the southeast.

Although shells kept bursting in and around the sandpits all morning, there were no casualties in my section. No doubt about it, an escape like this was a true miracle.

We started down a rather steep slope, walking single-file, ten feet apart, and could see another single file formation of troops on the move in the valley bottom. On reaching lower ground, my gun section was suddenly fired on by an unseen enemy machinegun.

Immediately, we dropped into the nearest shell hole, keeping low while the bullets swished overhead. One of my pals, Private Kenny, a tall good-looking young man was hit and we presumed him dead at the time. However, after the war, I met him on the streets of Calgary, fully recovered.

We found out later, this persistent enemy bombardment was being made by the German rearguard, to protect the retreat of their main forces. In actual fact, the German troops were retreating. Since the allies weren't aware of the enemies' retreat, an order came for our section to move back, set up our machineguns in readiness for a counterattack. When we of "J" Battery got our gun set up, I was #1 on the gun. Private Walker (from Ontario) was supposed to be #1. Having been in the war, previously, he'd been wounded and was back for a second round of duty. He had a great deal of experience with machineguns, but now he was feeling ill, so I took the #1 position.

From our new post, we had an extensive view of the valley and the *Hendrecourt Road* in particular. The machine-gunners who'd been shooting at us all morning, were firing from a row of trees along that road. Enemy shellfire died down as soon as it got dark, but we still had to 'stand to.' No sleep for any of us that night!

I recall standing at my post, taking in the clear skies, the moon, stars, and enemy flares lighting up the trees along the *Hendrecourt Road*. The sight was unreal! On toward midnight, we received word that we would be relieved before daylight. Sure enough, the relief unit did show up—on time for a change. After explaining where the enemy was located and what had happened during the night, our outfit moved out through the trenches. We then followed the *Arras-Cambrai Road* for eight kilometres until we reached *Tilley*. Lorries and limbers passed us going in both directions. Since it was still pitch dark and no lights were allowed, more than once we had to jump out of the way of fast-moving vehicles to avoid being run over. About this time we were able to load our machineguns and tripods onto a limber wagon, but we still had to carry our rifle, 40 rounds of ammunition, a full kit bag and haversack, our gasmask, bayonet, entrenchment tool, greatcoat, mess tin, along with a web harness to which everything was attached.

The perfectly straight road to *Tilley* had been the main target of artillery fire and had been blown to pieces as were the trees that lined the ditches. Finally, we came to trenches that had been occupied by the enemy only four days before. From these lines, German troops had looked out on *Arras* for three years. Yet they were never able to take the city. We soon found suitable places to rest, threw off our equipment, lay down, and slept like logs.

The next morning was August 29th, after breakfast, we packed up leisurely and walked a kilometre into *Tilley*. We didn't feel like marching; we were still worn out from nine consecutive, almost totally sleepless days and nights. We arrived at a camp of bow tents in *Tilley* and spent the rest of the day sleeping.

Then came a welcome and completely unexpected surprise. Private Hughes (from Liverpool), and I were ordered to report for leave.

CHAPTER FIFTEEN

Troops were entitled to a Paris leave every six months or a 'Blighty" leave every 10 months. I was scheduled to take my leave the previous March, but it was cancelled due to the big German push that spring. After Private Hughes and I received notice of leave, our first stop was at the paymaster's office where I drew 120 francs (about $70.00 or 15 pounds). Then on we went to the quartermaster's office where I received new puttees.

Our orders were to take our rifles and all our equipment with us, leave the works at the YMCA in London to be picked up on our return to France. Taking these items out of France was a precaution to keep military items from falling into enemy hands.

Hughes and I needed to get to the railhead at Agnez-le-Duisans before dark, so we caught a ride on a motor lorry which was already carrying officers' bags and three other men to *Warlus*. This only took us halfway. At *Warlus* we ate a skimpy meal at an army cook kitchen, shaved, got cleaned-up, and waited for another lorry that never came. So, we had to walk the rest of the way, getting to *Agnez-le-Duisans* after dark. We'd missed the train, but we slept on the floor of an army hut and thought it was wonderful to be under a real roof.

We heard that another 'leave' train would pull out at 9 am the next morning. Down we went where other soldiers (also on leave), had congregated. These men were from various other regiments.

This was August 30th, and after a short wait, a 'leave' train backed in and we climbed aboard. We were tightly packed into an old wooden French coach with plank benches to sit on. It certainly wasn't a fast train; it took four hours to the first stop at *St.Pol*. We didn't get going again until 4 pm. After passing *Hesdin*, I gazed out the window hoping to see the machinegun camp at *Aubin-St-Vaas*. 'Couldn't see it for trees. Still, knowing the camp was there brought to mind the pleasant days we'd spent at that camp.

Eventually, we arrived at *Boulogne*. By this time, it was 9 pm. We marched down to a rest camp near the waterfront. Here we were given meal tickets and a bed for the night. The next day, August 31st was my 25th birthday. At 8 am we were crowded onto a transport and were soon on our way across the English Channel. The water was choppy, and I sat on a coil of rope most of the way across. I knew I'd be seasick if I tried to move around. As before, two destroyers accompanied the transport across the channel, one on either side. We arrived at the quay in *Folkstone* shortly before noon and immediately boarded a passenger train for *London*. I couldn't help admiring the lush English greenery. What a contrast to the war zone in France!

At 4 pm, Private Hughes and I stepped off the train in *London*. We were met by some lovely ladies serving troops with hot tea and cookies. Then we went over to the "Maple Leaf Club, where Canadian troops could stay for one night only. Here we left our rifles and equipment in a tagged locker. I did some letter writing on Sunday morning, before deciding to see something of the city. I'd never stayed in London before, so wanted to visit all the places I'd heard about, but never seen. I walked down Kingsway and stopped off at the Australian YMCA, had lunch, and hung around there for an hour.

Photo credit: William Lees's collection

On Monday I went to the Grosvenor Gardens which was directly across from Victoria Railway station. It was a beautiful spot, full of flowering bushes and colourful flower beds. In the center of the gardens was a building resembling a one-story Swiss chalet that was very popular with the troops: Canadians, Australians, Americans, and Imperials alike. Soldiers could go there anytime, day or night, and get a good meal served by young women in pale blue uniforms. The whole atmosphere had a cozy feel. There was no rush or confusion. Men liked to linger, mainly because it was a good place to gain some sense of normality after being in those nightmarish, frontline trenches.

There was a nice surprise waiting for me when I stopped in for a noon meal. I ran into my old friend, Private Turner. He'd been with the 191st the same time as I had. He'd also been drafted to the 50th with me and was still with that battalion. We had lots to talk about, remembering the walk we'd taken in the rain to *Haslemere* with Swabey and Peat. And we both knew Private Tompkins who'd been killed in action in January. Thus, we exchanged condolences at losing our common friend.

From then on Private Turner and I kept company while we were in England, Private Hughes having gone up to *Liverpool* to visit his folk. We had dinner in Hampton Court, took the #11 bus, then changed to a streetcar and sampled what pleasures London had to offer. Perhaps the most memorable event of our stay in *London* was renting a rowboat and rowing down the *Thames River*. What a difference a few days meant! In a matter of days, we'd gone from fighting a war to this peaceful cruise on the *Thames*. We also visited several landmarks: Westminster Abbey, the Parliament Buildings and Big Ben Tower.

Although we would like to have stayed longer in *London*, we needed to go north to visit family. Turner was going first to *Nottingham* and then on to *Manchester*, the latter being my destination. It was dark when the train reached *Nottingham*, but as this was Turner's former hometown, he knew his way around. First, we checked in at a local YMCA for bed and breakfast, then went to a Hippodrome (a variety show), the likes of which were immensely popular in England at the time. Early the next morning, we spent some time walking around the city with Turner pointing out various sights of interest as well as relating incidents that happened when he lived in Nottingham as a child. I wanted to see Nottingham Castle. Unfortunately, it wasn't open for visitors until 10 am the next morning, and we had to be at the train station by 10:30 am sharp.

The train left *Nottingham* on time, traveling by way of the scenic town of *Monsaldale* in the Peak District. It was a beautiful trip and very soon we reached *Manchester*. After a good meal at the YMCA, Turner went on his way to *Urmston*, ten miles west, while I went ten miles north to *Blackley*, a suburb of Manchester where my relatives lived.

The family members I visited in this area were my uncles, John, Richard, Alfred, Robert, Peter, James, Arthur and my Auntie Jennie (Jane) and cousins, Sarah-Ann, Maude, and Harry and Leonard Loftus.

Uncle John was a keen gardener. He had a garden behind his house, plus an allotment nearby. Uncle Richard also had an allotment—all vegetables—on a piece of farmland that had been subdivided as part of the war effort. Uncle Alfred's enterprise was a greenhouse, and he treated me to some of his home-made wine, a product of his own home-grown grapes. Then there was Uncle Robert up Old Road, Uncle Peter down Moston Lane and two other uncles I didn't know as well. All of them considered it their patriotic duty to grow as many vegetables as they could.

One of the places I liked to frequent was *Boggart Hole Clough* a lovely peaceful wooded park in *Blackely*. On one occasion Cousin Harry accompanied me to Heaton Hall on an electric train. This stately property had been owned by the Holland family since the middle ages, but lately it was thrown open to the public. During WWI, the park was a training camp for the Manchester Regiment while the hall itself was used for a military hospital. Another evening, Uncle John took Auntie Jenny and me by tram to the Manchester Hippodrome (another variety show), staged downtown. And yet another day, Cousin Leonard and I went to visit the Belle View Gardens and saw a wonderful outdoor presentation of the 'Fall of Lucknow.' A gorgeous sunset in the west made the show all the more impressive.

The thing I liked best about wearing an army uniform was I was dressed for any occasion, whether it be a casual event or attending St. Peter's Parish Church with my aunt Jenny. On Monday, cousins Arthur and Maude came from *Leigh*, 20 miles away, to visit with me and Uncle James' family. The next day, cousins Sarah Ann and Maud accompanied me on a walk down Crab Lane to Crumpshall Park and a water well named Pike Fold Well. Here, an excellent spring of ice cold water bubbled up to form a meandering stream. How good it felt to be walking with the young ladies and listening to the cheery songs of thrushes, wrens, and warblers. After a while, we circled past the old Crumpsall Workhouse, the CWS Biscuit Factory, and were soon back on Crab Lane.

September 14th, 1918: Far too soon it was time to leave my relatives and return to France. Auntie Jenny made a delicious noon meal, then Uncle Robert and Cousin Harry escorted me to the railway station. In my mind, I can still see the concerned look on their faces as I waved goodbye. The train reached *London* at 5:30 pm and I stayed overnight at a hotel run by the Salvation Army (opposite Grosvenor Gardens). It was now Sunday the 15th, and I decided to spend an extra day in *London*, enjoying the Maple Leaf Club and Grosvenor Gardens. This time, I didn't run into any old acquaintances, but I did see a military policeman who asked to see my pass. After studying it for a few minutes, he said, "You ought to be in France by now." Then he said, "For a small sum of money, I can fix things up for you."

"Nothing doing!" I snapped. "I'm already on my way back to France."

CHAPTER SIXTEEN

On the night of September 15th, 1918, I collected my rifle and equipment at the Maple Leaf Storage in *London*. Then early the next morning (6:18 am), I left *London* by train, arriving in *Folkstone* at 10 am. It took nearly two and a half hours to cross the English Channel and I disembarked at *Boulogne* around 12:30. On leaving the boat, I joined other troops returning from leave and walked with them to *Saint Martin's rest camp*. The next day was spent at *Boulogne*, waiting for a train to take me back to the war zone. While waiting I mailed a postcard to my sister, Evelyne, who never received it. Possibly, whatever I wrote was against regulations. In which case the letter would be confiscated.

At 9 am on September 17th, the troop train left *Boulogne* and I travelled the same route as previously, except in reverse: *Etaples, Saint Pol,* and finally detraining at *Dainville* near *Arras*. Here I inquired as to the whereabouts of the 2nd Battalion CMGC and was told the battalion had already left *Dainville* for the front. So, I stayed on the train until it reached *Boisleux*. I got off here and began asking after the 50th Battalion. No one knew where they were. By this time, it was well past sunset, so I looked around for a place to stay overnight. Apparently there had never been a rest camp in this district, so I kept walking until I came to the Imperial Tank Corps lines and slept there in a small tin hut with another soldier who shared his rations with me.

I decided the best thing to do would be to go back to *Dainville* and try to trace the 50th from there. It rained all night. The next morning, I got on a train with a lot of excited Scottish troops who were just starting their leave. How I envied them! After walking all

193

over *Dainville*, I discovered the Divisional Headquarters were at *Warlus*, so I headed for *Warlus*. Once at the headquarters, I got a very stingy meal and was told the 50th Battalion was up the line at *Chérisy* (15 kilos from *Arras*), about 20 kilometres away from *Warlus*. What a goose chase! I shouldered my bags and equipment and started walking.

I walked through *Dainville* again and onto *Arras*. Although I had seen *Arras* from various front lines, this was the first and last time I ever set foot in the city. Although *Arras* had never been in German hands, the city was badly shelled and was truly a pitiful sight.

I kept trudging along, seeing very few civilians. However, I ran across an elderly Frenchman who had set up a fruit stand. In spite of having very little money left, I was able to buy some grapes from him and later bought chocolates, cookies, and cigarettes at a YMCA along the way.

When I was taking a break, another soldier from the 1st Division Infantry came along. He was an interesting fellow to talk to, and we walked together for about two kilometres. Then he went his way and I caught a ride with a lorry that was going in my direction. Just as I thought I'd never find the 50th, I recognised a long, straight road. I'd seen this road four months earlier when it was behind enemy lines and being strafed by Canadian artillery. So, I left the lorry when it was opposite *Monchy-le-Preux and* set off walking again. I angled southeast until I came to *Guémappe*. This town had really been through hell. There was nothing left except a freshly painted sign marking what had been the town center. Otherwise, the whole town had been levelled. Not one building or even a wall remained standing.

I walked on from that wretched place, finally coming to the outer edge of *La Sensée River Valley* and then on to *Chèrisy*. Presently, I saw a man wearing a red arrow on a blue shoulder patch. He directed me to "J" Battery Headquarters. Here I turned in my pass, and although I was four days overdue, nothing was said about me being late.

September 18th: My section was in what was called 'surface hollows.' These hollows had been the frontline when I left to go on leave. It was now the current reserve line. I joined the other men in my section just as they were heading for a bath parade. They had towels slung over their shoulders and were marching to *Hendrecourt-lès-Cagnicourt,* a distance of three kilometres. The baths were very crowded, so much so that many men (myself included), left without actually taking a bath. But I did get a change of shirts and underwear.

The day after I arrived, we had a pay parade. Having come back from leave stone broke, I was truly grateful for the 20 francs I received. It was always a godsend to have enough money to buy chocolate bars and cookies at the "Y". At dusk the same day, we marched forward through *Hendrecourt-lès-Cagnicourt* and the town of *Cagnicourt* where we came to two patches of trees connected by a German communications trench. A few German-made huts had been built in the woods. Some of the troops quickly moved into dugouts while my buddies and I took over the huts. I shared a hut with Private Pat Halley, a tall, well-built, good-natured fellow from Vancouver, B.C. We had just settled down when an enemy shell sizzled past and split a nearby tree. Halley said, "I think we'd better get back into a trench and try to locate a dugout."

On the other hand, I wanted to stay put, so I said, "No, I'd rather sleep in a hut than a smelly dugout." I barely got the words out of my mouth when another shell exploded between our hut and a tree that was only a few yards away. We dived out of the hut in record time and made for the dugouts.

In the nearest trench, we discovered a dugout with a caved in entrance that other men had passed up. The entrance had been cribbed-up with planks that had fallen sideways. Between Halley and I tugging and pushing, we were able to reposition the planks and unearth a 5' X 6' hollowed-out area. We slid into it and found some German picks and shovels inside, indicating the enemy had been improving their defences when they were driven out. But now, shells were falling thick and fast with explosions that fairly shook the earth around us. Gradually, the shelling became sporadic, so we could creep out and inspect the damage.

The trenches we manned were two kilos from the front line. Although there seemed to be a lull in shelling, we still had to be ready to move forward if and when we were ordered to do so. We could plainly see at least six enemy observation balloons in a line on the horizon, and we were warned to keep out of sight of these in daylight hours.

Since we hadn't received orders to move forward, we stayed in this location for five days. We'd seen a YMCA in a dug-out, after we passed through *Cagnicourt*, so three of us young fools took our chances, left the dugouts, and quickly made our way down to the "Y" in hopes of buying something filling. On the way, we came across a battery of four '5.9 guns' located behind a row of trees. These were allied machineguns—four men to a gun—actively engaged in firing at the enemy. When given the command, the guns would fire one after another in rapid succession.

When we felt confident enough to stand upright, we walked the rest of the way to the "Y' where we found a long line-up of men waiting for supplies to arrive. Presently, a lorry pulled up and several boxes of merchandise were unloaded. In a few minutes, the queue began to move forward—very slowly. My two companions and I were about 40th in line. We were talking among ourselves, wondering if the goodies would run out before we got any. Just then an enemy shell exploded in a building across the plaza. We were covered in dust and smoke as bricks and lumber spewed in all directions. Most of the men raced for cover, but since my friends and I were now at the top of the line-up, we stayed put and bought the regular: chocolate bars and cookies.

Late on Wednesday, September 25th (after dark), we were marched to a spot near one of our own observation balloons. According to a map, this was the northeast end of the *Drocourt-Queant* switch trench system. Again, we saw another whole area pock-marked with shell holes and strewn with mounds of muck, rubble, and bone fragments. And once again, we were short of rations. We were told to clean ammunition, but most of us didn't. A raw wind was blowing, and we were cold, hungry, and fed up. To make matters worse, just as it was getting dark, angry black clouds rolled in. Lightning flashed across the sky and rain came down in torrents. At the very worst time, when thunder was crashing around us, we got orders to move forward. We went past *Cagnicourt*, past *Buissy*, along a ridge toward *Baralle*—all this marching in rain that continued to turn the road into a sea of mud.

The new frontline extended along the *Canal du Nord*. As we approached the canal we were cautioned not to talk because the enemy had listening posts not far away. Neither were we to light matches or smoke. We learned an offensive was coming off in the morning. In this allied attack, our ("J" Battery's), assignment was to create a barrage at various points, targeting crossroads that were within machinegun range. Visibility was nil. It was still pitch dark and raining.

Limbers brought up ammunition, so all night we were kept busy carrying ammunition across broken ground to the gun locations. Platoon officers were making the rounds with clinometers. They were preparing machineguns, shoring them up for indirect firing at distant targets. There was also a battery of Stokes guns set up nearby.

After I'd made four trips carrying machinegun ammunition, another fellow and I were sent with a message from our platoon officer to the signallers' unit at *Cagnicourt*. And then, wonder of wonders, the rain stopped. The moon came out from behind the clouds, as the two of us made our way beneath dripping branches. It was dangerous walking in the moonlight, but much easier to follow the narrow trail through the trees. We found the signallers' unit. We delivered the message, then made our way back to our platoon officer, with a response.

Our #13 platoon guns were located along a trench that had been held by the enemy a day before. The trench crisscrossed over a hill directly above *Baralle*, north of *Buissy*. Since there were no dugouts here, the only cover we had was a pillbox, and this was being used by signallers as an observation post.

The night of September 26th was relatively quiet with only an occasional explosion, but we knew what was coming—the big Allied push—and we nervously awaited zero hour.

On the morning of the 27th, just before daylight the allied attack began. First came a bolt of gunfire, then another, and another. Then several more came all at once until the whole line was alive with explosions that lit up the southern, western, and northern sky. We worked our machineguns frantically in the opening barrage. Then we 'stood to', awaiting orders, ready to move forward to support our infantry. A shell exploded in the trench we were in, but none of our men were in that particular bay at the time.

The first half-hour of the battle was still in darkness, but as the sun began to rise an early morning mist covered the valley. Still, the big guns pounded away. At the lower end of the trenches was a battery of 5.9 guns. Similar to our section, they'd taken part in the first barrage, but now they were waiting, tense and alert.

My unit held this position most of the day. Around ten in the morning, the fog began to lift. And from this spot, we were able to watch the progress of the battle. I recall seeing several formations of Canadian infantry advancing up a hill in the vicinity of *Bourlon.* At one-point, light German field guns were firing point-blank into the Canadians who were doggedly pressing forward in an attempt to surround the enemy.

The signallers set up two large telescopes and were con-stantly sending messages to dispatch runners to report the progress of the battle. When not in use, we could use the telescopes. I took a turn peering through the glass and could see *Bourlon Wood* and the village of *Bourlon*, also *Cambrai* which was partly hidden by high ground, but the spires and chimneys set the city apart. And then there was *Oisy-le-Verger* with her red brick buildings and spires rising out of a greyish-green forest like mystical apparitions.

Around four in the afternoon, a dozen or more bedraggled, enemy prisoners trudged past us. A sign of victory, we thought. They were under escort on their way out.

An hour later a sergeant came by to tell us to get ready to move—but not forward. Our battalion would be relieved after dark. We were then taken out of the line and moved back to a point west of *Cagnicourt.* Here we stayed overnight in shell holes, scattered over quite a distance. Private McNeil and I were on ration duty.

Stumbling into hollows and over debris in the dark, it took us over an hour to locate the sergeant who was in charge of 'dry rations' for the day.

The next afternoon, we moved forward again, crossing open fields in full marching order, every nerve in our bodies on the alert. To be in the open like this was suicidal; we could be attacked at any time with no place to take cover. In reaching the *Canal du Nord,* we stopped to rest. Here engineers were erecting a temporary wooden bridge to replace the concrete bridge that had been blown up. A short distance away was a pontoon bridge and over this came more German prisoners. One of our machine-gunners, Private Beckman, had German parents. He'd learned German at home and spoke to the prisoners, saying they were lucky to be leaving the war zone because millions of Americans were coming to support us.

We were soon on our way again, crossing the pontoon bridge in the opposite direction and entering *Sains-lès-Marquion.* The village had been the target of Canadian guns the previous day, so it too was badly torn up. Here we were told to make our billets the best we could among the ruins. Private Halley and I found a big brewery cellar with a dome-shaped roof. After shovelling bricks and other clutter aside, we camped on the floor. There was plenty of room in this cellar. Sometime later, several other machine-gunners moved in with us as well as a section of signallers. The more the merrier!

Obviously, German troops occupied the cellar only hours before we got there. We found sundry articles of German equipment: potato-mashers (grenades) and the like.

The next day being Sunday, we had church parade in a field on the opposite side of the canal. And in the afternoon, we had clothing parade with each of us receiving a brown sweater. The sleeves of mine were much too long, so I shortened them with my bayonet.

In an attempt to familiarize ourselves with the surrounding area, Private Halley and I went out later in the day. We first came to the canal where a trench had been cut into the canal bank. The enemy had been located here only a few short hours before. In the trench were German rifles, machinegun belts, and ammunition.

Later we came upon the Canadian machine-gunner Headquarters (CHGH), situated in what appeared to be a badly shot up church with a beautiful mosaic floor.

We were still at *Sains-lès-Marquion*, when the YMCA arrived and opened their canteen in the remains of a house. Opposite this, was an open field where burial parties were bringing in the deceased and placing them side by side in long rows. Since many of the casualties were Canadians, we went up and down the rows to see if we knew any of the dead—a sad business to say the least.

It rained steadily all day Monday. Regardless, I made several trips to the "Y" with my buddies. Standing still, waiting for another bomb to drop was too nerve-wracking.

In the very early hours of the next day (about 3:30 am), we machine-gunners got marching orders. By then it had quit raining. Both moon and stars were hidden in clouds and the road was wet and sloppy. We climbed over hilly ground that had previously been occupied by our infantry during the first day of the attack. Here we were halted for the rest of the night. We took out our groundsheets, rolled up in our greatcoats, and tried to snatch a little rest. But sleep didn't come easy; it was a miserably cold night.

In the morning, we discovered we were within four or five kilometres of *Cambrai* and could plainly see the topmost part of the town: the church spires, chimneys, belfry, and roofs of buildings. This ancient city lay on the banks of the *Scheldt (Escaut) River*. It had been the Duke of Wellington's headquarters and was now under heavy gunfire with devastating fires set in Cambrai by German arsonists. As the German troops retreated, they left a rearguard of machine-gunners to cover the withdrawal of their main forces. (That is what machine-gunners did; they held their posts until killed or captured.)

I counted six guns in the vicinity, with dead machine-gunners still at their posts. They looked to be fresh recruits, young, chubby faced with the look of innocence. No doubt they'd been rushed in for the emergency, teenagers who hadn't enough training to know how to dig themselves in.

Germany was certainly scraping the bottom of the barrel now, sending young boys out to be slaughtered. For the love of God, why did Kaiser Bill keep fighting?

Each young lad was wearing a greatcoat and full equipment. Each had new boots, fastened to his pack. Among other things they all carried fresh loaves of bread. We Canadians had been on extremely short rations since the big drive started. Hunger overrode our scruples, and we helped ourselves to the loaves. I was lucky to get one for myself. It was dark brown in color, quite heavy, and slightly sour. I found it so filling that I couldn't eat more than a quarter of an inch slice at a time. The loaf lasted me ten days, and by the time I finished it, I'd begun to enjoy the strange tangy taste.

On October 2nd, German troops still controlled *Cambrai*. This city was scheduled to be the next allied objective. In the daytime, we could see vast columns of smoke rising from two separate quarters of the city and at night *Cambrai* was outlined in rings of fire. So much burning going on seemed to indicate the enemy intended to pull back, which was a mixed blessing.

On one of my walks with another soldier (I forget his name), we came across a dead Canadian soldier in an open field. He was very blonde, looked to be in good health and we could find no sign of what had caused his death. On another hike, Private Halley and I came across a British army greatcoat. Halley felt in the pockets and pulled out an expensive-looking watch. As there was no one around to claim the timepiece, Halley gladly kept it.

For the next few days, we didn't have much to do because the allied drive had spent itself out. I continued to hike, and on one of my forays, I ran across a derelict British tank bogged down in a swampy area of *Bourlon Wood.* No doubt it was abandoned when the enemy drove the British out in 1917. Afterward, when I told Private Walker about seeing the tank, he wanted to see it for himself, so we both went back to have a good look.

Once again, we were fortunate in that the weather was warm and the enemy barely shelled our area. Had there been more shelling, our chances of survival would have been slim because we were billeted in such shallow trenches. We had to have men posted to watch for gas attacks twenty-four hours around the clock. One night when I was on gas-guard, I was able to watch the fires burning in *Cambria.* As mentioned before, the city was still occupied by the enemy, and it appeared many of the buildings were on fire. In fact, the Germans must have had an incendiary squad at work in every town, because during the night, I counted ten outlying communities ablaze.

****

The Bigger Picture: October 8-9th, 1918. Germany's strongest defence on the Western Front, the Hindenburg Line, was broken by the Canadian troops who proceeded to surround the city of Cambrai. Canadian troops under General Currie took the northern side. The 2nd Canadian Division secured the crossings, while the 3rd Canadian Division entered the city from the northwest to find the German army had deserted the city, leaving their rearguard behind to suffer the consequences. Although the Germans succeeded in burning whole areas of Cambrai, the rapid advance of the Canadian saved much of the city.

****

CHAPTER SEVENTEEN

On Tuesday night, October 8th, we heard the Allies were organizing a massive push to run the German troops out of *Cambrai*. The next day, being October 9th (at 3:30 in the morning), we machine-gunners were given orders to move forward. We marched as far as the *Arras-Cambrai road,* rested for an hour in abandoned farm buildings, then took to the road. After awhile, we came to a shallow trench near the *Douai-Cambrai road.* Here we set up our machineguns with two men stationed at each gun. Our orders were to fire on any enemy plane that came within range, which we did.

At noon we had great news: German armed forces had withdrawn from *Cambrai,* leaving nothing but rearguard machine-gunners to cover the retreating troops. It was late in the afternoon when we got moving again and around 5 pm we passed through *Neuville Saint Remy*, a suburb of *Cambrai*. We didn't go into the city, but marched north under a high-arched bridge and stopped at a partly demolished brick church. Thinking we were going to be billeted here, we began to clear bricks and mortar from the church basement. However, around midnight, we got our marching orders. So, we gathered up our equipment and on we went through heavy smoke. Some of the buildings we passed were still smouldering. After some time, we came to *Escaudpeivres,* halted at a white-washed dwelling, and "J" Battery crowded into this small house for the night.

During the wee hours, the Germans started shooting and the shells were exploding in close range. Presently, one shell came crashing into the house next door. There was a huge bang then a loud grinding of masonry and splintering of wood as the building collapsed. The next morning the house was still burning, so another fellow and I took our rations over and stirred up the coals. Soon we had a real bonfire going with enough heat to fry our bacon and toast our bread.

After eating, we continued our march to the crest of a hill. From here, we looked down on a valley where the small town of *Naves* was located. On the far side of the valley was a ridge of dense trees where German troops were thought to be digging in. We were warned to be extra cautious as we were definitely under enemy observation. With this latest warning in mind, we made our descent into the valley, striking off in the direction of *Naves,* but stopping short of the town. We came to a cut bank and were directed to "fall out." While waiting to move on, Private McNeil and I discovered an accordion in a dugout which enemy troops had recently vacated. Several of us tried our hand playing a tune, none too expertly, so we left the accordion where we'd found it.

The Germans likely heard us, because moments later they began to lob shells at us. This hastened our steps, and we quickly set off marching through the outskirts of *Naves*, but not entering the main part of town. Once we were about a kilometre beyond the town limits, we halted at a twelve-foot cliff adjacent to a sunken road. Here we set up the machineguns and were put on a two-hour rotation, taking turns manning the guns, shooting in the direction of the incoming shells. After I'd taken my turn, some of my pals and I went to work improving our billets in the cliff wall.

We had just finished eating our noon meal, when a cavalry squadron of about thirty men, came up at a gallop and stopped to rest their horses. With the sun reflecting off their brass buttons and their sleek mounts, they made a dazzling sight. Several of the riders rode over to the cliff wall for a short chat. When their leader gave the command; the men spurred their horses, and they were off and running.

Anxious to know how they made out, Private Halley and I climbed the bank and got down on our bellies to watch. We saw the cavalry leave the road, watched as the horses tore across an open field. Apparently, they were heading for the far ridge of trees, where we'd been told the enemy was digging in. They never made it. As they reached the middle of the field, enemy machineguns opened up. Immediately the column was transformed into a struggling mass of men and animals. Some horses dropped in their tracks; others plunged head over heels, while a few riderless horses made frantic dashes away from the carnage. Neither Halley nor I could tell whether any of the riders survived, but we thought they hadn't. Even at this distance the whole grassy area looked red.

Presently, a cavalry commander rode up with a few men. They hadn't been with the first riders. He asked us to fire some 'bursts' across the valley at the enemy who slaughtered the first group of cavalry riders. So, we did. We fired several rounds, but at this range we doubted we were successful, especially with our high trajectory meant to shoot down planes. However, in firing these rounds, we unwittingly disclosed our exact whereabouts, and immediately the enemy began firing at us. Shells were raining down thick and fast. Private Halley dived across the road and squeezed into our dugout, and I followed suit. We barely had time to get in the dugout, when a shell exploded in the very spot we'd been standing, less than a minute before.

Later, another detachment of cavalry came up. While resting their horses, they told us the other squadron should not have gone forward when they did; someone had blundered. They were supposed to wait until the 5.9s softened up the enemy machinegun nests. When this second group of riders went on their way, neither Halley nor I bothered to find out what happened to them. Witnessing one gruesome scene was one too many.

I believe the devastating cavalry charge witnessed by Private Halley and I, was the last of its kind on the Western front. These old-fashioned cavalry charges were no match for machineguns. They had no place whatsoever in modern warfare.

That night, we saw several more towns burning, the closest being *Avesnes-les-Aubert, Iwuy,* and *Rieux-en-Cambrésis.* At that time, Canadian 5.9s were firing into *Iwuy* and *Rieux* hoping to rout the enemy. The next morning, shelling of the sunken road (where we were), became more frequent. Worse still, the enemy began using deadly gas. We wore our gasmasks. Once again, we couldn't eat breakfast as our rations had absorbed the gas fumes.

Mid-morning, a company of the Duke of Devonshire's Regiment marched past, followed by a battery of Light Artillery who stopped to rest their horses. The latter had three guns with ammunition carriages and each gun was pulled by three teams of horses, and a rider with each team. The officer in charge left the horses and climbed up on the bank to observe the valley below. At the same time, one of the riders dismounted and walked over to Halley and I. He held up a cigarette. "Got a light?" he asked.

Surely, the smoker's guardian angel was looking after him. No sooner had he lit his cigarette than an enemy shell exploded right in the middle of his gun team. The six horses and the two riders who stayed on their mounts got the full force of the blast. I ran over to the wreckage, intending to drag the men out, but there was no hope. Neither of the men had any chance of surviving. The first man had lost a hand and part of his face. He died just as I got there. The second had blood pouring from his abdomen and was begging for water. I gave him a sip from my water bottle and the regular line: "You're lucky to have a nice Blighty," but I doubt he heard me. He quit breathing a minute later. Of the horses, two were killed outright; and the other four had to be shot.

Enemy shells were still pounding our area and my three companions, Halley, and two others were getting nervous. "We're moving to a safer spot," they told me.

Once again, I was in favour of staying put, but I relented, "If you fellows are clearing out, then I'll come, too," I replied.

We dug a deeper trench, dragged our equipment into it, and had just settled down for the night when we got our marching orders. The relief battalion had arrived, and we barely had time to round up our belongings before we were on our way out. It was dark when we set off. Due to the enemy being in close proximity, we didn't march in any kind of formation but zigzagged in single file. As before, we kept a good distance between one another, so fewer men would be killed if a bomb fell between us. We ended up walking as far as *Escaudoeuvres* where "J" Battery crowded into an upper room of a château that was relatively free from shell damage.

On the 13th of October, I decided to go to *Cambrai*, a distance of two kilos. Having seen the burning of *Cambrai* from a distant hill, I wanted a closer look. The enemy had vacated the city four days earlier, and this might be my last chance to see the city. Not finding anyone willing to go with me, I went alone. By now most of the fires had burned themselves out, and already engineers were hard at work tearing down brick walls that were in danger of crushing pedestrians. On some streets, all of the buildings had been burned, while others were still intact with very little damage.

Soon, I came to the city center where I viewed the Place D'Armes, and the Hotel de Ville, the latter with its roof torn away. Most of the buildings in the square were in ruins. Engineers had put up notices on two of the buildings warning people to stay away, as the Germans had placed time bombs inside. I walked across the square to a theatre where posters indicated German troops had been entertained there only days before. I found many doors ajar and went into several buildings. Homes were fully furnished but in total disarray. The whole city had been stripped of its spirit, so to speak. I had never seen anything like it, nor do I wish to see anything like it ever again.

Cambrai, as William Lees saw the city on October 13, 1918

Credit: Chronide/Alamy Stock Photo

Before Cambrai was burned.

Postcard from W. Lees's collection

Cambrai after bombing and fire. Photo credit #10004847

Archives of Ontario C 244-0-0-10-37

October 14th: From this time until war's end, the 2nd CMGC continued to advance behind our first-line infantry units. We were the second line of defence. We left *Escaudoeuvres* late one afternoon, marching through the village in a haze of smoke. Then on we went through *Ramillies*, never stopping to rest until we reached a place called *Cuvillers*. There was a German ammunition dump at *Cuvillers* which contained antiaircraft shell cases, gun shells, and loose bundles of cordite. Just for something to do, some of us lit the cordite and warmed our hands over the blaze. I also unearthed six live German shells and defused them with my army knife. I gave four of the shells to my friends and kept two for myself to take home as souvenirs.

Just as it was getting dark, we moved on again. Eventually, we located an outfit of Imperial machine-gunners. Our orders were to relieve them. Earlier, when we met the Imperial at *Escaudoeuvres*, our "J" Battery agreed to make a swap. The Imperials would carry our ammunition boxes in trade for our ammunition belts. This turned out to be a bad deal for us. Our belts were new and spotlessly clean, whereas theirs were old and caked with mud and grime. When we collected our ammunition boxes from the Imperials, the boxes looked like they'd been rolled in the mud, too. We had some pretty unsavoury things to say about the Imperials when we had to clean up their filthy mess.

We were now camped less than a kilometre from *Paillencourt*, an abandoned village. Supposedly, we were on the front line, yet this was a strange front line. Nobody seemed to know where the enemy was. We could hear gunfire in the northwest. As well, an occasional rocket flare lit up the night sky. Other than that, the district was unusually quiet. We were told there was some active fighting going on near *Douai* and also some intermittent shelling in the area we had just come from.

While at *Paillencourt*, I shared a dugout with three others. It was four feet deep and six feet square with a covering of metal sheeting. As things turned out, this was the last time we machine-gunners were billeted in dugouts. After *Cambrai* was liberated, the war became one of forward movement and the old trench warfare came to an end.

We scouted around the immediate vicinity, finding more dugouts at the edge of a field next to the road. Here the Germans had fitted out their dugouts with blankets and mattresses, doubt-lessly taken from homes in the village. We considered packing a couple of mattresses back to our dugout, but they (like those I'd seen in the *Cambrai* area), had been defecated on, making them unusable.

When no other activities were scheduled, Private Walker and I hiked over to *Paillencourt*. On the way, we came across several British soldiers who had recently been killed. The burial parties had not yet made their rounds, so there they lay exposed to the elements.

Walker and I went to *Paillencourt* a second day. This time I was able to find some postcards in a deserted 'parmacie'. Postcards made good souvenirs as they took very little room and were light to carry. While in the drugstore we spotted a safe in an upper room. As we were sizing the safe up, two more machine-gunners came into the store, and together we attempted to open it, but even with four heads scheming and forty fingers twiddling, the lock won the day.

Later on, a couple of our men attempted to take an undam-aged mattress to their billets. No such luck! Two officers stopped them and made them take the mattress back where they'd found it. But we didn't return to our billets without some spoils of war. On the outskirts of *Paillencourt* we discovered a large garden of pota-toes, peas, and carrots. And since fresh vegetables were luxuries we never had, we ate our fill and took an armload back to our billets. After our foray became common knowledge, other fellows visited the garden and helped themselves, too.

It rained heavily the next morning, so most of the time we stayed in our cold, wet dugouts. When the rain let up, Private McNeil and I hiked down to *Canal de la Sensée* where we found some German grenades (potato mashers). We pulled the firing pins on a few and tossed them into the water, one after the other, hoping to see some fish come up to supplement our scanty meals, but we didn't have any luck. It was obvious; the Germans cleaned every fish out of the canal.

That night we were on the move, but I must say we made some very strange manoeuvres. First, we marched a short distance to a v-shaped corner where we stopped and stood around, not knowing if we were coming or going. Two hours later, we did an about turned and marched back on the same road we came in on, right past the spot we'd been billeted in. Then on we went to a small field near the canal. Although there were dugouts at the field's edge, we didn't use them. We preferred to lie outside under the stars for the rest of the night

The next morning, we marched back to the billets we occupied when first coming to the *Paillencourt* area. Here we waited until noon before moving forward again. We crossed the canal over a temporary wooden bridge, the enemy having blown up the concrete bridge. While we were taking a short rest break, a shell made a direct hit on a brick building close to where we were standing. No one was injured, but we were covered from head to toe with dust and particles of brick. Expecting more of the same, we dashed for cover. However, no more shelling occurred. We decided this was a parting shot from the enemies' retreating rearguard.

We continued marching, double-file until we arrived at a small village called *Wavrechain-sous-Faulx*. Here "J" Battery was billeted in a barn that was heavy with the scent of newly cut hay. This suited us fine. A soft bed of fresh hay was much to be preferred over those clammy dugouts. Although the village had only minor shell damage, all of its civilians had been evacuated. We literally had the town to ourselves. I took a stroll down the streets and enjoyed the silence. I also went into a building I assume was the village priest's residence by the well-stocked library of religious books. I also watched two officers (from my machine unit), busily cutting a fine-looking oil painting out o a gilt picture frame. Watching them, I was reminded of an old saying, "The true test of a man's character is what he'll do when he knows he won't get caught."

We left *Wavrechain-sous-Faulx* on a Sunday. After marching through a farming community, we reached *Wasnes-au-Bac,* and my section was billeted in a very small house close to the canal. After taking off our equipment, we set to work hunting for firewood. Any scrap of wood to burn in the stove would do. Then we'd be able to heat up our rations and warm our hands and feet. It was October and evenings were cooling off. How we longed to be warm and dry.

While billeted here, I noticed two middle-aged Frenchmen singing as they walked into the village. They were returning from enemy-held territory and belting out their National anthem with great gusto. One of the men, a very thin fellow, would sing snatches of the Marseillaise. Then he'd turn and shake his fist in the direction of the retreating Germans. The Frenchmen (the first we'd seen in many days), had grim tales of hardship under German occupation, stories interpreted through two machine-gunners who spoke the French language.

The Canadian machine-gunner Corp Band visited each machinegun battalion to entertain us with a medley of rousing band music, something we all enjoyed. At *Wasnes-au-Bac*, the band members stayed in the village church, which was very dirty as it had been used as a horse barn by the German cavalry. There were no seats, but the soldiers stood clapping, and cheering enthusiastically in the muck.

On October 22nd, we left *Wasnes-au-Bac* at eight o'clock in the morning (passing a large German airdrome with two German fighter planes abandoned on the runway) and arrived at *Émerchicourt* (still in France). Here the soldiers of our gun crew were housed in two upstairs rooms in a large apartment building. The rooms were fully furnished with cook stoves, several chairs, and wonder-of-wonders, real spring mattresses. Strange as it seems, no one scrambled to claim the beds. No, we chose to drag the mattresses onto the floor and sleep that way.

The next morning, we were instructed to take our guns and ammunition back to the horse transport lines. This move could mean only one thing: the big brass weren't anticipating an immediate attack from the enemy. A most welcome sign!

It was a cold, bleak morning when we packed the limbers with the machineguns and ammunition that we'd been carrying—thankful to be rid of such heavy burdens. That evening, a band concert was on hand to entertain us in a roomy barn. Four large beams reached from one side of the barn to the other. As the barn filled with soldiers, men scaled up the supports to sit on the beams and crowded all over the hay and straw. Every square inch of the barn was taken up, and an excellent concert followed. While at *Émerchicourt*, regular activities were carried out such as drills and work parties.

I recall one day when five of us went on "fatigue duty" to clean and swab down limbers. It was a warm sunny day—a day of good-natured camaraderie—the kind that helped weave us into a loyal team. Laughing and talking were the order of the day.

On October 25th, the Prince of Wales arrived for inspection. We machine-gunners had to be in top shape: buttons and boots polished, clean-shaven, etc. We were given a brisk session of squad drills in hopes of smartening us up, and were still being drilled, when Prince Edward rode up on a horse, accompanied by a top-ranking British general. The Prince wore the uniform of a British army officer. As he came to a halt in front of us, I heard him ask, "Is this a regular parade, or have the men been got out for my inspection?" I never heard the answer, but my guess is our officer said it was just an ordinary performance.

The MG Corps band were playing opposite the saluting point. They accompanied us with trumpets blaring as we marched past to salute the prince. We then formed a hollow square, were given the order to 'stand at ease' before being dismissed.

Another day, we went on a bath parade to *Aniche,* the place where we finally got rid of the millions of trench lice that had plagued us night and day. The sanitation Corps brought up a mobile fumigating boiler where our uniform, shirts, and underwear could be deloused. Men were given a skimpy shower, barely enough time or water to soap up and rinse off, but the treatment worked. What a relief; no more lice—and that was all that mattered.

CHAPTER EIGHTEEN

The enemy had been constantly retreating since October 14th, 1918. This being the case, we machine-gunners never again had to actively defend a line or position. Consequently, we suffered far fewer casualties than if the situation had been reversed. Had the enemy been advancing, then we machine-gunners would have held our positions in order to allow our main body of troops to escape.

By October 31st, the front line was now 20 kilometres to the east with the enemy continuing to retreat. Every now and then we'd see German prisoners trudge by. Some were walking wounded, all were war weary, empty-eyed, and discouraged.

German prisoners of war Credit: public domain, Wikipedia.

In spite of the enemy drawing back, army life for us machinegun operators continued as before. There was more rifle practice and more work parties. And there was also entertainment. One evening the Ack-Emma concert party staged an event in a severely bombed iron-works factory. Bricks, mortar, twisted iron girders, and all sorts of rubbish cluttered the floor. Planks were set up on top of this clutter to accommodate the troops while the stage itself was perched on a pile of debris at the far end of the building.

We also had time to visit the surrounding country. While hiking one day, I came across some English propaganda brochures that had been tied to small balloons and floated over enemy lines when the wind was right. The leaflets were intended to reach the enemy and weaken their morale. They consisted of crude sketches relaying a message that Germany couldn't possibly win the war. One showed American planes coming to join the Brits. This was a stretch of imagination as no airplane had ever crossed the Atlantic Ocean in 1918, nor would one until two Englishmen, John Alcock and Arthur Brown, made the first Atlantic crossing by plane in June of 1919. Another sketch depicted a dark-faced German giant, holding a club over the Belgium woman he'd just beaten down. Other leaflets had maps of the Western Front with the frontline marked in red at different dates, showing how Allied forces were advancing. All captions were in German, but any person of any nationality could easily understand the message: Germany give up and go home!

On Monday, November 4th, we heard we'd be leaving *Émerchicourt.* We'd been there for twelve days and had enjoyed our stay. We'd had proper sleeping arrangements; the food was palatable, and we were free of those dreadful lice. So, we were leaving with mixed emotions: sorry to be leaving, yet eager to see what lay ahead.

Eight lories came to pick us up. There were between 200 and 260 men, all carrying equipment. After twenty kilometres, we came to *Petit Forêt*. Here, we left the lorries and spent the night in unoccupied houses. In the morning we were on the road again. That night we stayed in miners' dwellings in *La Sentinelle*, a suburb of *Valenciennes*. The next day, we left the suburb in the pouring rain and were billeted in a church in the middle of *Valencienes*. I remember trying to sleep on the church's cold stone floor. Not a great experience!

November 7th, we marched out of *Valenciennes* shortly after noon, and were immediately hemmed in by the high volume of military traffic. There were two endless columns: marching soldiers, guns, ammunition wagons, motor lorries, horse-drawn limbers all going east (as we were), up the line. An equally long procession of lorries, wagons, despatch riders, and German prisoners were going west—down the line.

Marching through crowded streets was extremely frustrating. We marched less than a mile and were held up for half an hour. When we started up again, we were stopped within a few hundred feet. It took a long time to reach *Onnaing*, and that town was only 5 miles from where we'd started in *Valanciennes*. It seemed like the whole population was out watching the troops. Obviously, overjoyed at being liberated, they were shouting, cheering, and clapping. One elderly man had a wicker basket full of white clay pipes. As a sign of welcome, he was handing these out to troops as they marched by.

After a great many stops and starts, we detoured around the heavy traffic and cut across a farmer's field. Then, after a short-unhampered march, we came to *Quarouble*. The most impressive feature of this town was a huge water-filled crater, the result of coal mining activity. After leaving this town, it began to get dark. Up ahead, we could see the large slag heaps of another coal mining community which turned out to be *Quievrechain*, a village located on the Belgium border. As we approached the village, the residents came out en masse to welcome us in. We were the first Allied soldiers they'd seen, the enemy having only just left the day before. This time, we machine-gunners were billeted in private homes. In most cases, the family who owned the homes gave up one or two rooms to accommodate us.

It wasn't long before the residents were telling us stories about the 'Allemands," the invaders, and begging for our cap and shoulder badges for souvenirs. Some of us complied and gave our hard-earned badges away. In return we were treated to hot tea and cocoa. A white-haired homeowner lived in the house where my unit was stationed. Evidently, he'd been a soldier in the war of 1870 between France and Belgium and was only too proud to show us the many war medals and ribbons he earned.

The very next day we crossed the *België*, a stream that marks the border between France and Belgium.

At long last we were actually in *Belgium*. This was great! Soon we entered the village of *Quiévrain*. Rows of houses lined the streets, and almost all had black, yellow, and red National flags flying from upper rooms. We marched a little farther where we saw some Royal Engineers in the process of digging up and defusing a landmine that civilians had pointed out to them. Shortly after, we stopped to rest near some miners' cottages. Immediately, the owners ran out to welcome us and generously handed out steaming cups of hot coffee which were very much appreciated.

We resumed our march toward the front line with the rumble of distant shell fire coming to us sporadically. We came to *Élouges,* a larger village than we'd seen so far and were billeted in an upper room overlooking the *Place d' Armes*. We also looked down on the marketplace where four dead German soldiers lay, receiving the curses of Belgium citizens who bore a deep hatred for German occupation. During the night, the enemy began shelling *Élouges.* The explosions came intermittently like the low rumble of thunder, spaced farther and farther apart until by daybreak they'd given way to a welcome silence. At breakfast, we were surprised to find the CMGC Band had caught up with us. This was November 9th (seven in the morning). The sun was rising in a bright blue sky, and after a full 'marching order' parade, the band led us down the main part of the city in a 'column o' route'. Within minutes the whole population of *Élouges* was either out on the streets or waving from windows. They were smiling, laughing, shouting, and waving hats and handkerchiefs. Never was there a more thrilling ovation!

We'd been given extra ammunition to carry as it was thought we might need it. That made the going a little more difficult since we were already carrying our equipment etc. Yet the band played on.

Coming to the village of *Dour* we approached a Catholic Convent. Several nuns came out to greet us, bringing baskets of handmade medallions. The mediations were fashioned from bright blue cloth attached to discs of cardboard. They were complete with safety pins to secure them to our shirts and a verse, that read, "Blessings on the soldiers of our brave allies."

Although we were supposed to be keeping step with the band, there was quite a scramble to get one of these unique medallions. I got four and gave three to friends who were reluctant to step out of line. Everywhere we looked there was jubilation. On one residential street, a homeowner was in the process of raising an unusually large Belgium flag.

We kept marching right out of town, led by the band, over hill and dale, through a wooded area where a footpath took us to *Warquignies.* Once again, the band played and crowds lined the streets, cheering and clapping. Both the residents and soldiers were in high spirits. One young lady danced up to our officer, Lieutenant

Marshall, took his arm and kept step with him. Of course, this brought catcalls from the rest of us, but the lieutenant didn't seem to mind. He was grinning from ear to ear.

When we arrived on the village green, we took off our equipment, piled arms, and were free to rest for a couple of hours. We were given a small ration of mulligan—not enough for marching men. Some of the men went searching for something to keep their stomachs from rumbling. One man came back with a loaf of freshly baked brown bread. Seeing this, two friends accompanied me to the bread maker's residence. At first, the woman of the house was reluctant to sell us any baking, but after offering a favourable price, we got three more loaves.

At a nearby estaminet, the proprietor started giving free glasses of cognac, but as more and more soldiers came for a complimentary drink, the owner's business sense kicked in, and he began charging one franc per glass.

While standing by our stacked rifles, I saw another dozen prisoners-of-war being escorted on their way out. Like all the rest, they wore a cowed expression, were dirty, ragged, and looked as if they'd reached the limit of their endurance. Most of us machine-gunners watched silently. We knew full well we could easily be in the same predicament; we never knew what our future held from one day to the next. The villagers reacted differently: jeering, scoffing, and catcalling in their own language. We couldn't make out what they were saying but knew by the gestures it wasn't the least bit flattering. We were told the German troops left only a matter of hours before we arrived.

About the middle of the afternoon, we left *Warquignies* and were on the march again. Darkness came as we approached a mining town with electric lights. Streetcar rails ran down the main street. The enemy left town a very short time before our arrival. So, out came the residents, cheering, whooping, and chanting, "Anlais,

Ingleesh, Vive las Anglais!" Apparently, they'd never heard of Canadians.

To our great disappointment, we were kept marching through town, and away from the glitter of those wonderful electric lights. Another few kilometres down a country road, and then a halt was called (in total darkness). Once more, our venerable leaders tried unsuccessfully to figure out where we were and, more importantly, which direction we were supposed to be going. It was a long wait, so several men (myself included), went over to a house with a light in the window and asked if the coffee pot was on. For our brazen request we were rewarded with hot coffee. We were tired out, what with packing machineguns as well as our regular equipment and rifles, so hot coffee was refreshing and very much appreciated.

Presently we got the order to 'fall in", and we were off again, slugging it out in silence for another three kilometres which brought us to another village. This one was in total darkness, not a light to be seen. Once in awhile someone would be awakened by the sound of marching men; a door would open, and a sleepy head would poke out. Otherwise, the whole town was asleep.

We soon came to what was evidently the older part of town. Here chalk-white houses were set back at various angles from a narrow cobblestone lane. At last my section halted in front of a small house and we were informed it was to be our sleeping quarters. Just as we were settling down for the night, the sergeant came in with a list of names for guard duty. Sure enough, my name, as well as Private Hughes and two others, were on the list. Up we got, reluctantly took up our rifles and equipment and went back out into the night. The other two men were sent in one direction, while Hughes and I went in another to stand guard in front of an old stone church with a shoulder-high, stone wall. The 30-foot strip between the church and wall was filled with graves. Gazing at these and listening to the boom, boom of big guns, may have been disturbing, had it not been for Hughes recounting every minor detail of his stay in hospital at Buxton the previous year.

The next morning was November the 10th. We were getting ready for another forward march when suddenly we were under attack. Enemy gun and shellfire were being directed at us from somewhere near the village of *Nouvelles*. 'J' Battery was instructed to do some indirect firing in that direction, while the infantry manoeuvred into a position to attack. My section of the battery was standing at the ready, while Lieutenant Marshall's section and his second in command, Lieutenant Scott, set up their gun in an open field. They had just begun to direct their fire at the enemy when an enemy shell made a direct hit. As we watched, both lieutenants were enveloped in a cloud of smoke. Lieutenant Marshall came out unscathed, but Lieutenant Scott was badly injured and died minutes later. As far as I know, Lieutenant Scott was the last machine-gunner killed before Armistice Day which (unbeknown to us), was les than 24 hours away. It seemed so unfair, that Lieutenant Scott should go through the whole ugly war and lose his life a few hours before war's end.

Later, that same day we resumed our advance with a bitterly cold wind blowing. We continued in an easterly direction and were about two hours and a few kilos behind the infantry. At last we came to a clump of elm trees and took cover in them, swinging our arms and stamping our feet to keep warm. In the meantime, the men in charge of finding billets went ahead to a nearby town. When the scouts returned, we marched into the village of *Noirchain*, ten kilos from *Mons*. Our gun crew was housed in a tiny front parlour of a private home. This didn't leave much floor space per man, but we were tired enough to sleep anywhere. And so, we slept, completely unaware that tomorrow would bring amazing new

CHAPTER NINETEEN

For the past few days, there had been rumours of an armistice, but we hadn't paid much attention to such talk, putting it down to wishful thinking. However, the next morning, Monday the eleventh, our company was called out on parade. We thought it strange that we were being allowed to appear in caps and tunics, instead of full uniforms. Yet we weren't wondering long. When the Commanding officer strode out, he was holding a copy of General Foch's Orders For The Day, which had been forwarded to all Commanding officers along the Western front. The officer began to read, "…at 11 o'clock on the morning of the eleventh day of the eleventh month, hostilities will cease on all fronts. All troops will halt at the positions attained at that hour and await for further orders."

On hearing this, we all took a deep breath, then let it out, cheering, yelling, and slapping our buddies on the back. What a day! What fantastic news! When order was finally restored, the C.O. made a second announcement. "Men, this a special occasion to celebrate!" He then commenced issuing rum rations all 'round.

It was 9 am when we marched out of *Norchain.* We passed a battery of 5.9 guns in a field, already under gun-covers. Although the war had two more hours to go, no more gunfire was heard. When we reached the village of *Ciply*, Belgium, it was eleven o'clock. The Colonel then gave a short speech, telling us, "The war is officially over. Armistice has now come into effect." He added that army discipline would be maintained as before.

Billets had been arranged upstairs in a private home for our gun crew. This house had a cosy atmosphere, and the owners made us feel at home. They were soon telling us about the battle in 1914 when British soldiers retreated from house to house, shooting at the advancing Germans who were in the process of taking *Ciply*.

After lunch, when I couldn't get anyone interested in walking three kilometres to Mons, I set out on my own. Along the way I stopped to rest under some elm trees and found myself staring down at several dead Germans, their bodies twisted, their blood not yet dry. Even if they were supposed to enemies, my heart felt heavy as I turned back to the road and hurried on my way. Half a kilo more and I reached the older part of *Mons*, where I saw an amazing number of flags: the Belgium National flag and Allied flags, hundreds of them, waving from upper and lower windows. Crowds had taken over the streets, moving in one direction, toward the market square or Place d' Armes. So, I joined the throng. Every so often, I'd see a German soldier who'd been killed in the last minutes of the war. People didn't bother to stop, but merely gave the cadavers a look of contempt and kept walking.

As I wandered around, I overheard some English-speaking men say General Currie was going to make an official entry into *Mons* that afternoon. Sir General Arthur Currie affectionately called old 'Guts and Gaiters,' was considered one of the most respected commanders on the Western Front. Unlike many officers who graduated from university, Currie had a limited education. He began his army career in 1897 as a prewar militia gunner, then rose in the ranks to be the first Commander of the Canadian Corps. He had even been knighted for his bravery by King George V.

So now I knew the reason this large crowd was gathering in the market square and certainly wanted to see the general for myself. First, I needed to find a good vantage point. Seeing civilians climbing up to window ledges on the Hotel de Ville, I went with them and soon found myself clinging to an iron railing on a second-floor balcony. Minutes later, the carillon in the old belfry began pealing: Brabanconne, Belgium's National anthem, as well as Marsellaise, the French National anthem. This was followed by other lilting patriotic music. A gentle breeze caused the music to rise and fall, making the anthems even more grand. A few minutes later, the whole gathering began singing in a remarkable expression of patriotism. They were thankful to be free after four long years of oppression. However, General Currie didn't appear at this time. I'd have to wait until 4 pm for his grand entrance.

Later in the afternoon, the mayor, the city council, and other prominent townsfolk made their appearance in front of the Hotel de Ville. The band was still playing and the bells still ringing. In due time, General Currie arrived at the head of the 3rd Division Infantry Battalion. He was riding a sleek bay horse and the 3rd Division was looking their best for the occasion. Several staff officers accompanied the general on horseback. There was also a contingent of British Lancers in the cavalcade. On reaching a position opposite the mayor, the general dismounted and the mayor gave a welcoming speech followed by a prayer of thanksgiving. To this, General Currie replied in French. Then, after much cheering and clapping, the people once again broke out in jubilant tones, singing their national anthem. The troops had formed a hollow square for the ceremony, then regrouped and marched away.

Some of the people began to leave. Obviously, the largest November 11th event was over, so I climbed down to see what the rest of the town had to offer. My only purchases were postcards portraying views of the city. I attempted to buy bread but couldn't find any to buy. One shopkeeper told me it was illegal to sell bread to soldiers. No doubt this rule was put in place when Belgium was under German occupation. One helpful person directed me down a back alley to a working-class home. At first, the lady of the house said she didn't have any bread for sale, but then she gave me a motherly look and said. "I make waffles, yes?"

That suited me fine. Before long, she presented me with six full-sized waffles. When it came time to pay for them, both the housewife and her husband refused to take my money. So, I thanked them profusely and went on my way. I ate three of the waffles on the way back to our billets. Of the three remaining, I gave one to Private McNeil, one to Private Hughes, and ate the last one myself. Nothing had happened while I was gone. The official brass hadn't missed me, and the men had been sleeping.

****

The Bigger Picture: The armistice was not a peace treaty as such, but a declaration acknowledging Germany's defeat. On November 8th, a German delegation headed by Matthias Erzberger, crossed the devastated French war zone (under escort), and boarded Ferdinand Foch's private train which was parked on a siding in the Forest of Compiègne, France.

The German officials were shown a Paris newspaper confirming the abdication of the Kaiser and ordered to sign the treaty containing what the Germans felt were harsh Allied conditions. However, they signed the agreements at 5 am on November 11th and Armistice came into effect (Paris time), on the eleventh hour of the eleventh day of the eleventh month, 1918.

****

On Tuesday the 12th, I was on 'limber-washing fatigue' with a few others. We did the cleaning in a small slow-moving creek. We were finished by noon and had the afternoon off. I told Private McNeil about my exploits in *Mons*, so naturally he was anxious to come with me when I went a second time. All the flags were flying as before, but there certainly wasn't the rowdy celebrating I'd seen on the eleventh. Still, the people were congenial, especially to men wearing a khaki uniform.

On November 13th, we (#3 company), left *Ciply* and marched to *Frameries*, north of *Noircain*. Again, this was another coal-mining town with dwellings attached to one another in long rows on either side of the street. Our men were housed on the ground floor of one of these buildings. Having been behind enemy lines for four years, the town had not been shelled. All the same, the buildings were rather dilapidated and covered with coal dust.

On November 14th, after a lengthy march (with full equipment), we were billeted in a mental institution. An extension of the main building was still under construction and that's where we stayed. Four of us crowded into one very small completely empty space. We barely had room to breathe, but it was a roof over our heads, so we didn't grumble. While we were at the asylum, several British soldiers (POW) came in. They had been captured some time ago by the enemy and recently rescued by Allied troops. On the backs of their tunics were black numbers on grey circular patches. We were interested to learn which prison camp they'd been detained in. However, they were too physically and emotionally drained to talk, so we directed them to the cook kitchen.

November 15th found our battalion marching into *Mons*. We were here to watch the official entry of the 2nd Army Commander, General Horne, into Belgium.

The Canadian Corps was part of the 2nd Army, and we machine-gunners were dismissed as soon as we reached the Place d' Armes which was packed with soldiers and civilians. The event that followed was much like the one I'd witnessed when General Currie rode into Mons, except General Currie rode a bay horse and General Horne's horse was pure white. Otherwise, the formalities were basically the same.

The next day, November 16th, any man who still had outdated 'web' equipment, was sent to the quartermasters' store to exchange his light-weight webs for new leather gear. This was in order for all machine-gunners to be dressed alike. Strangely enough, the new leather equipment was stored at the undertakers. Down we went to make the exchange. We not only found our new equipment but were confronted by rows and rows of wooden caskets with dead German soldiers inside. It seemed the war was over, but death still hung heavy in the air.

On Sunday the 17th, we were marched to an open field for church parade. After the service the adjutant spoke to us, telling us that we—of the 2nd Battalion CMGC—were one of the Battalions chosen to take part in the Army of Occupation in Germany. Our battalion was to march behind the enemy soldiers, making sure they returned to Germany, after which we would occupy a stronghold in Germany. This was to ensure Germany was complying to the newly signed peace treaty. Soon we would leave *Mons* and march in easy stages into Germany to a 'bridgehead' on the *Rhine River*. A few of the men said they'd rather go straight home now the war was over, but most of us agreed to the proposal. I, for one, wanted to see something of Belgium and Germany, two countries I'd never seen before.

Later that day, I walked to *Mons,* to explore parts of the city I'd missed on my first two visits. Perhaps the most interesting sight that day was the Belfry of *Mons* which has been an important land-mark since the 17th century. It was open for inspection that day, so I went in. A wooden stairway led to the third-floor bell tower where approximately eighteen bells of varying sizes hung. While admir-ing the bells, I was joined by another machine-gunner. Together, we climbed another flight of stairs to the top balcony. What an amazing view of the city from that height: quaint red-roofed houses, crooked streets leading away from the Grand Place de Mons, green wooded hills, and a perfectly straight canal extending from *Mons* to *Conde.*

Still later, I ran across an old acquaintance, a Welshman named Tempest. I first met Private Tempest at the machinegun training school in *Aubin-St-Vaast*. In earlier years, he'd been an engineer in a gold mining camp in *California*. Since his stint in the machinegun training school, he'd been drafted into the 3rd Battal-ion CMGC. Consequently, he was one of the first Canadians to en-ter *Mons* in the early hours of Armistice Day. I was happy to see him again. We compared our past months' experiences and later took in a movie together. Unfortunately, we lost contact with one another and never met again.

Later that evening, we heard that our battalion was to com-mence our long march to Germany the very next morning. The rea-son we'd been delayed in *Mons* this past week, was to let the Ger-man troops have a head start. Keeping us apart was a calculated move to avoid any unpleasant incidents between us and those we still considered to be our enemies.

On the morning of November 18th, approximately 900 men of the 2nd Battalion machine-gunners left *Mons,* going in an east-erly direction. It was full marching orders with each man carrying his rifle and 40 rounds of light gun ammunition. Bringing up the rear were the machineguns and machinegun ammunition loaded onto horse-drawn limbers. The first five kilometres we marched through a forested area on a long, straight road. After that we entered open country with clumps of trees here and there. After 16 kilometres steady-going, we reached *Roeulx*. We were very tired and were billeted in small homes, one-gun section (six men), to each residence. After the regular meal of mulligan, another man and I were detailed to bring food rations from a railway station a kilometre away. We found our way to the station with no trouble, but what a desolate place to wait. A raw wind was blowing, and the building was rundown and draughty. The rails were rusty and there were holes in the platform. We waited for over an hour, but no ration train ever showed up. So, we left, feeling like failures when we delivered the bad news to our hungry companions.

A family of five lived in the house where we were billeted: an elderly lady, a middle-aged man, his wife, and two boys, 16 and 18 years of age. Later in the evening, the two sons entertained us with accordion music, while their parents told us how they'd been forced to work in a factory when they were under German occupation. They also pointed an accusing finger at Britain for bombing a number of railways and coal mines in the area.

The following morning, we had a short parade in the morning and were told to rest the remainder of the day. With an order like that, we should have known the days ahead were going to be taxing. However, Private McNeil and I played deaf. Disregarding the order, we hopped on a civilian streetcar bound for *Houdeng*, four kilos away. We had barely stepped off the streetcar when we ran slap dab into our adjutant and another officer.

"What are you doing here?" the adjutant queried.

"We wanted to see the sights," I said lamely. It was a poor excuse that produced a cold stare.

"Turn around and go back to your billets without delay," the adjutant said gruffly.

So, that was pretty much the end of our adventure in *Houdeng*, not counting our brush with some very aggressive children.

While we were waiting for a streetcar to take us back to *Le Roeulx*, a mob of kiddies surrounded us. They wanted one of our shoulder badges and they weren't going to take "no" for an answer. What a ridiculous situation to find ourselves in. Here we were supposed to be brave Canadian soldiers; we'd faced the mighty German army without flinching but being swarmed by a bunch of aggressive kids was downright scary. Quite simply, we didn't know what to do. After considerable pestering, Private McNeil finally gave in and traded one of his 'Canada' shoulder badges to a young girl for an inexpensive jet broach. And then the fun began with me as their victim. I kept telling them, "No, no more souvenirs!" But the threats and roughhousing persisted until a streetcar came to our rescue.

That night, the homeowners invited us into the kitchen for coffee and a light lunch which was much appreciated. Once again, they entertained us with accordion music and then handed out 'visiting cards' Apparently, presenting us with these special cards was considered the correct thing to do in polite society.

For the reasons given above, we continued to mark time at *Le Roeulx*. This was for our own safety as emotions were still running high with the German people. Many simply could not accept the fact the war was over, and they had emerged the losers. Snipers, loyal to Kaiser Bill, were said to be roaming the countryside looking for their enemies—us.

At eight in the morning of November 21st, we left *Le Roeulx*, passed through *Houdeng,* and arrived at *La Louvière* at noon. Once again, townspeople flocked out to see the Canadians, cheering and waving. Once in the town center, we piled arms and stood at ease waiting for the cook kitchen to come with our noon meal. As we waited, a prosperous-looking man stepped out from the crowd with two large jugs of steaming hot coffee. This was just what the doctor ordered. It was November and the wintry weather chilled us to the bone. We were happy to see our rations arrive, but disappointed to find less food than we expected. We could have eaten three times as much as we got. However, another generous citizen called us over. He was bailing out hot pea soup and even dished out seconds. As a result, our stomachs were well satisfied when we resumed our march across Belgium.

As we travelled farther inland, people stood in their doorways, and although smiling and friendly, they were more restrained than those who greeted us earlier. By Friday evening we had reached *Godarville,* a small village where Private Robertson, two others and I were billeted on *Rue de Chapelle Street* in a large upper room facing a railway. From now on, at the end of each day's march, we were issued two grey woollen blankets for overnight use. For troops who were used to huddling under a greatcoat, two blankets were opulence. The next day the blankets were tightly rolled and placed on limbers to be taken with us and used the next night.

Bright and early on Sunday morning, the troops left *Godarville*, and reached *Courcelles* by twelve noon. Another long route march followed. Along the way we saw more evidence of British bombing. Finally, we arrived at *Wangenies* and once again were billeted in private homes. We'd marched 18 kilometres that day.

We didn't lose any time in this town, but started off early the next morning, passed *Fleurus,* and entered *Keumiée* where we had a lunch break. On the road again, we were treated to an extensive view of the *Sambre River Valley.* We dipped down into the valley, where we saw our first riverboat. We passed *Jemeppe-sur-Sambre*, crossed a bridge, and came to *Mornimont* where the residents had acquired a supply of German flare pistols and flares. As we approached, the residents began shooting the flares off as a way to celebrate their freedom from German oppression.

All told we had marched 14 kilometres that day, compared to 18 the day before. We were beat. But no sooner had we found our billets, than I was called out for picket duty with three other men. We didn't appreciate the job. After tramping 32 kilometres in less than 40 hours (up and down hills), we were in no mood for picket duty. Besides, we hadn't eaten anything since noon.

The next morning broke cool and misty. We packed up, left *Mornimont,* crossed to the north side of the *Sambre River* at *Moustier*, and continued on through farming communities towards *Namur*. Approaching the city, we saw outer forts with four trench systems and vast lines of barbed wire entanglements. We could also see the city's most prominent landmarks: The Citadel (just beyond the confluence of the *Sambre* and the *Meuse River*), and the Cathedral with its domed roof. Many allied flags were flying in the breeze, and once again residents flooded onto the streets to give us a rousing welcome.

After marching through the city, we crossed the *Meuse River* on an ancient seven-arched, stone bridge. This was the only bridge connecting the suburb of *Jambes* to *Namur*. One kilometre farther, and we came to *Jambes* where the whole Battalion was billeted on two streets. "J" Battery (mine) lodged on *Rue d' Enhaive* (street), in a house owned by a kind-hearted family, Louis Tonneau and his wife and two grown children. Louis was in his mid-fifties, had a ruddy complexion, and a dark handlebar moustache. He was a locomotive engineer on the railway that ran between *Namur* and *Dinant* (Belgium) and *Givet* (France). He had a thirty-year-old son who also worked on the railway and a younger daughter who was a seamstress and lived at home. During our conversation, the family showed us pictures of a devastating flood that occurred the previous year. One picture showed their home completely surrounded by river water which had risen twenty feet above normal. They also told us about food shortages and abuses under German occupation.

The next day was November 28th, and although Christmas was almost a month away, we received our Christmas pay. While I was waiting for the paymaster to get to the "Ls" (for Lees), I walked down to the wharf and watched a number of boats travelling up and down the river. One small motorboat was towing six barges. Then my attention was drawn to a pile of trash. On further inspection, I found a German belt and buckle in the rubble. The buckle was engraved with the words 'Gott mitt uns.' When translated, this means the same as the inscription on our own belt buckles, 'God With Us.' It is hard to imagine a loving God pitting one god-fearing nation against another." I rescued the German buckle and took it home as a reminder of why we should strive to keep the peace at all cost.

CHAPTER TWENTY

After receiving our Christmas pay, Private McNeil and I set off for downtown by way of the railway bridge, the shortest route. We found a large department store open for business, went inside, and I bought three broaches with the name *'Namur'* imprinted on them as gifts for folks back home.

The next morning, we left *Jambes* at 8:00 am, but perhaps not as professional as the big brass would have preferred. Private Campbell, one of our machine-gunners, had been drinking and hadn't sobered up yet. He was in bad shape, whooping and staggering about. What to do about that? We had to keep moving. So, two men were ordered to carry Campbell's rifle and equipment while two others (one on each side), were ordered to guide him down the road. Around noon, he sobered up and wouldn't speak to anyone.

Since leaving *Namur*, the country had noticeably changed from flat meadows to rolling hills. Most hills were bare of trees with some very steep inclines. At one point, we passed a fort-like military defence post in the small town of *Maizeret* in the *Meuse Valley*. The roads in this part of the country varied from hard-packed clay to beaten grassy trails. Once we were actually walking on bare rocks. We passed through a dilapidated little place called *Thon* before reaching day's end at *Bonneville,* an equally poverty-stricken farming village. Here we were billeted in houses that at sometime or other had been whitewashed, but certainly not recently.

The six men of my gun section were housed with a Mr. and Mrs. Walton who weren't nearly as friendly as the Tonneau family in *Namur*. After we got settled, Private Robertson and I were sent to a farm a kilometre away, to pick up the blankets that were previously dropped off by the limbers.

At noon the next day, we packed up and under full marching order, we began a long 22-kilometre march—the longest so far. The region we were passing through was sparsely settled, and folks didn't pay much attention to marching troops.

Again, it was uphill and down, from narrow closed-in valleys to the picturesque town of *Haltinne*. It was after sunset, and we men expected to stop for the night at *Haltinne*, but the only stop we made was to allow two of our men to go on leave. They fell out of line and the rest of us kept marching. By now it was very dark.

One of the men began singing, "There's a long, long trail a winding into the land of my dreams." It seemed so appropriate the whole company broke into song. We didn't quit singing until we were approaching (what I believe was), the town of *Évalette*. At this point, we were facing another steep hill and needed to save our breath for another challenging climb. Up we went, through mature trees, then down the other side and into the town of *Havelange*. Finally, we stopped here for the night.

Twenty-two kilometres had been a hard day's march and tempers were wearing thin. My section roomed in an estaminet where beer and wine were sold by day. Since it was after hours, we could only look longingly at the bottles in the shop window and snarl about the proprietor's lack of service. There was a large wall map in one of the rooms. It drew our interest, and we speculated on our probable route from *Havelange*, Belgium to Germany. At this time, we didn't know for sure if we were going to Bonn or not.

Before long we'd all settled down for the night. My bed was two benches drawn together. For a pillow, I stuffed a sweater in my tin helmet. After spending nights in dugouts, sleeping on a bench was no hardship. The next morning, we woke up to a light snowfall, but that didn't stop us. We were on the road as soon as we'd eaten breakfast. After marching several kilometres, the snow vanished, and we continued southeast, toward *Luxembourg*. The hills were higher here and well timbered. At the foot of one ridge, we came upon an unexpected spectacle. At least 150 German-made tin helmets were lying on the ground, obviously tossed away by disheartened enemy soldiers.

We stopped in a grassy meadow for our noon meal. The sun was shining in a cloudless sky, yet the breeze had a touch of frost. After eating, we carried on, crossing a bridge over the *Curthe River*. This river was about 60 feet wide with clear water flowing over a bed of pebbles. After a steady march through gently rolling hills, we arrived at the small railway town of *Barvaux*. Here we were billeted in a long, two-story brick building which was unoccupied and unfurnished. This had been another 22-kilometre march. Fatigued, we curled up on the wooden floor and slept well into the next day.

This part of Belgium lies in the county of *Luxembourg* and was the most scenic we'd come to so far. My eyes were drawn to a solitary gorse covered hill that loomed up in the east. The day after we arrived, I hiked to the top of it, and the view was amazing.

After 'rifle inspection' and eating our noon meal two other fellows and I walked downtown, which wasn't really a town at all, just a small collection of houses. There were no shops, but one house had a few groceries and knickknacks on display in its front window. I went in and bought a Christmas card; nothing else. Along the way, we saw a sign stating the altitude was 150 metres above sea level (about 492 feet).

The next morning, we lined up on a cinder track at the railway station and started our day's march from there. The evening before, the weather had been cloudy and dull. Now it started to rain, a regular deluge that turned yesterday's fine dust into dark grey mud. To avoid the quagmires ahead, we took a side trail that ran parallel to the main road. This led us to a spring that flowed into an irrigation ditch. The rain stopped momentarily, and we were happy to see such lovely spring water, so we dumped out our stale water and refilled our bottles with the pure spring water. What a treat!

However, about the time we joined the main road, the rain came down in torrents. Although we were wearing our groundsheets, they didn't give much protection and our packs were twice as heavy when wet. The road went on and on (up and up). When the terrain eventually levelled off, we found ourselves in the little town of *Grandmènil*. We thought we were stopping here for the night, but oh, no! We marched right down main street and out the other side. Presently, we came to a halt in a farmer's field, where grumbling among the ranks grew to a crescendo. Here we were like drowning rats in pouring rain, and there wasn't even a tree to duck under.

After a while, the lieutenants got their bearings, and we set off again. We went about two more kilometres to *Oster-le* (something or other) and stopped at some deserted farm buildings. "J" Battery took shelter in an old brick feed barn that was half full of musty hay. I was among the unlucky devils sent to the limbers to get the blanket rolls. As could be expected, the outside blankets were soaked before we got back to the barn, but we carriers made sure to secure inside dry blankets for ourselves. It rained steadily all night. There was more muttering and cursing when we had to stand in line in the rain to get our rations.

By the next morning, the rain had stopped, and we resumed our march in wet clothing. It was a seemingly endless trek of climbing through forests with very few cultivated fields. Midday, we arrived at *Baraque de Fraiture*, a town on a hilltop with an elevation of 650 metres (2130 feet). From here there was a striking view of bare hills rising one after another as far as the eye could see. We didn't stop very long in this hilltop town. The good news was from here on, the grade was downhill. Later in the afternoon, we reached *Salmchâteau* situated in a narrow, canyon-like valley. Again, we didn't stop but continued in a southerly direction until we came to *Bovigny*, Belgium, six kilometres from the German border. We had come 28 kilometres that day and were happy to stop for the night here in *Bovigny*.

After our regular mulligan meal, a good many of the troops (myself included), were billeted in a bleak stone church. It was cold and damp as most stone churches are, and I had a difficult time getting to sleep. We were beginning to move around in the morning: some men dressing; some shaving, and others folding blankets, when a priest came thumping down the stairs, preceded by a boy ringing a bell. The priest was an overly plump, middle-aged, sour-looking fellow. Although we didn't understand his language, his message was only too clear; he wanted us out! He wind-milled his arms, then made motions to shoo us away. We weren't overly impressed with his antics. With a few snide remarks in his direction, we left as quickly as we could. None of us were anxious to catch pneumonia in that miserably cold church, anyway.

December 6th, 1918: This was the day that we of the 2nd Battalion were expected to cross over the border and enter Germany. The Commanding Officer's instructions were simple. We were to cross the border in flying colors. After all, we were the mighty conquerors, and by golly we'd better look the part.

The sergeant in charge of the flags took them out of their canvas bags and gently unwrapped them. The colors were bright and spotless, ready to make us proud. However, that was not to be. A heavy mist turned into a fine rain. With no sign of the weather clearing, the colors were returned to their bags and the march into Germany resumed. Although we appeared to be going through dense pines, we couldn't see much on account of thick fog. At length, we came to the village of *Beho* and realized we hadn't reached Germany yet—we were still in Belgium. There were more flags in evidence in *Beho*--more than we'd seen elsewhere on our recent march. Along with the flags was a huge banner reading, "Welcome To Our Brave Allies."

When we were within 100 yards of the border, we were ordered to halt and stood at ease until a lieutenant came walking towards us. He said that our battalion commander had just been over the Belgium-German border on horseback and found there was only a certain place for Canadian troops to cross into Germany. The line itself was marked by two posts (six feet apart), for each country.

So much for making a grand entry! We crossed the line without fanfare and could finally claim to be in Germany.

About two kilometres farther we came to a small German village. After marching through this town, we carried on for two kilometres and stopped for lunch at the edge of a potato field. One of our men got the bright idea of digging for potatoes. Soon the camp cooks provided sacks and about a third of the machine-gunners began scratching for spuds until we had enough to last the week. The farmer himself came out, stood watching for a few minutes, then threw up his hands and walked back to his house.

The mist cleared. Once more we began moving. Although we could see farm buildings, there was never any sign of humans.

This road went under a fine-looking railway bridge which appeared to have been constructed recently in order to rush soldiers to the frontlines. From this bridge, it was no more than a kilo to *St.Vith,* a fairly large town. In a place this size the residents couldn't all hide indoors, so we saw some unhappy looking civilians on the streets. However, there was not a single-solitary uniformed German soldier to be seen anywhere. We were always mindful that the German people still regarded us as 'the enemy,' and every so often an officer would warn us to exercise caution. "The German people still hate us," he said. "They could turn on us at a moment's notice. Keep your mouths shut and for God's sake don't stir up trouble."

In *St.Vuth,* we machine-gunners occupied a vacant section of a stone building. Some buddies and I had a room which we reached by way of a stone staircase. About the time I was settling in for the night, my name was called (along with eleven other poor devils), for guard duty. My shift was 6 pm to 8 pm; 12 pm to 2 am, and 6 am to 8 am. 'Not much chance to get a decent night's rest with a schedule like that.

While on duty, I faced an imposing looking building with huge glass windows. The curtains were drawn back, so I could plainly see a party was in progress. Uniformed nurses were entertaining German officers. They were cuddled up, laughing, drinking, and smoking—having a great old time. They certainly didn't act as if they had just lost a war. I shook my head. This didn't make sense. We Canadians were supposed to be the victors. And what were we doing? Skulking around in the shadows like underdogs, cold and dripping wet, watching those we defeated having the time of their lives.

Since then, I've wondered if the party was intentionally staged to humble us. If so, it did the job. After six hours on night duty, morning came far too early. Regardless, we started marching

245

early the next day, changing directions from southeast to northeast. Road markers showed the distance in kilometres and hectometres, and since the markers began at *St. Vith*, it was easy for us to keep track of the distance we traveled.

From the very beginning, we'd known one of our Infantry Battalions were a day's march ahead of us. We were about four kilos out of *St Vith* when we overtook a soldier who had 'fallen out' of the infantry column. He was sitting at the side of the road. Farther along, we saw another, then another, then two more, followed by a large group of infantry men and a sergeant busily taking the names of deserters.

Farther along, another officer was taking names of a larger group of men. If the war was still in progress, deserters would have been court-martialled—perhaps even shot. We never did hear what actually caused so many men to abandon ship or what happened to them after the fact. Since it wasn't our problem, we kept marching. Yet, seeing this weird sight, led to speculation. Were we troops being asked to do more than we were capable of doing?

Several kilometres past *St. Vith*, we came to the neat little town of *Schönberg*. We marched a kilo past the town and stopped for lunch: Mulligan (of course), and some dry rations saved from the day before. Jam came in two-quart cardboard containers and was a day's ration for twenty men. When eating, I always kept an eye on who had the jam box. Otherwise, it might not get passed around and I could lose out.

With lunch over, we set out again only to discover we were faced with climbing more steep hills. The men began to tire. Many called for a rest as no end to the hills was in sight, but we were ordered to carry on. And so, we did, for another half hour, when we came to a collection of houses. We halted to rest in a narrow street. A young woman leaned from her window to give the closest troops a cup of coffee. Soon, her coffee pot ran dry, so not everyone got a cup. Similar to the story of the 'Fox and Grapes,' we unlucky ones claimed the coffee was probably poisoned.

The march was resumed through open country. Darkness was setting in when one of the advance parties came back to tell us where we'd be stopping for the night. Some on called out, "How much farther?"

"About a kilo," he answered. This was far from the truth. We went on and on, with dry tongues hurling disparaging remarks after the man who deceived us. A long while later, we came to *Arbruthen*, a well lit-up factory complex, and these buildings proved to be our billets. We had marched a full 30 kilometres that day, carrying very heavy loads. To a man we were hungry and tired to the point of nausea. The watery mulligan was not nearly sustaining. Some men complained to their officer about having hunger pangs. The officer promptly took them back to the kitchen for a second helping.

That night our beds were three tiers of cots with only wire mesh to lay our blankets on. Yet, we were so drained we made the best of it and slept well into the next day.

Sunday, December 8th: On looking around the complex in the light of day, we realized we were at a munition factory. The facility appeared to be recently built and all the machinery was shiny and new. There were great stacks of unopened oil drums and rolls of barbed wire. It wasn't completely vacant as several civilian caretakers were on hand to see nothing was stolen.

We were allowed to rest all day. Perhaps our officers wanted to avoid the kind of revolt we'd seen the previous day with the infantry battalion. When not sleeping, I spent my time addressing postcards to my English relatives and writing to Evelyne in Canada. Other men were doing the same: mailing letters home.

At 8 am the next morning we packed up and were marching by 8:30 am. First, we backtracked for nearly two hours before resuming our line of march. Very soon we were swinging downhill from the high country and entering a well-treed canyon with terraced slopes. Later, we came to *Stradtkyll* along *Kyll Creek*.

The number of large, attractive homes was baffling, until we learned this region had been one of Kaiser Bill's favourite hunting grounds. This was part of the *Ardennes Hill Country*, eighty kilometres west of the Industrial Rhineland. This day's march took us through rolling evergreen terrain that reminded me of Alberta's foothills. We ate our lunch at the edge of a farmer's field near the village of *Dahlem*.

Twenty-two kilometres after our morning's departure from *Arbruthen*, we came to *Blankenheimersdorf* where we were billeted for the first time in German homes. "J" Battery (mine) filed in through the kitchen to a back room with benches around the inside walls. A long table had been placed in the center of the room and an organ sat at the far end. The room was filled to capacity when it came time for supper. The owner was a solid-built, middle-aged farmer who readily conversed with Private Beckman, a machine-gunner who could speak German. Both the farmer and his wife were very pleasant and sold some large oval loaves of brown bread to three machine-gunners.

We didn't leave our comfy quarters in *Blankenheimersdorf* until 10 am on December 10th. In less than two kilometres we came to another town with a similar name, *Blankenheim*, an ancient town with many crooked streets, Elizabethan style houses, and thatched

248

cottages. Most of the homes were painted white or a warm yellow with black trim. We saw very few people on the streets as we marched through town.

Minutes later we came to *Tondorf,* where buildings were built so close together, we had trouble squeezing between them. We didn't stop until we reached a densely wooded valley where we ate our noon rations. Our next interesting sight was the attractive old-world town of *Münstereifel* with its ancient walled fortress. We complained to our commanding officer, saying we'd marched far enough; we needed to stop here, but no such luck. We kept going until we came to *Iversheim.* We had marched 25 kilometres that day.

"J" Battery's men were billeted in a house in a back alley where we tossed and turned, trying to get to sleep on yet another cold stone floor.

The following day, December 11th, we continued marching until we reached *Arloff* and stopped to rest near a church. While there, several friendly German kiddies (no older than six or seven), walked boldly up and began speaking to us in German. One chubby little fellow was drawn to my rifle, fingered it while chattering like a little chipmunk. He was asking about my rifle, but not understanding the German language, I couldn't give him an answer.

We moved on and after some time we came to a hill where we could see far and wide—a view that took in at least six towns and cities. *Cologne* could be identified by the twin towers on her cathedral. However, the closest city was *Bonn* which we suspected was our final destination. *Bonn* and the *River Rhine* looked to be one day's march away. Other towns we passed through were *Euskirchen, Palmersheim, Odendorf,* and finally *Niederdrees* where we were billeted in a residential area. This had been an easier day. To this point we'd covered only 12 kilometres. Unfortunately, the limbers had thrown our blankets off somewhere in the city. Another fellow and I were detailed to get the blankets, so we hiked all over town—at least another two or three more kilometres—before we found them.

After that I spent most of the day with Private McNeil, sitting in the front window, lazily watching the traffic go by. There wasn't much traffic to speak of, just a few civilians and an occasional horse and cart.

We left this quiet little town at 8 o'clock the next morning, went through a factory town named *Rheinbach,* then *Meckenheim*, before turning north toward *Bonn.* Presently we were marching on a trail through the woods and stopped to rest among the trees. Farther along, it began to rain, and we were allowed to duck into a factory shed at *Röttgen* until the shower was over. From there, we went to *Ippendorf,* a town situated on a low ridge overlooking *Bonn.* That's when we realized we were actually going to Bonn and getting closer with every step.

Once in *Ippendorf*, we stopped at a cinema hall where we spent the night. We had marched 15 kilometres that day. We attacked our new quarters with zeal, stacking chairs down the center of the hall, and cleaning the place up so we could bed down on the floor. I had only just wrapped a blanket around my aching body in anticipation of a good night's rest, when I was called out to join a fatigue party. This time we were detailed to clean limbers, two men to a limber. We cussed our luck. If we'd been allowed to wait until the next day, the rain would have done the job for us.

December 13th: In the morning our orders were for a general cleanup. Everything: clothes, brasses, and boots had to look sharp. This was the day we'd march through *Bonn* and cross the mighty *Rhine River.* All forenoon, the theatre was a hive of activity as our men polished, scrubbed, and cleaned. When at last the march started, the heavy mist plagued us all morning, then erupted in showers. Throughout the day, the rain continued in varying degrees. At times the drizzle almost ceased, only to start up heavier than before. Yet upward and onward! From *Ippendorf,* our route lay along a narrow lane that sloped down to a street paved with cobblestones. Here we halted and formed two-deep. After fixing bayonets and sloping arms in regulation order, we resumed the march with the polished bayonets glistening in spite of the dull sky. Soon we machine-gunners were marching on a broad highway, lined with upscale homes and beautiful flower gardens. The highway was called the *Poppelsdorfer Allee* and went in a straight line from the suburb of *Poppelsdorf* to the center of *Bonn.* I could feel the excitement building—at last we were entering the enchanted city of *Bonn.*

During the march, our machinegun officers were required to make sure German civilians (of military age), exhibited the same respect for our armed forces as they would for their own. That is to say, remove their hats and stand at attention. When one of our officers, Lieutenant Marshall, noticed a man wearing a cap, he stepped out of line, snatched the offending cap off the man's head, and threw it into a water-filled gutter.

Now, the streets were very crowded. What remained of our Infantry Battalion (those who hadn't deserted), arrived the day before, so they were off duty, mingling with the crowd of civilians. Once again, it was noticeable German army uniforms were non-existent.

A fine rain was still falling when we (2nd Battalion of machine-gunners), reached the bridge over the *River Rhine.* It was a beautiful bridge with a huge steel arch supported by castellated piers of an old German design. A double streetcar track crossed the bridge but wasn't active on this day. No civilians were allowed on the bridge until we troops crossed it. As we approached the far end of the bridge, we could see General Currie, the Canadian Corps Commander, on horseback. With him were other high-ranking officials. As we marched past, we turned to salute the officers. It was a heart-stopping moment, one to remember with pride.

After clearing the point of salute, we halted in *Beuel* (a suburb of Bonn), to unfix our bayonets. We then resumed our march past the factory town of *Hangelar* and the small community of *Menden.*

Darkness fell, and the rain continued, leaving huge pools of water on the road. Not to my liking, because when the order came to halt, I was left balancing on two rocks in the middle of a deep puddle.

About this time, I think we machine-gunners were asking ourselves, "Just how much more could our tired bodies tolerate?" It had been a taxing day and we were all ready to quit and go home. Not for the first time it occurred to me that in wartime we'd carried backbreaking weights; we'd survived inhumane conditions; we'd been shot at and seen our comrades die. Now, in peacetime (while our enemy rested comfortably at home), we were being pushed beyond our limits. I wasn't alone with these thoughts. Above the whistle of a cold north wind, I could hear the mutterings of my companions.

When at last our leaders figured out where we were going, we moved on until we could see the lights of a fairly large town, which turned out to be *Troisdorf,* situated near the outer perimeter of the Cologne bridgehead. It was now 10 pm, very dark and raining. We marched down main street to a large industrial building enclosed in a tall woven-wire fence. Later, we learned this had been a munitions factory.

We came to a halt at the side of the road and stood shivering in the pouring rain while one of our befuddled leaders went into the main building to see if this might possibly be our billets. Finally, what seemed like a lifetime, our dry-looking benefactors came out with smiles and we were herded into the compound like so many wet sheep. Then, at long last, we passed the main building and arrived at eight wooden huts. Oh, so these were our new billets!

Our energy returned after we'd dried off, eaten supper, and discovered a storage room filled with woollen blankets. Each of us took three blankets for ourselves. After spending several months with no bedding, three blankets were like winning a jackpot.

The next day we had an even greater find in another storage area—real beds and mattresses. We treated ourselves by taking these amazing beds into our huts, and then sleeping on them for much of the following day. Oh, how we needed the rest! From November 18th (when we left *Mons* in Belgium), until we arrived here in *Troisdorf* on December 13th, we had marched 340 kilometres. This averaged 20 kilometres a day for 17 days. We didn't know it then, but *Troisdorf* was to be our final destination, and was one of the three occupation zones east of the Rhine.

The munitions factory at *Troisdorf* (where we were now stationed), had evidently been built after the war began. Everything looked new. In front of the main building, small trees faced the road and had recently been planted. In the back, the huts we occupied looked new and were clustered around a one-story structure that held a dining room and cook kitchen. The bathhouse was the largest and best equipped we'd seen during the war. It was fitted with fifty porcelain bathtubs, fifty porcelain showers, and fifty porcelain sinks and toilets. What luxury!

The following day we had pay parade, and for the first time, we were paid in German marks—50 marks per private. Then came our hour-long PT exercises, something we'd have every morning while we were here in Germany.

After supper, Private Hisey, myself, and two other machine-gunners took a streetcar five kilometres to the village of *Seigburg*. As the streetcar made its way along *Colnerstrasse* (main street), two sentries lurched down the aisle demanding to see passports for all passengers. We four Canadians looked at one another and shrugged. We didn't have passports or passes. When the sentries came to us, all we could do was nod, say, "Yes sir," and fumble in our pockets for the passports we didn't have. Finally, the sentries gave up and moved on. Later, when headquarters became more organized, passes were issued and had to be carried at all times when we were away from our billets.

It was dark by the time we reached *Seigburg*, but stores were still opened. We did some window shopping but didn't purchase a thing. Hisley and I started walking back to *Troisdorf*. However, we soon realized we didn't have time; we needed to be in our huts before 'lights out.' So, we hopped on a streetcar—the last one going to *Troisdorf* that night—and barely made it back under the wire.

The next day was December 16th, and we heard Commander-in-Chief, Sir Douglas Haig, would arrive during the morning for inspection.

When the time came, we were paraded out of the compound and onto the main road, forming a single line on each side of the roadway. Two Infantry Battalions were also brought up from their billets near *Cologne* to take part in the ceremonies. It was a cold, windy day. As a result, we were allowed to 'fall-out', so we could exercise to keep warm. More than an hour later, the General's automobile was seen in the distance. We lined up again. General Haig's car reached the first troops; the General got out, stopped briefly to speak to our commanding officer, walked past the machine-gunners and was gone. The whole affair lasted less than ten minutes.

CHAPTER TWENTY-ONE

On December 23rd there was a nice surprise waiting for me. I received a Christmas parcel from Sister Evelyne. More goodies to share with my pals. And then on Christmas Eve, it began to snow, making a beautiful white Christmas similar to the ones I'd enjoyed in Alberta. Our huts were made festive by nailing spruce boughs over the doors and adding colourful streamers.

December 25th: Christmas morning we had a church service in a cinema hall. Then, at one o'clock the whole battalion filed into the big dining room for Christmas dinner. The dining hall was beautifully decorated, too. The battalion officers, who were scheduled to have their Christmas dinner later in the day, acted as waiters for our tables. They began by giving each man a nose-cap of rum. This was the last rum ration issued to the 2nd Battalion.

What a meal! There was roast pork, mutton, potatoes, carrots, Christmas plum pudding, apples, oranges, and maple sugar, and each man was given two bottles of beer. We'd been told we'd get a carload of turkeys which I presume was waylaid by higher ranking officers, because the turkeys never came. However, we couldn't grumble; we had more than enough to eat that Christmas. After dinner, Private Hisely and I took a long leisurely stroll around the factory area to walk off the effects of overindulging.

On January 5th, four other fellows and I got passes to go to *Bonn* to take in an Orchestral Concert at the Stadt Theatre. We took the electric railway which was a novelty in itself. The Divisional Orchestra played some excellent selections from Beethoven and Handel. (Incidentally, Bonn was Beethoven's hometown.) Another day, I went by train to see the ancient ruins of *Drachenfels Castle* in the mountainous area of *Königswinter* which was across the river

257

from *Bonn*. I'd heard a lot about this castle but was surprised to find the road to the castle was blocked off and guarded by sentries. *Drachenfels* was in the Neutral Zone, so we soldiers were forbidden to visit the famous ruins. What a disappointment!

Another day I applied for and was given a pass to spend an afternoon in the 2,000-year-old city of *Cologne*. I caught the 12:30 train. In half an hour I reached the west side of the river, walked across the *Hohenzollernbruckle Bridge* to the world-famous *Cologne Cathedral (*Kölner Dom) which is truly amazing. Taking over 600 years to build, its twin towers rise over 500 feet above the streets. I was soon inside, admiring magnificent stain glass windows and the many faceted, arched ceiling. I found a spiral staircase that led to one of the towers, climbed to the top, and was treated to a spectacular view of the city. Tourist shops nearby offered postcards of the city, so I purchased several as reminders of a perfect day's adventure.

Two days later, we had another pay parade which netted me 30 marks. In 1919, a mark was worth approximately twelve cents. About this time the British troops in *Cologne* released a newspaper of sorts, appropriately named '*The Watch on the Rhine*.' It was only a few skimpy sheets of paper, but we appreciated any news of the outside world. Another milestone was that we Canadians were allowed to seal our outgoing letters. 'No need to have them censored now the war was over.

On January 11th, 1919, I borrowed a used pass from Private Hisey and went by train to *Cobience* (Kobienz). About fifty miles from *Bonn, Cobience* lay at the junction of two rivers: The *Moselle* and the *Rhine*. As I sat looking through the train window, I saw a variety of landscapes: rocky cliffs, dense forests, the ruins of ancient castles, and small, picturesque villages. The scenery alone, as seen from a slow-moving train, made the whole trip worthwhile.

Cobience was a much larger city than *Bonn*. Across the river from *Cobience,* a modern fortress had been built on a 400-foot cliff. This was named *Ehrenbreitstein* and at one time was rated as the strongest fortification in all of Europe.

When I stepped from the train, the first thing I noticed was a very large number of American troops. It was noon when I arrived and I had a better than average meal of French fries, pork, and coffee at the American YMCA—all for four marks. I spent three hours in the city, bought a few more postcards, and had conversations with some of the Americans. The American military police struck me as hard-boiled and tough-talking when addressing their men. From what I learned from the US troops; they hated their own military police more than they hated the enemy.

On January 13th, I took a shorter trip to the ancient town of *Godesberg.* The *Godesburg Castle* was the castle we'd seen from a distance when we were approaching *Bonn,* so I was anxious to see the castle up-close. The caretaker of the castle charged me 10 pfennings to go inside. In return, his blonde daughter showed me around. The dark interior was unappealing, the dungeons even less appealing, and the view from the top of the round tower could barely be seen through the dusty cobwebs.

January 14th: In the morning we were lined up by companies in front of the dining hall for photographs, these after a ladder was carried out so the camera man could stand on the hall's flat roof and take pictures from there.

J Battery, 2nd Division, Canadian Machine Gun Corps,

taken at Troisdorf, Germany, January 1919.

William Lees, #895518, pin-pointed on the next page.

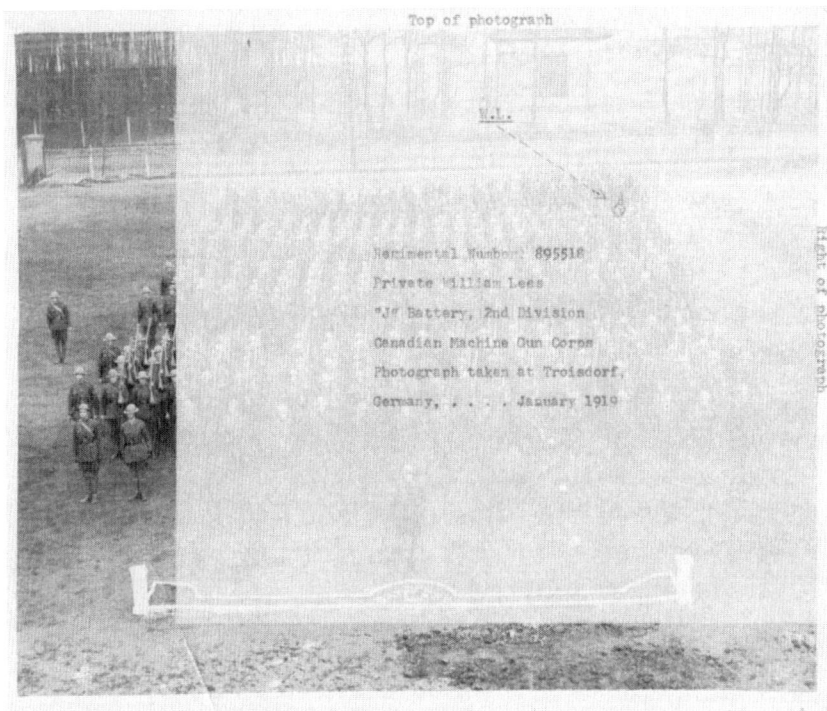

Top of photograph

V.L.

Regimental Number: 895518
Private William Lees
"J" Battery, 2nd Division
Canadian Machine Gun Corps
Photograph taken at Troisdorf,
Germany, ... January 1919

Right of photograph

Photos credit: William Lees's collection

January 19th, 1919 was a red-letter day. This was the day we were told the British Imperial Machine-gunners were arriving at *Troisdorf* to relieve us, the 2nd Battalion of Canadian Machine Gun Corp—my battalion.

But it wasn't until the morning of January 21st, they actually came. And then, at 4:30 pm, we gathered our belongings, left *Troisdorf* and marched down to *Seigburg.* We had been part of the Army of Occupation for five weeks. At *Seigburg*, a troop train was waiting to take us to *Florette, Belgium.* During the night we traveled via *Cologne, Air-le-Chapelle*, and *Herbesthal* where we crossed over the German-Belgium border. We then passed on the south side of *Liege,* then up the *Meuse Valley*, through *Namur*, and arrived at *Florette* as the sun was setting.

After getting off the train, we were billeted in different parts of the town. Some men were billeted close to the station. However, my "J" Battery had to march two kilometres up a narrow pass back in the hills, where we were housed in the office of a sand and gravel company. Although we didn't know it at the time, we would be billeted here in *Florette* for eleven weeks. Plans had already been made to keep us occupied while we waited to be sent back to Canada. Classes in mathematics, French, and several other subjects were given in the Catholic College, otherwise known to the troops as "Kahki College." The classes were held from 9 am to noon each day, except Sundays. Our afternoons were free.

From now on, formal parades were few and far between and discipline less rigid. During the coming weeks, Private McNeil and I walked from *Florette* to *Namur* on average of two or three times a week. It was six kilometres to *Namur*, and the road there followed the twists and turns of the river so that we often encountered riverboats of various sizes along the way. Boats and barges usually bore the names of their home ports, such as *Belgium, Holland, Antwep, Rottedam, Amsterdam*, and *Liege.* Occasionally, we'd walk across the *Meuse River Bridge* to visit the Tonneau family at *Jambe.* These were the folks who had been so good to us seventeen weeks before, when our gun crew was marching to Germany, and we were billeted in their home.

Early in February, there were several days of snowy weather when we troops were content to stay in camp. However, I'd put in an application for a three-day leave to go to *Brussels* (the capital and largest city in Belgium). The leave was to start on March 1st. I had barely received the pass when I became ill. My gums were extremely sore and my teeth so loose it was impossible to eat solids. Whether this condition was caused by an infection or by consuming too many chocolate bars, I'll never know. Since I wasn't able to bite or chew the medics put me on a liquid diet.

What to do about my three-day pass? I might never have another chance to go to *Brussels*, so why not go? I went by train and arrived in *Brussels* at 9 pm on Wednesday, March 5th. That night I slept at the YMCA. In the morning it was eggnogs and tea for breakfast, and then I joined a tour of the city which was sponsored by the "Y". I visited the Palace de Justice, the Palace du Roi, and Hotel de Ville where the Duke of Wellington danced before the Battle of Waterloo. I would love to have gone out that evening but felt too weak. So, I stayed in my room drinking eggnog and cocoa (hot chocolate). On Friday, March the 7th, I was feeling somewhat better, so joined another YMCA tour. This time we went to *Antwerp* and took in the Zoological Gardens and the Cathedral Art Gallery, where Ruben's best paintings were on display.

Two weeks later, on Saturday, March 22nd, when I'd regained my health, I accompanied other Canadian troops on a special train that had been reserved for us to go to watch the Canadian Corps Sports Games in *Brussels*. I wasn't as keen to watch the games as I was to go sightseeing. So, another like-minded fellow and I left the sport's fans at the station and took the streetcar twenty kilometres to *Waterloo*. After getting a brief look at the town, we walked another four kilometres south to *Mont-St. Jean*, where Napoleon was defeated. A short distance back from the road, sat a one-hundred-and-fifty-foot pyramid, holding the famous twenty-foot Belgium Lion Monument. It was mind-boggling and nothing would do but we had to climb the two hundred and twenty-six steps to the very top. There was also a nearby war museum crammed full of archives collected from the Napoleonic battlefield. There was far too much to see in the time we had. I'd gladly have stayed longer, but we had to be back to billets before the final bell.

Across the road from where we were billeted was an iron-gated cave entrance. On March 16th, forty of the "J" Battery machine-gunners (including myself), lined up for a group picture on a grassy spot in front of the entrance to the caves.

William Lees: back row, standing, second from left.

Photo credit: William Lees's collection, taken at Florette, Belgium

The caves captured our interest, so a few of us located the gatekeeper and asked him to give us a tour of the caves, which he did. We walked and crawled from one cavern to the next, seeing the most amazing formations of stalactites and stalagmites. Surprisingly, the caves extended underground for six kilometres. They were the most unique caverns to be found in all of Belgium. Apparently, in 1814 there were more than 20,000 refugees living in these underground caves.

Another highlight was a concert put on by the Battalion Theatre Company on March 18th at the Convent. It was an excellent performance.

Finally, on Tuesday, April 8th, after eleven weeks at *Florette*, the 2nd Battalion CMGC got orders to pack up and board a troop train heading to *Le Havre*, France. In spite of the pleasant times we'd had at *Florette,* we were anxious to go home. And so, with a goodly amount of joking and frivolity, the 50th Battalion happily boarded a troop train bound for France. We were travelling in boxcars, 20 men per car, not the best conditions for traveling, but that was how it was. We had only a one hour-long break for supper in *Mon*, before we were off again. During the night, we crossed the battlefields without getting a last look at the trenches where life had been so uncertain. From *Arras*, the train went by way of *Aubigny* to *St. Pol*, then south via *Frevant* and *Canaples* to *Amiens*. Finally, we arrived at *Le Havre* which was the port of embarkation for England.

We waited in *La Havre* for three whole uneventful days. Finally, at 5 pm, Sunday, April 13th, we boarded a troopship, and crossed the English Channel to *South Hampton*. The crossing took seven hours. After that, we stayed out in the harbour until daylight. While we waited, we were fed a breakfast of tea, a chocolate bar, and one lone bun. Then we were given a lunch bag with sausage rolls, cheese, biscuits, and another chocolate bar to eat later on the train. The train we took went through *Winchester, Working*, and *Giuldford* on the way to *Witley Camp*.

On Good Friday, April 18th, 1919, eight-day passes were issued to all machine-gunners. This was to be our final leave before we returned to Canada. I used my leave to do what I liked best— go sightseeing. While visiting, over breakfast, Sergeant Copping, and I decided to go to the Zoological Gardens and Madame Tussaud's Waxworks. Then in the afternoon, we went to *Saint Paul's Cathedral* to view the Canadian Battalion flags which had been deposited there for safekeeping during the war. These flags would be returned to the various battalions when the battalions left England. Later we took a walk across *London Bridge*, returning by the same route because the sidewalks and roadways were far too crowded with pedestrians and motor vehicles to manoeuvre easily.

At 10:30 pm that evening, I walked to *Kings Cross Station* where I boarded a train for *Edinburgh*. It was too dark to see anything, so I slept until I arrived in *Edinburgh* at 8 am on Sunday morning. That day I toured *St. Gile's Cathedral, Holy Rod Palace, Edinburgh Castle,* and *Forth Bridge*. I stayed overnight at the YMCA on Princess Street. Bright and early the next morning, I went touring again and visited the Sir Walter Scott Memorial before catching the train to *Glasgow* where I booked in at the "Y" hostel on Suachihall Street and stayed overnight.

Tuesday morning, I met an Australian soldier from *Perth*. Together we caught a motorbus at George Square and went to *Aberfoyle* in the Trossachs. The weather was sunny and mild, and I was pleased to get a glimpse of *Loch Lomond* which lay about two miles to the west of the motorway. My companion and I spent the day browsing through *Aberfoyle*, a delightful city in which I could easily have spent several more days. However, at 5 pm we caught the bus back to *Glasgow*.

We would soon be leaving for Canada, but before I did, I wanted to visit my English relatives one last time. With that in mind, the next day, I took the 10:30 am train to *Manchester*. I traveled by way of *Carlisle, Lancaster* and *Preston* and arrived in *Blackley* (via way of Manchester), in the early afternoon. I was fortunate to be able to visit the family in *Blackley* and *Moston* that afternoon, then went on to *Leigh* to see Aunt Lizzie.

On the afternoon of April 28th, I left for *London* and arrived at Witley Military Camp after stretching my eight-day leave to an even better eleven-day leave.

The machine-gunners soon got word that a Victory March of Overseas Troops was scheduled to take place in *London* on May 3rd, 1919. The 2nd Battalion (my battalion) was required to contribute one hundred men for this military pageant. I was honoured to be one of the soldiers selected.

After practicing rifle positions and marching (something which had been neglected since the Armistice), we machine-gunners were sent by train to *London* on May 3rd. We then marched from Paddington Station to Hyde Park where we overseas troops were assembled. As we ate our noon meal, each one of us received "*A Message to You from the King*," which read: *The Queen and I wish you God-speed, and a safe return to your homes and dear ones. A grateful Mother Country is proud of your splendid services characterized by unsurpassed devotion and courage.*

Victory March, Canadian Machine Gun Corps Battalion Wm Lees is one of the soldiers marching in the above photo. May 3rd, 1919.

Photo credit: William Lees's collection

We lined up in order of march with the forces of five overseas colonies, taking part: *Australia, New Zealand, South Africa, Canada*, and the separate territory of *Newfoundland*. As we arrived at the saluting point in front of Buckingham Palace, each unit in succession was given the order, "Eyes right." For the first and last time, I got a good look at King George and Winston Churchill. Queen Mary, whom I'd seen before, was at the king's side. Opposite the

King and Queen were wounded soldiers. They were given the honour of watching the ceremonies on raised benches in front of the palace. All streets, all sidewalks, and all windows overlooking the military parade were packed with cheering people. At one point an exuberant teenage girl yelled, "We're proud of you, Canada!"

After coming to a halt at Australia House, we machine-gunners sloped arms, marched down Oxford Street and returned to the Concentration Grounds in Hyde Park. The entire route covered five and a half miles. Next, we machine-gunners were dismantled, served tea and a light lunch. We were also given a three-day pass and were now at liberty to either stay in *London* or go anywhere on the British Isles. We were "Free!" How we loved that word. Having been constrained for so long, we appreciated freedom all the more.

I chose to go by rail to *Bristol* to see the city and the area around the *Severn River*: the Clifton Gorge, and the suspension bridge 200 feet above the river. I also took a tram to *Avonmouth* on the Bristol Channel, where I could see the coast of *Wales*.

On May 7th, I got back to Whitney Camp. I think every Canadian was getting bored with camp life and longed to go home. Finally, on May 14th, we got our final orders to pack up our kit bags, carry our rifles and line up on the parade grounds.

Leaving *Witley*, we marched to the railway siding where a troop train waited. After two hours of slow travel, the train arrived at *Tilbury Docks* (east of London), on the *Thames River*. Here we machine-gunners joined other units, and boarded the troopship, Minnekahda. Again, we waited several hours before slowly sailing down the Thames estuary, out to the English Channel and from there to the open sea.

I took nine days to cross the Atlantic. The ocean was moderately calm and on this ocean voyage, there were no enemy submarines to worry about. We arrived in *Halifax Harbour* on May 22nd. However, the 2nd Battalion CMGC was not demobilized until May 29th, 1919. At the armouries in *Toronto,* we were ordered to turn in everything but the army uniform and greatcoats we stood up in. I had intended to keep my rifle (#64251) as a keepsake, but I didn't take it apart in time.

Pat Halley and I were going west together. He was bound for *Vancouver* and I was going to *Calgary.* But first, we wanted to visit *Niagara Falls*. We went by boat to *Queenston*, then by electric train to *Niagara Falls*. We crossed the river bridge above the American falls to Goat Island. There we saw an iron stairway descending to the foot of the falls. We took the stairs down to a fenced-in boardwalk. This went under the falls. Neither of us hesitated; we had to go under the falls. In a hut nearby we found several slickers, but no waterproof pants. We put the slickers on, then fought our way under the rushing water. There was a tremendous downdraft, especially when we came to the Cave of the Winds. Here the swirling spray took our breath away. Later, when we walked down the main street, we were conscious of passers-by staring at the two former soldiers with the dripping pant legs.

Once more on the train, we travelled west, awed by the sight of the *Rocky Mountains* which we hadn't seen for 27 months.

Pat Halley and I parted company in *Calgary*. Then, I was on my own. I walked downtown *Calgary*, purchased a suit for $70.00, and returned to the homestead.

This was Tuesday, June 5th, 1919, and I was just an ordinary civilian again.

Canadian soldier, William Lees,

To Whom It May Concern

This is to certify that 895518

Pte. W. Les

has served with the

Canadian Machine Gun Corps.

in the 2nd Battalion

from Aug 4th 1918 to Nov 11th 1918

with Honour and Distinction.

He Has Been Honourably Discharged.

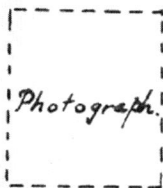

A Bentinck
Brigadier. General
Commanding Cdn. M.G. Corps

JG. Weir
Lt. Col.
Cdg 2nd Bn C.M.G.C.

Photograph

Wounds
Awards

DEVAMBEZ. G.

CANADIAN EXPEDITIONARY FORCE

DISCHARGE CERTIFICATE

200120

THIS IS TO CERTIFY that No. *995518* (Rank) *Private*

Name (in full) *William Lees* enlisted in

the *191 As Battn*

CANADIAN EXPEDITIONARY FORCE at *Red Deer* on the *20*

day of *December* 19*16*

HE served in *2nd Battn C.M.G.C. France*

and is now discharged from the service by reason of Demobilization. Medical Unfitness.

THE DESCRIPTION OF THIS SOLDIER on the DATE below is as follows:

Age *25*	Marks or Scars *Nil.*
Height *5 ft 9 ins*	
Complexion *Medium*	
Eyes *Grey*	
Hair *Brown*	

William Lees
Signature of Soldier

Date of Discharge

No. 2 DISTRICT DEPOT
24
MAY 25 1919
TORONTO

Issuing Officer
O.C. No. 2 District Depot.

Rank

Date *May 29* 19*19*

N.B.—As no duplicate of this Certificate will be issued, any person finding same is requested to forward it in an unstamped envelope to the Secretary, Militia Council, Ottawa, Canada.

M.F.B. 39,
1049-D.P.-300M-11-18.
H.Q. 1772-39-882.

273

Epilogue

In my mind, I can still see my father smiling and telling me in his humble way, that his little blue book, *My Adventures During WWI,* would be of little interest to anyone else.

In fact, he echoed that sentiment on May 11, 1965, when he wrote, *"I am engaged in my spare time in typing out those 'war experiences' again, just a few pages now and then and should finish them this summer. There will be about 300 pages altogether of absolutely no literary merit whatsoever, sprinkled all through with grammatical errors, done primarily for my own spare-time amusement, as it were. I don't expect anybody (including my relatives) to be the least bit interested in them, but it is interesting to me."*

How wrong he was in making such a statement. Interest? Oh my gosh! I never imagined that looking more closely at his life (when he was a Canadian soldier), would be such a rewarding experience. What an honour it has been to mentally walk through war-time England, France, Belgium, and Germany with my dad—all when he was an energetic and daring young man. These past few months of writing and studying a soldier (who just happens to be my dad), ranks at the very top of my list of wonderful memories. Father returned to France to visit his brother's grave in the summer of 1930 and again in June of 1969, an even fifty years after he returned to Canada.

No one knows better than I do, how indelible the horrors of war were written on my father's soul. Below the surface lay emotions so raw, mental pictures of death and dying so real, he was haunted by the trauma for the rest of his life.

One day when I was hounding Dad for answers, he said, "I thought I'd come through the war unscathed. Then five years, almost to the day, the nightmares began and never left."

And yet, through all his emotional struggles, he rallied and became a strong, compassionate man with high moral values.

It would be remiss of me not to mention that we three daughters had an incredibly happy home life. Both our mother and father created a warm and loving environment in which to grow, learn, and love by their example.

Gertrude (Gertie) Morris-Mister Lees, wife of William Lees

*Seated: Gertrude (Morris-Mister) and William Lees
and #1ˢᵗ grandchild Patricia (Heringer) Alexander*

Back row, left to right: Daughters, Doreen, Annette, and Evelyne

William Lees

Brother John Edward Lees

Sister Evelyne Lees

Evelyne never married. She taught in rural schools in Alberta for almost 50 years, often riding horseback to the schools she served.

During the 1930s (the depression years), the only pay she received was produce from the gardens of her students' parents, often accepting a bag of potatoes as a month's salary.

School teacher, Evelyne Lees

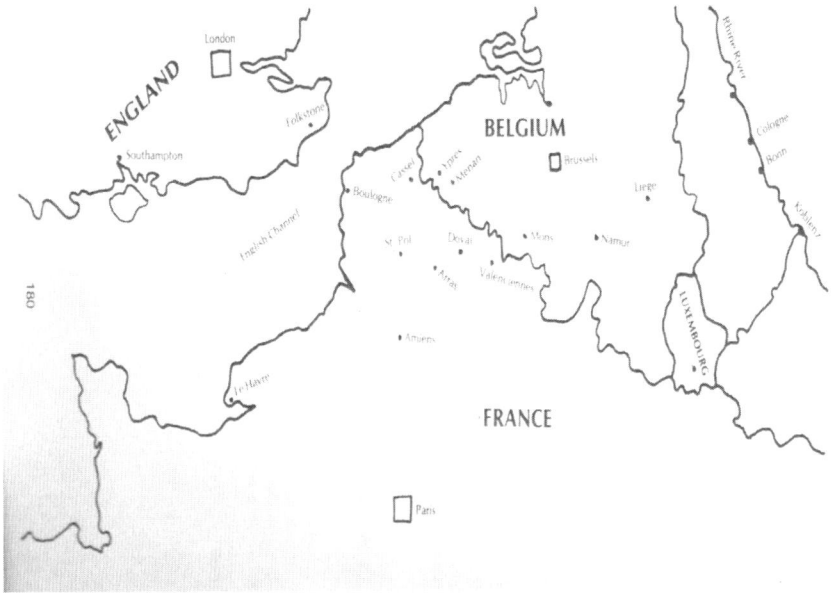

Map from William Lees's book "My Adventures During WWI

INDEX OF PLACE NAMES

(trace Williams's footsteps)

FRANCE

Aire, 88
Albain-St-Nazaire, 135
Alberta Camp, 135-137
Amiens, 165,167,169,
175,176,267
Arras,54,57,60,78,81,85,127,
145,153,154,157,176, 183,
185,186,193,194,205, 265
Aubigny,265
Aubin-SaintVaast,159,161,
164,188,233
Auchel, 144
Avion,46,77,80,81,124,125
Bailleul,153
Boulogne,47-49,188,193
Boves,170
Bourlon,199,203
Bruay, 52,88,117-121
Busnes,117
Caëstre,111-114
Caix,172,175
Calonne,51,52,115,149
Cambrai,121,154,183, 185,
199,202, 203-214
Canada Camp, 147,149
Canaples,164,265

Canal du Nord,197,200
Canche River,49,161
Casblain-Châtelain,144
Cassel,90.91.94
Carency,57,80,135
Cayeaux,171,175
Château d' Acqand,60
Château-de-la-Haie,63,71,75,
77,79,80,121,133.146.147
Chérisy,194,195
Cite-St. Pierre,146,147,
Cuvillers, 212
Dainville,176,193.194
Dickebusche,111,116
Divion,52,146
Eecke,113
Émerchicourt,217,220
Escaudpeivres,205.209,
212,213
Estree-Gauchy, 86,87,146
Flanders Plains,88,111
Frévent,164
Gauchin-Légal,52,53,87
Givenchy,73,82,124
Green Crassier,126
Guarbecque,88,89
Guémappe,194
Guisy,194,195

FRANCE (continued)

Belgium

Antwerp,263
Baraque de Fraiture,243
Barvaux,241
Bonneville,239
Bovigny,243
Brussels, 260,261
Ciply,227,228,231
Courcelles,236
Curthe River,241
Dour,223
Élouges,222,223
Évalette,240
Fleurus,236
Florette,259,260,262,265
Godarville,236
Godesberg,259
Haltinne,240
Havelange,240
Houdeng,234,235
Jambes,237,239,262
Jemeppe-sur-Sambre, 237
Keumiée,236
La Louviére,235
La Roeulx,234,235
Luxembourg,241 Maizeret,239
Meuse River,237,239,262
Mons,226,228,231,232,
233,253
Moustier,237

Mornimont,237
Namur,237,239,240,262
Noirchain,226
Nouvelles,226
Passchendaele,92,93,104,
123
Quiévrain,222
Salmchâteau,243
Sambre River,237
Wangenies,236
Warquignies,223,224
Waterloo,263
Ypres,88,90,92-97,103
110,114,116

GERMANY

NAMES OF MEN

William Lees sharing stories with daughter, Annette.
Picture courtesy of Evelyne (Lees) Heringer

About the writer/editor, Annette Gray

I feel truly blessed to have this opportunity to introduce you to my father, William Lees. He was a quiet unassuming man and a great mentor who taught me to believe in myself. "You can do anything you put your mind to," he used to say. "Believe in yourself."

Under his guidance, I became a writer with a great many articles published in both the USA and Canada. I have also authored seven other books: *Butterflies in the Dark, Mountains and Moonbeams, Twisted Heart, Twin Hearts, Rearview Mirror, Journey of the Heart-a true story, Westport's Tarnished Star–in defence of Johnny Behan.*

 A belated thank you, Dad!